Environment and Economy

B

For Kirk, Reed, Christopher, and Elizabeth

Environment and Economy

Property Rights and Public Policy

Daniel W. Bromley

BLACKWELL
Oxford UK & Cambridge USA

Copyright © Daniel W. Bromley 1991

First published 1991

Basil Blackwell, Inc.
3 Cambridge Center
Cambridge, Massachusetts 02142, USA

Basil Blackwell Ltd
108 Cowley Road, Oxford OX4 1JF, UK

Library of Congress Cataloging in Publication Data

Bromley, Daniel W., 1940–
  Environment and economy: property rights and public policy
Daniel W. Bromley
    p. cm.
  Includes bibliographical references and index.
  ISBN 1-55786-087-4
  1. Environmental policy.   2. Natural resources – Management.
3. Right of property.   4. Externalities (Economics)   5. Public
goods.   I. Title.
HC79.E5B75   1991
333–dc20   90-1262   CIP

British Library Cataloguing in Publication Data

A CIP catalogue record for this book is available from the British
Library.

Typeset in 10½ on 12 point Sabon
by Dobbie Typesetting Limited
Printed in Great Britain by TJ Press, Padstow, Cornwall

Contents

List of Figures

List of Tables

Acknowledgments

I have been concerned, for over two decades now, with property relations over natural resources. In this volume I pull together material that spans a part of that time, but containing ideas that have evolved over that full period of study, reflection, and writing. It is clear to me now, as I suppose it always has been, that natural resource problems are property rights problems; natural resource policy is property rights policy. While I do not claim to have addressed the full array of natural resource problems, I believe that I here offer a conceptual approach to the analysis of property relations concerning natural resources that transcends the particular examples under discussion. The applications will, I hope, show the reader how one might apply my framework to a wide array of important natural resource problems. With no less presumptuousness than any author, I suggest that the approach developed here is illuminating of the abiding policy issues we face in natural resource management.

I have benefited greatly, over the years, from the collaboration with – and counsel of – a number of fine colleagues and friends. Those with a special role to play in many of the ideas here include Paul Barkley, Richard Bishop, Benoit Blarel, John Braden, Michael Carter, Michael Cernea, Bonnie Colby, Ian Hodge, George Peters, Glen Pulver, Ford Runge, Warren Samuels, Allan Schmid, Kathleen Segerson, Basil Sharp, Martin Whitby, and Harald von Witzke.

Several chapters have appeared previously in a different form and I want to acknowledge my gratitude for permission to include those pieces here. Chapter 3 is a modified version of a paper that appeared in the *Journal of Economic Issues* in 1978. Chapter 4 is a much modified version of a chapter from a book that I edited for Kluwer Academic Publishers in 1986 (Bromley, 1986a). Chapter 5 is a revised version of a paper which appeared in the *Journal of Environmental Economics and Management* in September 1989. Chapter 9 is a revised version of an earlier paper in the *European Review of Agricultural Economics* which I co-authored with Ian Hodge of Cambridge University. Finally, chapter 10 is a modified version of an article which appeared in the *Journal of Environmental Economics and Management* in the summer of 1990.

As always, my secretary Mary J. Johnson deserves great credit for keeping the rest of my academic life in order while projects such as these detract from a decent level of attention and fastidiousness.

Finally, my wife Joyce offers the sort of encouragement and support that every scholar deserves. She shares my fascination with the evolution of institutional arrangements, and her wide knowledge of European history serves as a source of constant enrichment as I struggle with the social and economic dimensions of property, of rights, and of property rights. This is, in many ways, a joint project, and we dedicate it to our children who will, for better or worse, have more time to observe the property rights struggles that will surely occur over natural resources.

D. W. B.
Madison, WI

1
Property, Rights, and Property Rights

> . . . [all rights] . . . are conditional and derivative . . . they
> are derived from the end or purpose of the society in which
> they exist. They are conditional on being used to the
> attainment of that end.
>
> R. H. Tawney, *The Acquisitive Society*

1 THE INTELLECTUAL PROBLEM

There are few concepts within economics that are more central – yet
more confused – than those of property, rights, and property rights.
Many economists will invariably regard *property* as a physical object
such as a dwelling, a piece of land, or some such possession. They
will regard *rights* as something of interest to moral and political
philosophers. And they will regard the term *property rights* as some
vague but necessary condition for the "efficient" operation of a market.
With such inauspicious beginnings, small wonder that much of the
literature concerning property concepts in natural resource economics
and environmental policy is so incoherent. Different writers use the
same term to denote quite disparate concepts and ideas. To the extent
that scholarly progress requires clarity and consistency in concepts and
language, it is little wonder that progress remains elusive.

There can be no more important aspect of scholarship than the
concern for concepts and language. If we use the same words or terms
to describe fundamentally different fact situations, ideas, or phenomena,
then progress in understanding is impeded rather than advanced. As
but one example of this problem, it would be difficult to find an *idea*
(a concept) that is as misunderstood as that of the *commons* and

1

common property. The mischief to arise from the continuing failure to understand common property is perverse in both scholarly discussions and public policy formulation. On the former front, scholars will show no hesitancy to expound on the problems inherent in common property without the benefit of first defining *property*, and without betraying any understanding of the historical and contemporary facts surrounding common property regimes. On the practical side, scholars will show equal confidence in advising all who will listen about how to "solve" the so-called *tragedy of the commons*. This mischief is then perpetuated among politicians who, as Keynes put it, are often found to be under the thrall of some now-defunct economist. While this may be a bit strong, there is cause for serious concern when profound policy recommendations are predicated upon false problem definitions.

The economics literature is full of casual references to *common property resources* as if this were a universal and immutable classification – almost as if the prevailing institutional form were somehow inherent in a natural resource. Never mind that in one place trees and fish and range forage are controlled and managed as private property, in another setting they are controlled and managed as state property, in another setting they are controlled and managed as common property, and in other settings they are not controlled or managed at all but are instead used by anyone who so desires to use them. There is no such thing as a common property *resource* – there are only natural resources controlled and managed as common property, or as state property, or as private property. Or, and this is where confusion persists in the literature, there are resources over which *no property rights* have been recognized. The latter situation is one of *open access* (*res nullius*).

The key concept here is *property*. Property, as I will make clear throughout the remainder of the book, is a benefit (or income) stream, and a property right is a claim to a benefit stream that the state will agree to protect through the assignment of duty to others who may covet, or somehow interfere with, the benefit stream. Rights have no meaning without correlated duties and the management problem with open access regimes is that there are no duties on aspiring users to refrain from use. Property *is not* an object but rather is a social relation that defines the property holder with respect to something of value (the benefit stream) against all others. Property is a triadic social relation involving benefit streams, rights holders, and duty bearers (Hallowell, 1943). It is for this reason that, in subsequent chapters, I shall urge the abandonment of the term *common property resource* in favor of the more correct *common property regime*. Regimes, after all, are human artifacts reflecting instrumental origins, and a property regime is fundamentally instrumental in nature. That is, property regimes acquire their special character by virtue of collective perceptions regarding what is scarce (and hence *possibly* worth protecting with rights), and what is valuable (and hence *certainly* worth protecting with rights). Property is a social instrument, and particular property regimes are chosen for particular purposes.

The fallacy in traditional approaches to the commons is that writers have failed to understand the concept of property, they have very often treated a particular natural resource as if it had inherent characteristics that suggested it would everywhere be controlled under a particular type of property regime, and they have invariably failed to learn that the world is replete with reasonably successful common property regimes.[1] By successful I mean that (1) the natural resource has not been squandered; (2) some level of investment in the natural resource has occurred; and (3) the co-owners of the resource are not in a perpetual state of anarchy. In short, common property regimes exist and function very much like private property regimes and state property regimes. That is, some are not working very well, while others work very well indeed.

Once we have a better understanding of different property regimes we can begin to comprehend the richer tapestry that is environmental policy. We can see, for instance, that environmental policy is nothing if not a dispute over the putative rights structure that gives protection to mutually exclusive uses of certain environmental resources. Those disputed resources could represent the assimilative capacity of a river, they could represent the mutually exclusive use of certain pristine landscapes – say for urban development or greenspace – or they could represent the competing claims of a shrimp fishery and the desires of a chemical plant to find a cheap way to dispose of residues. These disputes may appear to be "environmental problems" but they are, in fact, problems of conflicting rights claims. To analyze such environmental problems is to confront, with full force, different interests that will make conflicting claims in order that they might have their interest given protection by a "right" (Bromley, 1989a).

Types of Rights

In thinking about rights and environmental policy it seems helpful to recognize two crucial aspects of rights claims. Recall that a right denotes a set of actions and behaviors that the possessor *may not* be prevented from undertaking. As we shall see in the following chapter, a right – by definition – implies a duty on the part of all others to refrain from preventing those actions or behaviors. Rightful actions are both permissible and inviolable, and actions intended to interfere with rightful actions are thus impermissible. Steiner (1977) calls a set of rights meeting these conditions *compossible rights*. If these conditions do not obtain then we have *incompossible rights*.

Incompossible rights may exist between different persons attempting to exercise *different kinds of rights*. The best example may be found in the controversy over various religious groups plying their recruitment trade in privately owned shopping arcades: one party has a right to attempt to save souls, while the other party has a right to determine the range of activities allowed on its private domain. Alternatively, incompossible rights may exist between different persons attempting to exercise *the same kind of right*. If there is room for only one of us to exercise our rights of free speech at the village square, then it is impossible for both of us to harangue the crowd at the same time. Hence, if the *same kind of right is claimed*, then denial of that right is based upon a denial of the validity of the *kind* of right invoked by both claimants. If *different kinds of rights are claimed*, then the denial is based upon a denial either of one person's claim or of the validity of the *kind* of right being invoked. In short, denial is based upon the denial of the *existence* of that particular kind of right, or upon the denial that that particular claimant in fact *has* that right. We have, as it were, a failure of claimed rights to prevail owing either to "existence," or to "coverage."

Much of natural resource and environmental policy is, I suggest, understood in these terms. Denial of claimed rights by existence occurs when two or more parties claim to have a right to a certain environmental quality parameter such as air quality, water quality, a scenic vista, or the nature of a particular landscape. Denial of claimed rights by coverage occurs when the dispute is over whether or not a particular claimant is, in fact, entitled to protection by the state.

Origins of Rights

Much of the literature on natural resources and property rights suffers, as well, from a lack of clarity on the origins of property rights. Economists are inclined to find Locke's views particularly compelling since, on this particular tack, the private appropriation of scarce and valuable natural resources is necessary and sufficient for a market to emerge among atomistic resource owners. Locke argues that prior collective consent is not required for individual expropriation of valuable resources. That is, he maintains that the absolute right to appropriation derives from the need for all to secure their sustenance, and from the right of all to the fruits of their own labor. These two conditions justify the private appropriation of the earth's bounty, quite prior to any social contract.

Kant challenged this position on two grounds – its universality and its necessity. Kant's position is that Locke confused empirical possession with *de jure* or intelligible possession[2] (Williams, 1977). That is, while physical appropriation is necessary for something to become my property – that is, for me to be able to control its benefit stream – it is not sufficient. Empirical possession cannot establish ownership. Kant argues that this confusion in Locke means that he (Locke) fails to see that a social convention – a social contract – is logically prior to real ownership. That is, only intelligible possession constitutes property.[3] If the necessity of a social convention is understood to be the core of intelligible possession, then two conclusions follow immediately from this fact.

First, and foremost, *all property rights flow from the collective* as opposed to flowing from some alleged "natural rights" that are claimed to be logically prior to the state. The contrast with Locke could not be more pronounced. Second, and logically deducible from the first, *property rights are instrumental variables*. That is, if the core of property is the external acknowledgment (that is, "social recognition") of the legitimacy of that particular claim by the "owner," then it follows ineluctably that property claims failing to win this external acknowledgment will not be recognized as legitimate by those forced to forswear interest in the benefit stream. Put more bluntly, if the collective fails to admit the social usefulness of a particular property claim, then it is delegitimized because it is regarded as non-instrumental.

Kant, unlike Locke and Hobbes, suggests that the true state of nature is something that man could never have experienced; it is therefore of special importance in understanding the origins of private appropriation. That is, not being able to experience a true state of nature does not render the concept useless in locating private property rights in the human condition. To Kant the state of nature has a moral – as opposed to an empirical – reality. That is, a state of nature in which the earth was in "our common possession" was followed by a similar postulate of a "social contract allowing private ownership of the earth and its produce" (Williams, 1977, p. 36). As one might expect from Kant:

The validity of property as a social institution does not rest on a fact of the external sensible world but rather on a moral imperative. This moral imperative is . . . "that it is a juridical duty to behave towards others in such a way that what is external (usable) may become the property of someone else". (Williams, 1977, p. 36)

As Williams notes, this leaves property rights hanging "on a very weak thread." Such rights depend, it would seem, on the presumption of goodwill of individuals to behave towards others in a moral way. Moreover, the mere *possibility* of some object being reduced to private appropriation is not sufficient for it to happen. The missing ingredient is the capacity of the collective to *coerce itself* – to exercise the "general will" as opposed to the "particular will." That is, merely exercising the particular will would deny the universality of property and so the reciprocal freedoms that would exist under the general will. So,

the constitution of such a society can only be founded on a will binding everyone subject to their freedom. It is not necessary that this contract exist in reality for the possibility of coercion into such a society to be made into a reality. For the existence of such an universal will sanctioning such use of force is an *a priori* idea of the pure practical Reason, and wherever civil society exists such an universal will has to be presupposed. The notion of such a contract must guide our behaviour in society, otherwise we would not be bound to leave another's property untouched. It is only through the reciprocal guarantee of ownership in the contract that ownership becomes a dependable status. Kant believes that this reciprocal obligation inheres as an idea of pure practical Reason in the very assertion of ownership, for the conditions under which I may own an object are those under which all others are potentially able to do so. (Williams, 1977, p. 37)

Kant regards property – the institution of ownership – as the essence of pure practical reason (Scruton, 1982). Property is an objective, but not an empirical, reality. Of course there has never been a social contract actually executed by anyone. But a civil society (*burgerliche Gesellschaft*) exists if and only if there are underlying tacit agreements recognized by all individuals capable of moral judgment. In the absence of such agreements civil society would cease to exist.

Natural rights to Kant are not the conditions necessary for establishing ownership. Rather, within the state of nature we have the natural right to compel – to coerce – everyone to enter with us into a society (a social contract) where property holding is sanctioned by positive legal powers. This "absolute moral demand" may be made upon humans in the state of nature.

So irresistible is this demand that even where the majority in the state of nature wish there to be no legal state this can still be seen as a one-sided opinion. It is our right . . . to force the majority to be free in a *burgerliche Gesellschaft*. This . . . argument . . . appears to stand on its head the usual natural rights argument. . . . The ground of all our rights is a civil (*burgerliche*) constitution. The state of nature then, of itself, confers no rights. . . . So with Kant natural rights, paradoxically, are only natural rights from the standpoint of an already established *burgerliche Gesellschaft*. This is what Kant means when he says the right to property within the state of nature is only provisional. The right depends entirely on the supposition that the claimant will enter with others into a civil society. And, in the last resort, he can be coerced into such a society. (Williams, 1977, p. 38)

In spite of what some are inclined to believe, Kant's deduction of property rights is not based entirely on the moral will but rather on the idea of a social contract allowing each individual to survive in a civilized society – of which property rights are essential instruments in the ordered relations he sees as the *burgerliche Gesellschaft*.

Summary

This Kantian perspective is congenial to the position to be followed here. In my view, the conventional Lockean understanding posits a too-restrictive and improperly dyadic notion of property rights. That is, the Locke-inspired position has individual property rights stand as the last bastion against a meddlesome state. And therein lies the obvious appeal of the Lockean vision to libertarian thinkers, whether economists or political commentators. In their terms, current property rights are some immutable and timeless *entitlement* that can only be contravened with difficulty, and then only if compensation is paid by the state to make the property holder whole. This dyadic perspective – the individual versus the state – is, almost by design, one that impedes social change. Libertarians, as suspicious of change as they are of the state, seek a rigid and stable world in which all change – inevitably initiated by a too-powerful state – must be resisted at every turn. One effective way to resist such change is first to sanctify the status quo property rights structure as the correct one, and then to demand that the state compensate rights holders for any change in the status quo. By then mounting an attack on the size of the public purse the strategy is complete. First deny the state the financial means to compensate rights holders for institutional change, second celebrate the status quo property rights structure as legitimate, and finally define all environmental matters as a struggle over the rights of private property as against the nebulous demands of some fringe environmental special interests (who are upper class anyway).

While life, in general, would be much more agreeable if there were no need for institutional change, reality is not inclined to cooperate. Population growth creates ever-increasing needs for sewage treatment, for solid-waste disposal, for more highways and housing developments, and for myriad goods and services seemingly prerequisite to the good life. Technology, too, is advancing in ways that are not always benign for environmental integrity. Finally, as individuals – and nations – become wealthier, tastes and preferences change in a way that attaches greater significance to non-material consumption. As a result, a quiet meadow, a scenic sunset, or a tranquil day at the water gains in value relative to rather more conventional commodities. An environmental economics – and a perspective on property rights – that starts from Lockean statics may feel good to some on personal philosophical grounds, but it is an analytical dead-end. Institutional change is inevitable in the real world and to hide behind some Lockean fiction is empty scholasticism at best, and intellectual malfeasance at worst. The job of the economist is to build models that will both reflect reality and illuminate the choices that collectives must inevitably make.

2   THE PLAN OF THE BOOK

My purpose here is to offer an operational theory of rights, property, and property rights with the intent of informing economic analysis and public debate about natural resource and environmental problems.[4] Our first challenge is to clarify language and concepts, and none is more important than the ideas of property and property rights. In chapter 2 I shall introduce notions of property rights and property regimes pertinent to natural resource policy. Here we shall see the critical role of rights and correlated duties in the Kantian logic of a social contract. The idea of a resource management regime will be introduced, and I shall elaborate on four general types of regimes: (1) state property regimes; (2) private property regimes; (3) common property regimes; and (4) non-property regimes (open access). This chapter will conclude with a discussion of property rights as policy instruments, a direct logical corollary of the collective interest in property rights via the social contract.

The rather straightforward view of property rights finds elaboration in the recognition that rights can be protected by different kinds of operational rules. Following Calabresi and Melamed (1972) I shall introduce in chapter 3 the protection of entitlements (rights) by property rules, liability rules, and inalienability rules. This greater detail in the ways in which an individual's interests can be given protection will be seen to offer important distinctions for innovative environmental policy. I shall also suggest a richer classification of the various types of externality problems common in the literature. Specifically, the externality problems of great favor among some writers tend to be rather straightforward problems between two parties, and instances in which the damage function is known. Small wonder, based on such examples, that many economists are so enamored of simple taxing schemes, or of letting the two parties bargain away the external costs. My point here is that most environmental externalities do not fit this simple two-party affair and so the textbook solution may often be inappropriate to the reality we face. While the simple externality models have nice heuristic properties, they are often highly misleading when applied to the real world.

In chapter 4 I pursue externalities in more detail, offering an examination of the full gamut of types of externalities – including technological, pecuniary, Pareto-irrelevant, Pareto-relevant, infra-marginal, ownership, technical, political, depletable, undepletable, and potentially relevant. This bewildering and overlapping taxonomy of externalities reflects differences in how externalities are experienced, how they arise, and the policy implications to flow from their existence. The student of natural resource economics may well be overwhelmed by these overlapping definitions and I hope to dispel some of that confusion here. Also in this chapter I address the widespread belief that in externality situations the initial assignment of property rights is immaterial for the ultimate outcome. This view, one enduring legacy from Coase's seminal work on social costs, matches the so-called "tragedy of the commons" in terms of pure mischief sown in the literature.

I finish the treatment of externalities by focusing, in chapter 5, on the problem of intertemporal externalities, and on the public perceptions of environmental uncertainty. In both instances the root of the problem is seen to be perceptions of rights and duties across generations, or perceptions of which party shall have the right to be free of residual risk in the face of uncertainty. I shall show here that the conventional way of framing the environmental choice problem – whether the externality is intertemporal or contemporaneous in nature – leads to incorrect policy recommendations. With intertemporal externalities, true efficiency is found by comparing alternative rights structures, including one option that gives the present generation a duty not to impose unwanted costs on the future. The usual view, inferring judgments of intertemporal efficiency and equity against the status quo rights structure, is seen to be inadequate and misleading.

In chapter 6 our attention turns away from externalities and towards resource management regimes, specifically those regimes in the developing world. Starting with the idea that the institutional setup of an economy is the very essence of a collective good, and that therefore this institutional infrastructure is a form of *common property* defining the choice sets for all independent economic agents, I suggest that the real and lasting "tragedy of the commons" is the gradual breakdown of institutional arrangements in the newly independent nation states of the tropics. First rapacious kings and princes, then alien colonial and imperial administrators, and finally often-inept national governments have all conspired to subvert or to destroy resource management regimes at the local level. With these institutional arrangements in disarray – and with conventional common property and private property rights having been delegitimized – it is small wonder that resource degradation occurs in the developing world. This is the real tragedy of the commons. Any property regime – whether private, common, or state – is an authority system. In the absence of consistent and coherent institutional arrangements, resource use is reduced to first come, first served. The *intelligible possession* of Kant gives way to the *empirical possession* of Locke and there is no authority except of the powerful. Intelligible possession requires social sanction and social legitimation. Colonialism and the modern nation state have sought, in most instances, to delegitimize traditional grounds for intelligible possession and to locate all rights in some alien source of authority – whether in a European colonial capital or in some new national capital. Nationalization of natural resources – and the attempt to control and manage natural resources from afar – is simply a form of domestic colonialism and leaves resource users and managers open to the whims of distant bureaucrats who believe that the solution to deforestation is to pass a law prohibiting the cutting of firewood. To set the people against natural resources only invites cynicism and lawlessness, and does little to protect natural resources. The record on this is now unexceptionable. Successful management of natural resources in the developing countries awaits the reestablishment of effective resource management regimes at the local level.

In chapter 7 I remain in the developing world, here challenging the received wisdom of late that the solution to natural resource degradation is to be found in the establishment of private property regimes in those areas where common property and/or open access are now the rule. I develop a model to locate the proper boundary between private property and common property and suggest that in most developing countries the existing institutional choice is *not incorrect*. This model turns on its head the conventional wisdom that private property regimes will lead to increased economic output. Rather, I start from the premise that economic potential will suggest the type of property regime suitable to a particular setting. Where resource degradation is present the problem is not that *private property is absent*, but that *common property is absent*. That is, open access regimes have replaced common property regimes for reasons spelled out in chapter 6, and the solution is to reestablish effective common property regimes. I conclude this chapter with a report of some empirical work in Nepal where we attempted to discern the willingness of villagers to contribute to a common property regime.

In chapter 8 I persist with the notion of property rights as policy instruments but return to the US setting to explore different perceptions of rights and duties from an instrumental perspective. I am interested here in the *implicit transfer* of rights among parties in a society – by which I mean a respecification of the bundle of rights in possession of the "owner" of a parcel of land. I also discuss, in some detail, the recent debates over efforts to sell (to "privatize") the public lands. Few initiatives of the Reagan Presidency (Star Wars aside) generated so much talk, and so little action, as the ill-fated efforts to sell federal lands in the western United States. I review the economic arguments for and against privatization, and discuss the various notions of "efficiency" implied by those advocating wholesale divestiture. In the end, the privatization initiatives failed for the very reasons that one might expect – they were the brainchild of a few zealous ideologues who failed to see that economic and political reality found the idea of public lands rather compelling.

In chapter 9 I turn attention to a different aspect of private property rights, this being the sanctity of private agricultural land. I argue here that agricultural producers have managed to capitalize on sentimentality over private land and rural fundamentalism to garner large "entitlements" in the form of price-support programs. Equally serious, any concessions made for environmental protection must be purchased by the public with side-payments or other financial inducements. In a word, modern agriculture epitomizes the Lockean notion – and the libertarian strategy – of forcing the state to pay for any modification of the status quo. If one started with a different structure of property rights, one where agricultural producers had to pay to deviate from certain environmentally sound practices, we would see a different constellation of products and environmental quality in rural America. As the developed world became less dependent on agriculture it would not be surprising to see sweeping changes in the presumptive property rights inherent in rural land.

The final chapter is devoted to a critical examination of efficiency as an "objective truth rule" for economic policy evaluation. By "objective truth rule" I have in mind the twin ideas of scientific objectivity and of "good" or "correct." That is, many economists are convinced that when something is said to be *efficient* it is a non-normative proposition attesting to an objective and value-free judgment. From this presumption of objectivity, economists then feel confident to offer up efficiency as the "correct" decision criterion by which alternative policies should be judged. I argue in chapter 10 that efficiency is neither objective (value free) nor necessarily the "correct" decision-rule for public policy. These are important points to make for obvious reasons. To regard property rights as policy instruments is to invoke a search for the efficient structure of property rights on the presumption that the efficient structure is an unassailable desideratum. If efficiency lacks scientific objectivity – as I maintain – then one must search for another "truth rule." The correctness of efficiency has always resided in its claim (or, rather, the claim made on its behalf) to objectivity. With that claim in doubt the way is clear to search for other criteria to judge new institutional arrangements (property rights).

I offer the notion of the *objective scientist* as opposed to the *objective science*. By that I mean that economists can analyze alternative institutional arrangements and in doing so they can perform their function in an open and careful fashion that makes their assumptions abundantly clear to others who may wish to replicate that work. In this way, the objectivity of the scientist becomes the important standard of good work. By trying to situate objectivity in the science, the conventional wisdom seeks to elevate economics to some exalted level so as to imbue it with invincibility. I suggest that it is far better to use economics not as a *decision-rule*, but as a *way of thinking* about environmental problems and choices. The public will appreciate us more, and we shall be more intellectually honest. It will not be easy for some to relinquish the accustomed high-priest role that fits so well. But there seems to be no feasible alternative.

NOTES

1 Though it would take us beyond the domain of natural resources, it must be understood that a private club is a common property regime. Such clubs, whether "country clubs" or more restricted collectives, are joint management regimes that control assets and allocate use rights among co-owners or members.

2 By "intelligible possession" Kant meant the social recognition of the property claim of the "owner." In my terms this is the triadic aspect of rights that recognizes the owner and the claim against all others.

3 See Sugden (1986) for an argument along Lockean lines that empirical possession constitutes property rights.

4 To some, the terms "natural resource" and "environment" may seem redundant. Our literature is not really very uniform in this regard. Some will regard *natural resources* as raw materials that we use in our daily lives: timber, oil, water, and manganese come to mind. The *environment* is then regarded as the whole complex of naturally occurring objects and processes that sustain life. I shall not be much concerned with these terms in what follows, using them in their rather more conventional sense. And therefore, while they may overlap somewhat, I do not regard them as exactly synonymous.

2
Property Rights and Property Regimes in Natural Resource Policy

Property has its duties as well as its rights.
Benjamin Disraeli, *Sybil* (1845)

1 INTRODUCTION

Public policy is essentially concerned with modifying the institutional arrangements that situate individual economic agents in the larger economic structure. That is, all individual action takes place within an institutional context that defines domains of choice. If electric utilities are free to emit sulfur dioxide into the air then other economic agents will have their choice domain defined – in part – by this fact. Those individuals concerned with the fate of forests or lakes will find a modified physical condition for those natural resources, and such conditions may well threaten the long-run sustainability of such resources. The electric utility will be inclined to suggest that it has always emitted sulfur dioxide, and therefore until told to do otherwise it has a "right" to those emissions. Those individuals who care about trees and lakes will probably object that the mere fact of traditional use of the airshed for waste disposal does not constitute a "right" for the electric utilities. Rather, it will be said that the electric utilities have had the very great advantage of being able to ignore the implications of their actions on others. Indeed, those who care about the trees and

14

lakes will probably suggest that *they* have a "right" to be free of the harmful emissions of electric utilities and other industrial polluters.

The example here of air pollution is quite incidental to the fundamental issue at hand, which is the actual and presumed rights structure that defines the positions of the two protagonists. If one is to understand public policy in environmental matters it is essential that we start with an exposition of the property arrangements that give rise to existing behaviors, and hence to confrontation with those who believe that their "rights" have been contravened.

2 THE CONCEPT OF RIGHTS AND CORRELATED DUTIES

A right is the capacity to call upon the collective to stand behind one's claim to a benefit stream. Notice that rights only have effect when there is some authority system that agrees to defend a rights holder's interest in a particular outcome. If I have a right in some particular situation then it means that I can turn to the state to see that my claim is protected. The effective protection I gain from this authority is nothing other than a correlated duty for all others interested in my claim. A right is a triadic relationship that encompasses the object of my interest (whether a physical object or a stream of benefits arising from fortuitous circumstances), plus all others in the polity who have a duty to respect my right. Rights are *not* relationships between me and an object, but are rather relationships between me and others *with respect to that object*. Rights can only exist when there is a social mechanism that gives duties and binds individuals to those duties.

When one has a right in something it means that the benefit stream arising from that situation is consciously protected by the state. The state gives and takes away rights by its willingness – or unwillingness – to agree to protect one's claims in something. Also note that to have *property* is to have control of a benefit stream. Property is the income stream. When I purchase a piece of land its price is a reflection of the present discounted value of all of its future benefit streams. By purchasing the land I am really purchasing the benefit stream – that is my property, the thing I actually own. Land is often called "property" in everyday usage, but the real property is the benefit stream that I now own, and that the state agrees to protect.

Returning to the air pollution example, the ability of the electric utility to discharge sulfur dioxide as opposed to spending money to purge its smoke of such compounds means that a benefit stream exists (in the form of cost savings) which the utilities now control. This benefit stream is manifest in the form of operating costs lower than if the plant were unable to discharge its sulfur dioxide.

Environmental policy is about rights and duties, and about benefit streams that represent "property" to various interests. I suggest that we might profitably approach environmental policy from a perspective that emphasizes the incidence of costs and the structure of institutional arrangements that permits the status quo to persist. This alternative approach would ask: (1) who is bearing unwanted costs? (2) what is the prevailing institutional setup (or rights structure) that allows this situation to persist? (3) who must bear the transaction costs necessary to resolve the situation? and (4) who gains and loses by this particular resolution of the problem?

This perspective tends to focus attention on the struggle over rights and duties as correlated ideas. This correlative nature was recognized at the turn of the century by the legal scholar W. N. Hohfeld (1913, 1917) who postulated four sets of dualities which he considered *the* essence of legal relations among individuals in a society. The correlates were picked up by John R. Commons and – with somewhat different terminology – comprised the basis of his analysis of collective, economic, and social relations under the jurisdiction of the Supreme Court, and also of the various types of transactions concerning economic quantities (Commons, 1968). Before turning to these four fundamental relations, I wish to draw a distinction between *legal relations* and a *legal system*. It is clear that no society can be considered as a going concern, to use Commons's terminology, in the absence of a certain degree of social order. The institutional arrangements of that going concern – its working rules – create the social order that allows it to function and to survive. The ways in which those institutions are promulgated and enforced constitute the legal system of that society. The societal recognition of a specific set of ordered relations among individuals is a legal relation.

When discussing the four fundamental legal relations we start with two individuals (Alpha and Beta). Recall that since legal relations are also group specific we might imagine Alpha to be a person (an individual) and Beta to be all other persons. Hence we have one social entity (Alpha) which may be an individual or a group against another social entity (Beta) which may be an individual or a group. The four fundamental legal relations are shown in table 2.1, with only a slight modification from the Hohfeld terminology.

In the Hohfeld scheme a *right* means that Alpha has an expectation or assurance that Beta will behave in a certain way toward Alpha. As examples we might note that Alpha has an expectation that Beta will not pick flowers from her (Alpha's) garden. A *duty* means that Beta must behave in a specific way with respect to Alpha and so duty binds

Table 2.1 The four fundamental legal relations

	Alpha	*Beta*
Static correlates	Right	Duty
	Privilege	No right
Dynamic correlates	Power	Liability
	Immunity	No power

Source: after Hohfeld 1913, 1917

Beta not to pick flowers from Alpha's garden. Notice that the dual of Alpha's standing is Beta's standing; Alpha has the right, Beta has the duty. The second correlate is that of *privilege*. Here, Alpha is free to behave in a certain way with respect to Beta. As an example we would say that the electric utilities (Alpha) are free to act in a way that disregards the interests of those who own trees and lakes (Beta). The dual of privilege is *no right* in which case Beta has no recourse if Alpha behaves in a certain way with respect to Beta – say by emitting large quantities of sulfur dioxide.

Turning now to the dynamic aspect, *power* means that Alpha may voluntarily create a new legal relation affecting Beta. That is, Alpha has the capacity to force Beta into a new situation that may be disadvantageous to Beta. The correlate of power, *liability*, means that Beta is subject to a new legal relation voluntarily created by Alpha. Finally, *immunity* means that Alpha is not subject to Beta's attempt voluntarily to create a new legal relation affecting Alpha. The correlate of immunity, *no power*, means that Beta may not voluntarily create a new legal relation affecting Alpha. The above scheme is perfectly symmetrical with respect to the position of Alpha and Beta. The legal relation is identical regardless of the position from which the relation is viewed (Alpha or Beta). The difference lies ". . . not in the relation which is always two sided, but in the positions and outlook of . . . [Alpha and Beta] . . . which together make up the two converses entering into the relation" (Hoebel, 1942, p. 955).

Two other considerations are important. First, individuals belong to more than one subgroup in a society, and we must expect that each subgroup will have its norms or codes of behavior. Some of these norms will be more imperative than others, and hence it may be that any one individual is subject to several sets of overlapping legal relations. We belong to a variety of organizations and associations that have their own constellations of legal relations. At work, or at play, we find a similar layering of these exposures and opportunities. Second, the four fundamental legal relations are reducible into two further categories which are either active (positive) or passive (negative). The right/duty and the power/liability relations are active in that they represent imperative relations subject to the authority of the state. On the other hand, the privilege/no right and immunity/no power relations are passive in that they are not themselves subject to direct legal enforcement. Instead, they set the limit of the state's activities in that they define the types of behavior that are beyond the interest of the state. As seen in the privilege instance, the state declares that it is none of its direct concern if Alpha imposes costs on Beta. In a sense, we have here legal relations that are statements of *no law*. Hoebel reminds us that in our legal system every right that Alpha has upon Beta is reinforced by accompanying pressure on courts to compel Beta to perform his/her duty.

Notice that policy prescriptions that suggest that we should "leave it to the market" imply that bargaining over environmental matters must occur against the backdrop of prevailing institutional arrangements. On the other hand policy prescriptions that imply a change from the status quo involve alterations in the prevailing institutional arrangements. It is no surprise that policy change is controversial.

Present environmental policy discussions reveal a great deal of interest in the concept of rights, in their establishment, and in their enforcement. It would be quite easy for the casual observer to gain the impression that the most important factor is simply that property rights be established. That is, one may conclude that who gets the property rights is of minor importance compared with the fact that *someone* has clear property rights so that volitional bargaining might begin over environmental disputes. However, this view is not only simplistic, but seriously mistaken. The literature growing out of the early influence of Coase and Demsetz would lead one to suppose that resource allocation – and therefore ultimate outcomes in terms of resource use – would be quite unaffected by which party to an externality was given the property right. All that is said to matter is that there be easy bargaining once rights have been allocated. It should be pointed out that this result hinges upon two very critical assumptions. The first assumption is that there are zero transaction costs in bargaining. In practical terms this requires that information is costlessly available to all parties to a potential bargain. It also means that the process of bargaining and contracting is absolutely costless. Finally, it means that there is perfect and costless enforcement of bargains that have been struck. If one or more of these conditions cannot survive close scrutiny then the outcome-neutrality of alternative initial rights assignments is quite impossible to sustain (Dick, 1976; Randall, 1972, 1974).

The second assumption regards wealth effects. Specifically, the alleged outcome-neutrality of alternative rights assignments is undermined by the realization that the wealth effects of alternative rights assignments can be significant indeed. Must recreationists buy out the presumed right of chemical factories to kill fish? Or must the factories buy out the right of recreationists to have pure rivers? The numbers of fish under these two initial assignments of rights will surely differ.

Environmental policy is further confounded by some of the contemporary language in such disputes. One sees repeated reference to the *private* benefits and costs in contradistinction to the *social* benefits and costs. That is, the individual takes actions whose private benefits exceed the social benefits, or whose private costs are less than the social costs. To label these effects private and social, however, is to miss the essence of environmental problems. What is at issue in environment disputes is the *private interest of one party (Alpha) as against the private interest of another (Beta)*. Either the interests of Alpha will prevail, or the interests of Beta will prevail. Note that Alpha and Beta need not refer to single individuals. Alpha could be all chemical factories along a particular stretch of river, and Beta could be recreationists who are concerned about fish. Both parties to a dispute will make a claim which they hope to have given protection as an entitlement by the state. That is, each party hopes to obtain a benefit stream that we call property. Recall that entitlements are structures of rights and correlated duties, and that power is the ability to impose a new entitlement structure on others. Also note that the standard formulation of private versus public (or social) gives the impression that environmental matters are characterized by the wishes of the individual against the wishes of the collective – and that government steps in to represent this collective interest. On this view it is easy to see how some believe that government is somehow "interfering" with the wishes of the individual in the name of some nebulous concern for the "public interest."

A more careful consideration would reveal, however, that environmental problems – because they are usually a matter of the private interest of Alpha versus the private interest of Beta – are more properly regarded as triadic matters; Alpha, Beta, and the state. To protect the interests of Alpha is to interfere with Beta, while to protect the interests of Beta is to interfere with Alpha. The state must do something, for to do nothing is to side with the party protected by the status quo property arrangement (Samuels, 1971, 1972). One party's government interference is another party's liberation. Put somewhat differently, when one party is constrained we can logically regard some other party as being liberated from the undesirable consequences of the prior situation.

The appeal of much standard environmental policy as presented in the economics literature is that it emphasizes process. That is, if we could but get the incentives right and then let volitional bargains ensue, all would – supposedly – be well. The engineering analogue is that of design standards. However, actual environmental policy is end-result oriented; it specifies, to a certain extent, the exact parameters of the acceptable outcome. The engineering analogue is that of performance standards. The conflicts arise when over-zealous economists claim that ubiquitous markets will solve all environmental problems, or when self-righteous planners and bureaucrats claim to know best about what should be done. Neither group will be explicit about the processes they advocate, each of which results in a reallocation – or an affirmation – of income (or benefit) streams among individuals in society, such reallocation or affirmation arising from the support for, or the suggested modification of, the structure of entitlements.

And this brings us back to my earlier assertion that environmental conflicts and policy are about the *incidence of costs and benefits*. The interest in deregulation and hence a greater reliance on the market suggests that these are not particularly happy times for those involved in policy reform aimed at environmental improvements. At the same time it would be a mistake of the first rank to assume that leaving things to the market will offer a solution to environmental conflicts that are characterized by (1) high transaction costs; (2) large and important nonmonetary benefits and costs; (3) uncertainty over the future; and (4) potential irreversibilities.

Markets are highly articulated institutional arrangements to channel individual initiative and avarice into putatively benign – but, if lucky, useful – directions. Markets are wonderful arrangements for those goods and services that conform to certain characteristics. Among these necessary traits are (1) highly divisible factors of production and outputs; (2) the absence of public goods; (3) the absence of externalities in use (no joint costs); (4) an absence of irreversibilities; and (5) a clear and precise structure of property rights. Unfortunately, many environmental matters are often characterized by (1) unclear property rights; (2) indivisibilities; (3) publicness, (4) contemporary or intertemporal externalities; and (5) irreversibilities. The preferred solution to environmental problems – though difficult to implement – would be a process yielding standards of performance that have been collectively (politically) determined, and then mechanisms for implementation that reward individual initiative, experimentation, and efficiency. This would entail a combination of collective choice and atomistic market processes where collective action has responsibilities for the larger social goals and then market processes are relied upon to achieve the most efficient implementation of those goals.

Put somewhat differently, economic theory cannot offer unique and *decisive* guidance on whether or not a particular scenic vista ought to be protected for perpetuity.[1] But once a decision has been made to protect it, then economic theory can offer important insights on efficient attainment of that goal. The problems arise when collective action becomes too specific, or when market processes are relied upon to decide whether the air should be clean, whether the homeless should be housed, or the extent of wilderness areas to be preserved. That is, concerns will be expressed when administrative rules become "too intrusive" in operational issues, and when the market has "too much" influence over the broader policy directions. It is, indeed, common to encounter planners who believe that operational issues are best solved by planning, just as there are economists who believe that the market can resolve all policy issues.

The fundamental policy problem in any economy is to determine the location of the boundary that divides the proper domain for collective choice from the proper domain for atomistic choice (the market). Research can be helpful if it is directed toward a determination of the attributes of certain land uses that carry special implications. That is, what are the attributes of different sites that hold important implications for non-owners? Are there available substitutes for these attributes? How great is the uncertainty surrounding the impacts on these attributes of current uses? How are social attitudes with respect to the environment changing? What are the policy implications of these changes? In what areas, and for which resources, is it absolutely essential that the larger public interest be protected? How should we define the public interest in environmental policy?

In one sense, *resource management regimes* have evolved over time in an effort to address some of these questions. Let us now turn to a discussion of four possible regimes.[2]

3   PROPERTY RIGHTS AND RESOURCE MANAGEMENT REGIMES

The above structures of right, duty, privilege, and no right operate within, indeed define, what I will call a *resource management regime*. Let me now become more specific by exploring the scope and nature of property rights inherent in four possible resource management regimes. The emphasis here is on regimes as human creations whose purpose is to *manage people* in their use of environmental resources.

Resource Management Regimes

A resource management regime is a structure of rights and duties characterizing the relationship of individuals to one another with respect to that particular environmental resource. Institutional arrangements are continually established (and redefined) in order to determine (and to modify) the scope and nature of the property regime over natural resources. Recall that property relations between two or more individuals (or groups) have been defined by stating that one party has an interest that is protected by a *right* only when all others have a *duty*. It is essential to understand that *property* is not an object such as land, but rather is *a right to a benefit stream that is only as secure as the duty of all others to respect the conditions that protect that stream.* When one has a *right* one has the expectation both in the law and in practice that one's claims will be respected by those with *duty*. And it is the essential function of the state to stand ready to refrain those with duty; if the state is unwilling, or unable, to ensure that compliance to duty, then rights are meaningless.

It is useful to note that much of the confusion in environmental policy stems from a fundamental misunderstanding of possible resource regimes. The "tragedy of the commons" allegory arising from the writings of Garrett Hardin has done much to confuse scholars and others, and hence meaningful progress in understanding resource management regimes has been stifled. One central purpose here is to expose the fallacy of received wisdom about group owned/managed natural resources. Among these regimes, common property carries the false and misplaced burden of "inevitable" resource degradation that properly lies with situations of *open access*. For some time now, Hardin's allegory of the "tragedy" has had remarkable currency among researchers and environmental policy makers. By confusing an open access regime (a free-for-all) with a common property regime (in which group size and behavioral rules are specified) the metaphor denies the very possibility for resource users to act together and institute checks and balances, rules and sanctions, for their own interaction within a given environment. The Hardin metaphor is not only socially and culturally simplistic, it is historically false (see Ciriacy-Wantrup and Bishop, 1975; Baker and Butlin, 1973; Dahlman, 1980). In practice, the "tragedy of the commons" metaphor deflects analytical attention away from the actual social arrangements able to overcome resource degradation and make common property regimes viable. Policy makers with incomplete knowledge of tenurial differences and systems of customary rights, encouraged by economists and others confused about the differences between open access regimes and common property regimes, may well attribute resource degradation to an assumed (but non-existent) regime of "common property." They will then often be led to reason that if only private property rights could be established the problem would be solved. Yet when resource degradation is observed on private lands – soil erosion, water pollution – the cause is assumed *not* to lie with the property structure at all, but is attributed, instead, to unduly high rates of time preference on the part of the owner, or some incentive problem that can be rectified with taxes or bribes. This asymmetry of logic – blaming the absence of private property in one instance, and slipping to alternative causal explanations when private property is present – obscures rather than clarifies the real issues involved.

For most purposes it is sufficient to consider four possible resource management regimes: (1) state property regimes; (2) private property regimes; (3) common property regimes; and (4) non-property regimes (open access). Each will be considered in turn.

State Property Regimes

In a state property regime, ownership and control over use rest in the hands of the state. Individuals and groups may be able to make use of the natural resources, but only at the forbearance of the state. National (or state) forests and parks and military reservations are examples of state property regimes. Shifts from state property to other types, or vice versa, are possible. For instance, the 1957 nationalization of much of Nepal's village forests by the government converted a common property regime at the village level into a state property regime.[3] The state may either directly manage and control the use of state-owned natural resources through government agencies, or lease the natural resource to groups or individuals who are thus given usufruct rights for a specified period of time. The "tree growing associations" in West Bengal (and elsewhere in India), consisting of groups of landless or marginal farmers who are given a block of marginal public land for tree planting, are examples of such usufructuary rights. The members are not granted titles in land, but the group is given usufruct rights *on the land* and *ownership rights* of its produce (Cernea, 1985).

State property regimes remove most managerial discretion from the user, and generally convey no long-term expectations in terms of tenure security. At the opposite "pole", as it were, we find individual property rights – most commonly referred to as "private property."

Private Property Regimes

The most familiar property regime is that of private property and hence there is not much need here for great elaboration. While most think of private property as individual property, note that all corporate property is private property, and yet it is administered by a group. There is also a tendency to consider private property as bestowing full and absolute control on the owner. However, it is well to keep in mind that an owner is faced with a number of strictures and obligations in the use of so-called "private" land and its related natural resources; few owners are entirely free to do as they wish with such assets. In light of this, only a few comments on private property seem appropriate at this time.

The fortuitous results emanating from the private control of land and related natural resources arise from the simple fact that the individual (or group) owner can make management decisions – and investments – in the full knowledge that good stewardship will return private rewards. There can be no mystery about this, and its appeal is practically as old as recorded history. There are only a few assumptions that render this particular property regime socially preferred under most circumstances. First we must assume that the owner chooses to manage well and to produce those things that are valued by society. As long as landowners produce wheat, tomatoes, trees, and cotton all is well. When landowners begin to produce marijuana, opium, and cocaine then the rather automatic beneficence of private property rights disappears. So, the compelling nature of private property regimes is moderated by the ends to which that particular property regime is put.

Secondly, private property is socially compelling as long as the general interests of the owner are rather in accord with the interests of non-owners. That is, if we assume that there are no untoward external effects emanating from the use of land and natural resources then complete autonomy properly rests with the owner. If soil erosion, polluting smoke, clangerous sounds, or insufferable odors emanate from a private property regime then, once again, the sanctity of that particular institutional setup will be under close scrutiny.

Thirdly, private property is socially useful as long as it is an inducement to industry rather than a substitute to industry. To quote Tawney in a historical treatment of private property:

> Property was to be an aid to creative work, not an alternative to it.
> . . . The patentee was secured protection for a new invention, in order
> to secure him the fruits of his own brain, but the monopolist who

grew fat on the industry of others was to be put down. The law of the village bound the peasant to use his land, not as he himself might find most profitable, but to grow the corn the village needed. . . . Property reposed, in short, not merely upon convenience, or the appetite for gain, but on a moral principle. It was protected not only for the sake of those who owned, but for the sake of those who worked and of those for whom their work provided. It was protected, because, without security for property, wealth could not be produced or the business of society carried on. (Tawney, 1981, p. 139)

The case for private property regimes, as with all property regimes, ultimately rests on judgments concerning its social utility.[4] Those who celebrate private property as some "natural right" will be hard pressed to defend private property regimes in parts of Latin America where over 80 percent of the land is owned by as few as 5 percent of the families. Would the defenders of this situation suggest that some individuals are born with a greater complement of "natural rights" than others? The very strength of private property regimes in land and related natural resources is also, it turns out, its greatest weakness. Private property is the legally and socially sanctioned ability to exclude others – it allows the fortunate owner to force others to go elsewhere. Additionally, we are often told that private property leads to the "highest and best use of land." With large segments of Latin America's best agricultural land devoted to cattle ranching while food crops fight for survival on steep and rocky mountain sides, skeptics should be excused if they challenge that particular conclusion. Private property is not necessarily theft, as Proudhon put it, but a good deal of theft has ended up as private property. This is especially true in the western world where European colonizers appropriated vast terrain inhabited by tribal peoples.

The obvious successes of private control of agricultural and industrial land is not being questioned here – except to the extent that the above assumptions can be said to be violated. But to suggest, therefore, that private property regimes are optimal for all natural resources is a *non sequitur*. While state property regimes are prevalent in natural resource management, there are a number of instances in which common property regimes may also be worth consideration.

Common Property Regimes

The third regime is the common property regime (*res communes*). First, common property represents *private property for the group of co-owners* (since all others are excluded from use and decision making).

Second, *individuals* have rights (and duties) in a common property regime (Ciriacy-Wantrup and Bishop, 1975). In one important sense, then, common property has something very much in common with private property – exclusion of non-owners. In that sense we may think of common property as *corporate group property*. The property-owning groups vary in nature, size, and internal structure across a broad spectrum, but they are social units with definite membership and boundaries, with certain common interests, with at least some interaction among members, with some common cultural norms, and often their own endogenous authority systems. Tribal groups or subgroups, or subvillages, neighborhoods, small transhumant groups, kin systems, or extended families are all possible examples. These groupings hold customary ownership of certain natural resources such as farm land, grazing land, and water sources (McCay and Acheson, 1988; McKean, 1986; National Academy of Sciences, 1986; Netting, 1976; Wade, 1986).

Corporate group property regimes are not incompatible with distinct individual use of one or another segment of the resources held under common property. For instance, in customary tenure systems over much of Africa the ownership of certain farmland may be vested in a group, and the group's leaders then allocate use rights on portions of the land to various individuals or families. As long as those individuals cultivate their plot, no other person has the right to use it or to benefit from its produce. But note that the cultivator holds use rights only (usufruct) and is unable to alienate or transfer either the ownership or the use of that land to another individual. Once the current user ceases to put the land to good use it reverts to the jurisdiction of the corporate ownership of the group.

Note that common property of this kind is fundamentally different from the land-based property regimes in collective farms or agricultural cooperatives prevalent in the once centrally planned socialist economies of Eastern Europe, and still surviving (although undergoing change) in the Soviet Union. Land in these entities does not belong to the members of the collective as common property. Rather, the land belongs to the state. The profound restructuring now going on within Soviet agriculture (similar in some respects to what has happened in China) reveals the impact of state property and its effects on management patterns for natural resources that are *not* common (or group) property. The most telling aspect is restrictions over the products of labor applied to those resources.

Contrary to such state ownership regimes, the customary common property regimes in the developing world are characterized by group/corporate ownership with management authority vested in the respective group or its leaders. In many developing countries, some of the resources in the public domain (that is, non-private land) are managed as common property, some are managed by the public sector as state property, and some are not managed at all but are, instead, open access.

Consider, if only briefly, the incentives that exist in a common property regime. This is important in view of the fact that a widespread fallacy would have us believe that the only incentive is to pillage and plunder natural resources. To the contrary, the correct understanding defines a common property regime by group ownership in which the behaviors of all members of the group are subject to accepted rules and open for all to see. It is not stretching the truth to say that in many cultures conformity with group norms at the local level is an effective sanction against antisocial behavior. A viable common property regime thus has a built-in structure of economic and non-economic incentives that encourages compliance with existing conventions and institutions. Unfortunately, in many settings, those sanctions and incentives have become inoperative – or dysfunctional – largely because of pressures and forces beyond the control of the group, or because of internal processes that the groups were not able to master; this will be elaborated in chapter 6. But that does not undermine the essential point that, in a social setting in which individual conformity to group norms is the dominant ethic, common property regimes have a cultural context compatible with and indeed vital for effective performance.

Essential for any property regime is an authority system able to ensure that the expectations of rights holders are met. Compliance, protected and reinforced by an authority system, is a necessary condition for the viability of any property regime. Private property would be nothing without the requisite authority system that makes certain that the rights and duties are adhered to. The same requirements exist for common property. When the authority system breaks down – for whatever reason – then the management or self-management of resource use cannot be exercised any longer and, for all practical purposes, common property (*res communes*) degenerates into open access (*res nullius*).

It is not just the property regime (joint possession) alone that explains compliance and "wise" natural resource use. The common property regime as a system is broader than the set of possession entitlements that is its core; it includes also use rights, exchange rights, distribution entitlements, a management subsystem, and authority instruments as means of management. When any part of this complex system is undermined or annihilated, the entire system malfunctions up to a degree at which it ceases to be what it was. It is indeed the management subsystem, with its authority mechanisms and ability to enforce operating rules and system-maintenance provisions that insures that the particular property regime is adhered to, and that its systemic integrity (or system equilibrium) is well protected, thus enabling it to operate in a well-balanced manner. This, in principle, is not different from the ways in which the other property regimes operate as systems. For instance, in private property regimes the owner/manager also relies on the authority of the state and its coercive power to assure compliance and to prevent intrusion by non-owners. If this (or other) authority would not be exercised, the private property regime too would collapse and would become open access.[5]

In common property regimes two problems may arise. The first is that a breakdown in compliance by co-owners may be difficult to prevent because this will entail loss of opportunity arising from changes elsewhere in the economy. If spreading privatization precludes seasonal adaptation to fluctuating resource conditions then overuse of a local resource may be necessary by members of the group. Secondly, if the modern state holds common property in low esteem – that is, if the state disregards the interests of those segments of the population largely dependent upon common property resources – then external threats to common property will not receive the same governmental response as would a threat to private property. The willingness of the modern state to legitimize and protect different property regimes is partly explained by the state's perception of the importance of the citizens holding different types of property rights. If pastoralists are regarded as politically marginal – a common occurrence in many parts of the world – then the property regimes central to pastoralism will be only indifferently protected against threat from others. If those threatening pastoralist property regimes – sedentary agriculturalists for example – happen to enjoy more favor from the state, then the protection of grasslands under common property against encroachments for cultivation will be haphazard at best.

Note that the best land in most settings has already been privatized and the worst has been left in the "public domain" – as state property, as common property (*res communes*), or as open access (*res nullius*). It is not legitimate to ask of common property regimes that they manage highly variable and low-productivity resources, and also adapt and adjust to severe internal and external pressures, when conditions beyond the bounds of that common property regime preclude the adaptation to those internal and external pressures. That is, the internal pressure of population growth may be impossible to resolve if traditional adaptation mechanisms – hiving off for instance – are now precluded by increased population growth *beyond the confines of the common property regime under study.*

Likewise, in many settings private property and associated fences are encroaching on common property regimes, thus preventing the traditional movements of a people and their livestock. In these circumstances it is hardly legitimate to blame the common property regime for increased use caused by encroachment. Private property regimes *appear* to be stable and adaptive because they have the social and legal sanction to exclude excess population, and effectively to resist, through the power of the state, unwanted intrusions. These powers have been eroded for common property regimes. To see the exclusionary aspect of private property, recall the effects of primogeniture. The dispossession of younger sons (to say nothing of *all* daughters) is regarded as a *costless* social process and therefore it looks as though private property is robust and adaptable. Private property in such a setting may work for the oldest son; but those with no rights in the estate may be harder to convince.

Common property is in essence "private" property for the group and in that sense it is a group decision regarding who shall be excluded. But when options for gainful and promising exclusion of excess population have been destroyed by surrounding political, cultural, or economic events, then those engaged in the joint use of a resource are left with no option but to eat into their capital. However, to blame this situation on their failure to create private property is absurd. Common property is *not* the free-for-all of open access resources. Individuals have rights and obligations in situations of common (non-individual) property, just as in private individual property situations. The difference between private and common property is not to be found in the nature of the rights and duties as much as in the number to which inclusion or exclusion applies. The difference is also in the unwillingness of the group to evict redundant individuals when that eviction will almost certainly relegate the evicted to starvation. In a sense, the group agrees to lower its own standard of living rather than single out particular members for disinheritance.

Finally, some will say that common property lands must be privatized in order to save them. Since there is no clear evidence that privatization reduces land exploitation when other economic incentives are left unaltered, this conclusion must be challenged. Moreover, since privatization will simply mean exclusion and the shifting of population elsewhere (to city slums or to other common property areas) the appeal of privatization as a solution is suspect.

Open Access Regimes

Finally we have the open access regime in which there is no property (*res nullius*). Because there are no property rights in an open access situation, it is logically inconsistent to assert – as many often do – that "everybody's property is nobody's property." It can only be said that everybody's access is nobody's property. Whether it is a lake fishery, grazing forage, or fuelwood, a resource under an open access regime will belong to the party to first exercise control over it. The investment in (or improvement of) natural resources under open access regimes must first focus on this institutional dimension. If property and management arrangements are not determined, and if the investment is in the form of a capital asset such as improved tree species or range revegetation, the institutional vacuum of open access insures that use rates will eventually deplete the asset.

Open access results from the absence, or the breakdown, of a management and authority system whose very purpose was to introduce and enforce a set of norms of behavior among participants with respect to that particular natural resource. When valuable natural resources are available to the first party to effect capture, it is either because those natural resources have never before been incorporated into a regulated social system, or because they have become open access resources through institutional failures that have undermined former collective or individual management regimes.

Those responsible for the vast literature on the so-called "tragedy of the commons," and on the problems of alleged "common property," have never bothered to understand the essence of property. They apparently believe that "property" is a physical object such as a forested area, or a piece of land, or a school of fish. By confusing the social dimension and the *concept* of property with a *physical object* it is then easy for them to imagine that open access constitutes "common property." That is, if fish are mistakenly thought of as "property," and if fishing is available to all who might be interested, then the "property" is thought to be "commonly available to all." It is this conceptual confusion that permits them to allege that "everybody's property (fish) is nobody's property (fish)." Since no-one owns the fish, it is said to be common to all. But of course property is *not a physical object but is instead a social relation*. On that correct interpretation, there can be no confusion about open access and common property. The four types of resource regimes are listed in table 2.2.

Table 2.2   Four types of property regimes

State property	Individuals have *duty* to observe use/access rules determined by controlling/managing agency. Agencies have *right* to determine use/access rules
Private property	Individuals have *right* to undertake socially acceptable uses, and have *duty* to refrain from socially unacceptable uses. Others (called "non-owners") have *duty* to refrain from preventing socially acceptable uses, and have a *right* to expect that only socially acceptable uses will occur
Common property	The management group (the "owners") has *right* to exclude nonmembers, and nonmembers have *duty* to abide by exclusion. Individual members of the management group (the "co-owners") have both *rights* and *duties* with respect to use rates and maintenance of the thing owned
Nonproperty	No defined group of users or "owners" and benefit stream is available to anyone. Individuals have both *privilege* and *no right* with respect to use rates and maintenance of the asset. The asset is an "open access resource"

Source: Bromley, 1989a

Property and Resource Management

A major distinction among the first three types of resource management regimes rests with the decision-making process inherent in each property regime. Specifically, the private property regime is usually regarded as one in which a single owner can decide what shall be done. Those inclined to regard private property as the most efficient institutional form for resource management and environmental protection will usually have this in mind. They would point out that even a well-organized common property regime still requires consensus among all the co-owners before certain actions can be taken. It is this *transaction cost* that will be blamed for the cumbersome nature of common property regimes – even assuming that the collective has managed to solve the problems of group size and free riding. It needs to be noted, however, that the very notion of "transaction costs" is culturally specific – one person's tedious meeting (a cost) may be another's most enjoyable activity (a benefit). That is, in some cultures, such meetings take on great social significance and become the venue for a wide array of useful social interactions.

In a situation of open access each potential user has complete autonomy to use the resource since no-one has the legal ability to keep any potential user out. The natural resource is subject to the rule of capture and belongs to no-one until it is in someone's physical possession. In the case of air pollution, all who wish to discharge their wastes are free to do so since no party has the right to prevent that outcome. The polluter has privilege, and others have no right. Only when air pollution is made illegal do erstwhile polluters have a duty, while others now have a right. Likewise, in an open access fishery, the fish belong to the first party to effect capture. There are no property rights in this regime, there is only possession. That is, property – *a social contract that defines an individual and an object of value vis-à-vis all other individuals* – cannot exist when an individual must physically capture the object before he / she can exercise effective control. Having *property* means not having to stand guard over something; the social recognition that gives property its content means that others have a duty to respect the owner's interest in the thing owned.[6]

With common property forests, rangelands, and fisheries, some natural resource degradation arises from population growth within the relevant social unit having rights to the resource. The entailed increase in the use of the given natural resource, though exceeding the ability of the renewable resource to sustain its annual yield, cannot be stopped because of the nominal right of every villager to take what he / she needs to survive. As a village grows, and therefore as the number of rights holders grows apace, the total demands on the physical environment and its resources will ultimately exceed the rate of natural regeneration. Failure to deal appropriately with the change in the size of the group affects the equilibrium and integrity of the system. If, for instance, the village believes that all of this larger population has a right to take what is needed, in a situation when the supply remains constant, then it is obvious that very soon no villager will be able to satisfy that right with anything other than what he / she can capture by being there first. Because of the decline of effective social conventions and institutions to regulate total use, a common property regime for the group becomes an open access regime for those within the group.

To improve the situation requires a reduction in total offtake entitlement (and in *actual* offtake) until the resource base can generate sufficient annual yield to meet the needs of the new (lower) harvesting, and allow for some continued regeneration. The obvious problem is to meet the reduced needs of those deemed to be excessive claimants on the resource base until that regenerative capacity is restored. Alternatively, if it is determined that the given resource will never be able to sustain the increased level of demands to be placed on it, then there must be some capital investment to augment it and its output. But capital investment in the absence of a *prior institutional solution* will simply assure that the new asset is squandered as the old one was.

Hence with open access regimes the necessary precondition for any successful policy prescription is that the property regime be *converted away from open access*. Whether it goes to private individual property, to common property, or to state property is a policy choice that will have to be made on the basis of the conditions at hand. Regardless of which specific regime is chosen, it will require work to establish a new set of rules. Those rules must be made known to all relevant individuals, and new management patterns and social authority systems must be established to assure that those new rules are followed.

As regards the comparative advantage of one institutional choice over another, note that to bring resources under a regime of individualized private property in the developing countries will often conflict with prevailing socio-cultural values. Depending on the nature of the asset – and on the socio-cultural characteristics of its users – it may sometimes be more appropriate to restore a common property regime than to attempt to promote privatization. Recall also that a common property regime at the village or subvillage (neighborhood) level constitutes *private property* for the group, with the attendant co-equal rights and duties for the individual members.

Obviously, converting open access situations to common property systems is a complex process that cannot be done by administrative decree. When such a process is attempted, the design of the change process must take into account a number of general variables and their local context. These variables pertain both to the physical environment and to the existing socio-cultural systems. There are at least four main sets of variables that are critical for such a process and they must be meticulously considered if this process is to be deliberately pursued. These variables are (1) the nature of the resource itself; (2) the supply-demand conditions of the resource; (3) the characteristics of the users of the resource; and (4) the characteristics of the legal and political environment in which the users reside (Ostrom, 1986).

Each of these sets of variables must be detailed and examined in a given context to determine at which specific values the variables would lend themselves, in a greater or lesser degree, to such a conversion in property regime. With respect to the nature of the resource, if open access is to be converted to an effective common property regime, then the existence of clear resource boundaries, small (manageable) resource size and scope, and accessible information about the condition of the resource are critical. With respect to supply and demand conditions, the resource's relative scarcity *vis-à-vis* the demand placed on it will be critical, as will situations in which some users have a sufficiently large stake in the careful management of the resource. With respect to user characteristics, the conversion from open access to common property will be facilitated in those instances in which the size of the user group is small, the users are reasonably homogeneous in important socio-economic characteristics, and the users reside in close proximity to the resource. Finally, it is important whether local users are prevented by the government from exercising local initiatives regarding management, whether they have prior experience with organizations for solving similar problems, and whether there are overlapping institutional arrangements and organizations that can complement the nascent resource management effort.

The introduction of a state property regime may sometimes be proposed to address the resource degradation problem. Indeed, a striking feature of the last two decades in the developing countries has been the rise of governmental authority for the management of local natural resources through central regulatory policies, new legal frameworks, project financing, and direct administration. However, most analysts agree that this shift in the locus of control has not resulted in effective natural resource management. It has, instead, simply weakened local customary regimes. This subject will be discussed in greater detail in chapter 6.

The *appearance* of environmental management created through the establishment of governmental agencies, and the aura of coherent policy created by issuance of decrees prohibiting entry to – and harvesting from – state property, has led to continued degradation of resources under the tolerant eye of government agencies. If the current degradation of state lands is to be arrested it will require that current practices of indifferent enforcement be corrected (Thomson, 1977) and that staffing levels and incentives be sufficient to administer and manage that domain which the government has taken unto itself. Unfortunately, most state property regimes are examples of the state's reach exceeding its grasp. Many states have taken on far more resource management authority than they can be expected to carry out effectively. More critically, management by such decrees and proclamations sets the government against the peasant when, in fact, successful resource management requires the opposite.

4   PROPERTY RIGHTS AS POLICY INSTRUMENTS

Economists, at least since Coase (1960), now have little difficulty in regarding property rights as factors of production; firms can buy and sell property rights just as they can buy and sell other factors. The obvious corollary of this view is that property rights are also policy instruments. That is, one can alter property rights among individuals and groups to accomplish certain desired ends. I have earlier suggested that environmental policy is, in essence, concerned with altering actual or presumed property rights among independent agents. One sees this interpreted in several ways. One view, popular in the "deregulation and privatization" fad of the 1980s, was to create private property rights in natural resources and then to "let the market work." This interest in the concepts of property and of property derives, I suggest, from the recent belief that government regulations had somehow been excessive. Those who have been speaking most enthusiastically on behalf of market processes seem to suggest that all that is needed is to establish property rights – by which they invariably mean *private* property rights – and then most of the activities in which government has been engaged can safely be taken over by individuals.

On the other hand there is a concern that this new-found interest in property rights is being used as a Trojan horse to discredit and to undermine collective action to deal with environmental issues. While economic concepts and language are being used, there seems to be a certain fear that much recent environmental policy is driven less by economic logic than by an ideological position that government is necessarily bad and that volitional bargains are necessarily good. While it *is* correct to favor clearly defined property rights in environmental resources, that is not the issue that must concern public policy. The issue of relevance is precisely one of *who will get those rights, and thus who will have the effective protection of the state to do as they wish?* Equally important, property rights indicate who must pay whom to have their interests given effect. Those most avid in their zeal for less government and more individualistic bargaining make a number of implicit assumptions to support their position. If one assumes perfect mobility of all factors of production and of all outputs, if one assumes perfect divisibility of the above factors and products (that is, lumpiness is precluded), if one assumes perfect and costless information among all participants to a possible bargain, and finally if one assumes perfect capital and contingent-claims markets, then economic theory suggests that the resulting allocation of society's resources will be Pareto optimal; there is no possible reallocation of any resources that would improve the utility of one member of society without decreasing the utility of at least one other person.

This happy state follows, logically, from the assumptions listed, and against this "optimal" allocation no government could do any better.

As if this were not convincing enough, the market celebrants add two more observations for good measure. They will admit that, of course, the initial endowment of resources – by which we mean property rights and wealth positions – will influence the ultimate distribution of welfare across members of society, but since economists as objective scientists are said to be precluded from passing any meaningful judgments on this matter, we must leave that to the politicians to worry about. They would claim that as scientists we can only assume that if the current distribution of wealth and rights were not acceptable it would be changed via political action.[7] The second observation, also deriving from the work of Coase, is that under the proper assumptions the initial assignment of property rights does not matter as long as volitional bargains are possible; the rights will go to the highest bidder and efficiency will be assured regardless. As suggested earlier in this chapter, for this last result to be plausible, two further assumptions are required. The first assumption is that all costs of transacting among individuals are zero. Transaction costs are of three types: (1) information costs; (2) bargaining costs; and (3) enforcement costs. It should come as little surprise that few economists consider this particular assumption to be very likely in the real world.

The second assumption for the Coasian result to hold is that the wealth effects of alternative rights assignments – and ultimate allocation – are zero. This requires that we ignore the obvious difference in my wealth position if I have something that you wish to buy, or if you have the same thing that I am forced to buy from you. The Coase theorem, of such great comfort to the market celebrants, is more properly called the Coase tautology. For it follows immediately that if wealth effects are assumed away, and if it is costless to engage in and to enforce bargains, then obviously the initial assignment of property rights is immaterial to the ultimate allocation of resources. With these required assumptions some might question the relevance of the Coasian results to the real world, and Coase himself went on to show how transaction costs and wealth effects modify his simplistic finding.

But the latter-day disciples of Coase, perhaps with a more well-developed ideological agenda, are not so circumspect. It is from these quarters that one hears bold pronouncements about the thoroughgoing wisdom of establishing (private) property rights and then letting the market work. We are told, for instance, of how the Audubon Society bought precious swamp lands in Louisiana and then proceeded to sell oil-exploration rights to petroleum companies; this is offered as proof that private markets are much wiser mechanisms for resource allocation than a government that was inclined to protect the swamp without letting in the oil producers. It is also offered as evidence that private entrepreneurs – even those as single purposed as the Audubon Society – will act in their self-interest and make everybody better off in the process. To the market advocates it is now known as "doing well while doing good."

But notice something critical about the Audubon deal – namely the matter of third-party effects. Specifically, what assurance is there that the bargain struck between the Audubon Society and a particular oil company bears any resemblance at all to the bargain that would be struck if the interests of others concerned about the swamp were taken into account? The particular deal being celebrated is evidence of only one thing – that it is possible for the Audubon Society to get the price and extraction conditions it wants for oil under its land. There is no assurance, nor can there be in this thin and attenuated market setting, that social welfare is enhanced by the sale of oil. We cannot even say that the agreed-upon price is socially correct: the Audubon Society and the oil company are hardly the full set of relevant interests regarding the marginal social value of another barrel of oil relative to a pristine swamp. It is, quite simply, a fallacy of composition to assume that this particular bargain represents social optimality.

Advocating transferable property rights so that volitional exchange can occur is the triumph of process, and it requires that we accept on faith the benevolent outcomes promised, but not proven, by the advocates of market exchange. What is left unsaid is that there are several ways in which property rights might be established, and then several ways in which rights might be given effect. One can have a property right that is protected by a property rule; it can be protected by a liability rule, and it can be a right that is inalienable. This matter will be developed more fully in the following chapter.

It matters very much in the real world of imperfect, costly, and asymmetric information among participants to a bargain who it is that obtains the initial assignment of entitlements, and the nature of that entitlement. When wealth effects are admitted it is easy to see that the initial assignment of rights is everything. If one needs to be reminded of this, imagine a pauper dealing with a millionaire, and ponder the resulting bargain under two different initial assignments of some valuable right – say access to the only water in a vast desert. To assign or allocate rights is also to assign or allocate power and the control over future benefit streams. A property right is, above all else, the ability to hold something off the market until a possible buyer meets the price that the owner is free to set.

The environmental policy problem is nothing but a struggle about who shall have control over the stream of future environmental services. That is, will that control reside with those who wish to dump their industrial or municipal wastes into the air or water, or will it reside instead with those who wish to see the natural environment maintained in some acceptable state of quality? To give an environmental organization such as the Audubon Society a property right which it chooses not to sell may appear to be no different from giving the US Department of the Interior ultimate control over the same benefit stream. But there is an important difference. There will be one aggregate level of environmental protection if the Department of the Interior has the property rights over unique habitats, and another if the Audubon Society has such rights. For the Audubon Society can only purchase as much endangered habitat as its budget will support. And who is to suggest that its budget, deriving entirely from private philanthropy, is of the socially optimal size? Moreover, who is to say that the Board of Directors of the Audubon Society speaks for the full citizenry in deciding what to purchase and to protect? Since when does a society deserve only as much environmental protection as can be purchased with private philanthropy?

I do not wish to imply that the Department of the Interior will give us the socially optimal level of environmental protection either. But the conditions are certainly different. The Department of the Interior, as a governmental organization, is politically responsible to the citizenry through legislative oversight. However imperfectly this may work, the presumption must be that the wishes of the full citizenry are more properly catered for than would be the case if environmental protection were left to the ability to pay by a few members of society given to philanthropy. I do not challenge the efficacy of individualized property rights as policy instruments to help us to avoid the waste inherent in uniform environmental standards. Marketable permits for air and water pollutants are very good examples of this approach. But let us be clear about what is at work here. We have a marginal arena in which trades can occur based on potential savings among similarly situated firms in an economic and ecological environment that is defined for them by a regulatory machinery that sets overall standards. The purpose of issuing transferable property rights is simply to facilitate the search for a more cost-effective way to achieve the predetermined – and collectively determined – standards.

5 SUMMARY

The understanding that property regimes – whether private property, state property, or common property – are complex constellations of rights, duties, privileges, and exposures to the rights of others would seem to advance the prospects for a more careful formulation of natural resource policy. It also helps to illustrate the conventional fallacy that considers "common property" as a free-for-all more properly understood as an open access regime. If this fundamental confusion can be struck from the vernacular much important progress would follow immediately. But the particular property regime is only part of the issue. An equally important part concerns the relationship between property regimes and the larger market processes that influence resource allocation.

The recent political climate has pushed to the fore the debate about market versus nonmarket processes, and in that milieu it would seem that a number of individuals are making strong claims for the wisdom and beneficence of thoroughgoing markets in managing environmental resources. These claims for volitional exchange are supported by appeal to a body of economic theory that is not made explicit, for if it were the appeal of the proffered solution would be clearly undermined. The advocacy of these optimistic solutions to environmental policy serves only to galvanize the concerns of a number of others who believe that, while markets may be fine for a few commodities, they may be quite pernicious in the management of natural resources. By promising too much for markets, the zealots have undermined the constructive role for bargained exchange in a restricted domain of resource management. There are obvious arenas within which market-like processes can enhance the effectiveness of environmental policy. My earlier reference to transferable discharge permits is but one example. Another area is in that of allocating fishing quotas among a set number of fishermen, or moving water from low-value to high-value uses. But if notions persist that thoroughgoing markets will properly indicate how clean our air or our water should be, then otherwise congenial people will understandably reject the advice of economists even for those areas where market processes are clearly advantageous.

NOTES

1   Of course economics can suggest how to assign monetary values to that scenic vista.

2   Some of the following material is a revised version of parts of Bromley and Cernea (1989). I am grateful to my co-author and the World Bank for permission to use this material here.

3   Some abandoned private forests were also incorporated into the newly nationalized forest domain.

4   See Becker (1977) for a discussion of the philosophical foundations of private property. His work is also summarized in Bromley (1989a). See Sax (1983) for a discussion of recent changes in perceptions regarding the social utility, in certain situations, of private property rights.

5   Wealthy (and even middle class) families in many developing countries often must hire their own private guards to protect their homes and belongings, a clear example of the inability of collective (public) measures to uphold rights and the correlated duties.

6   This important distinction between property as a social convention and property as mere possession has not been helped by recent theoretical literature. See, for example, Sugden (1986). Recall the Kantian distinction between intelligible possession and empirical possession.

7   I shall have more to say on this issue in chapter 10.

3
Entitlements by Property Rules, Liability Rules, and Inalienability Rules

> In any large group general rules, standards, and principles must be the main instrument of social control, and not particular directions given to each individual separately. If it were not possible to communicate general standards of conduct, which multitudes of individuals could understand, without further direction . . . nothing that we now recognize as law could exist.
>
> H. L. A. Hart, *The Concept of Law*

1 INTRODUCTION

In the previous chapter I was concerned to establish the conceptual basis of property rights through understanding such rights as correlates. One cannot logically have a right to something unless all others have a correlated duty. Conversely, when I have no rights it means that others enjoy privilege in that these other individuals are free to act without regard to my interests. When one has a right it means, above all else, that the collective has agreed to recognize and to protect one's interests in a particular outcome; this is what establishes the right. But of course rights – or entitlements – can be given protection in several ways. In this chapter I shall elaborate on these alternative ways in which the collective can agree to protect one's rights.

An earlier version of this chapter appeared in the *Journal of Economic Issues*, 12, 43–60, March 1978. I am grateful to the journal for permission to reproduce parts of it here.

I have yet another purpose here, and that is to suggest several considerations which will be helpful in gaining a more complete understanding of the myriad ways in which we impose costs on each other. To say that externalities are pervasive in a modern complex society is to be somewhat redundant. What follows, then, is an effort to focus analytical attention on the economic relationships among economic agents through a more detailed treatment of the concept of entitlements. Moreover, it also focuses attention on some of the important attributes of human interference that we call externalities. Rather than assume that transaction costs are low (or zero), rather than assume that only two parties need engage in the bargaining, rather than assume a unique damage function, and so on, I shall here evaluate different forms of human interference precisely for these attributes, for it is only out of a clearer understanding of the structure and assignment of property rights, and from a better understanding of the multifaceted nature of mutual interference, that we shall be able to develop meaningful advice on how to reduce externalities in an increasingly interdependent and complex world.

2   ON PROPERTY RIGHTS AND ENTITLEMENTS

According to some authors, property rights evolve to internalize externalities when the economic gains become greater than the implied costs to render the change possible (Demsetz, 1967). On such a view an externality is said to persist whenever the costs of change exceed the anticipated gains. Thus, if a factory pollutes a certain river and there is no action to change the situation, it must mean that the potential gains are less than the implied costs; once the gains increase – or the transaction costs fall – then there will be action to change the property rights and so internalize the externality. The policy conclusion that one reaches from this definitional approach to a "theory" of property rights is that what exists must be optimal, for if it were not, it would obviously change. That is, once society values clean rivers sufficiently with respect to the manufactured products made cheaper by the disposal services of the river, we shall see a restructuring of property rights such that firms may no longer dump their wastes. This justification of the status quo is convenient to those who are concerned with government "intervention," since it seems to provide a benefit–cost logic to the choice of alternative institutional arrangements. But we must take a closer look at such reasoning in order to obtain a better understanding of the distinction between various kinds of rights. To facilitate this enquiry I shall here talk of entitlements (or rights) protected under three different structures: (1) those entitlements protected by property rules; (2) those entitlements protected by liability rules; and (3) inalienable entitlements.

Under a type I entitlement Alpha may not take actions which interfere with Beta without the latter's consent; Beta has a right against Alpha protected by a *property rule*. Under a type II entitlement Alpha may proceed even though the action may interfere with Beta, but Beta must be compensated; here Beta's rights are protected by a *liability rule*. Third, under a type III entitlement Alpha is free to undertake actions which may interfere with Beta and Alpha can only be stopped if Beta buys off Alpha; here we say that Alpha's right is protected by a *property rule*. Finally, under a type IV entitlement, Beta may stop Alpha from actions which may interfere with Beta's interests, but must compensate Alpha for the cessation; Alpha is protected by a *liability rule*.

With this elaboration of rights, it is possible to see that we can draw out a number of implications for environmental policy. In those instances where Alpha may not interfere with Beta in the absence of Beta's prior consent, one sees the traditional private property right; my land is mine for my exclusive enjoyment, and no-one may use it without my prior permission. In some instances I may allow persons to cross my land for no compensation. In other cases various forms of tribute may be required, but regardless of the compensation, the purpose is clear – to gain my acceptance for allowing the other person to benefit from my property right. If I own a lake-front lot and access to the water, others may use my land for access only upon gaining my permission; here my right is protected by a property rule. This is called a type I entitlement (Calabresi and Melamed, 1972).

Now consider the other type of property rule. Assume that I live in a home separated from the lake by a piece of land upon which the owner decides to construct a fence, thereby blocking my view of the sunrise and the boats on the lake. The other individual (Alpha) possesses an entitlement to interfere with me and can only be prevented from doing so if I intercede and agree to provide adequate compensation. If a zoning ordinance emerges from some form of public action which prevents the construction of fences over two feet high without the consent of others, then public action has converted a type III entitlement into a type I entitlement; here we have extended the notion of private property from physical objects such as land to more intangible objects such as a view.[1]

Notice the difference in the incidence of transaction costs under the two types of property rules. In the first case (type I) those who wish to interfere with me must obtain my prior consent – the burden of proof is on them to see that the hoped-for action will not be seriously detrimental to me. That means that they must confront me individually (or as a collective) to seek my permission to do what they want. If this type I property rule governs fence construction, the would-be fence builders must approach me and be prepared to meet my reservation price for having my view blocked. If the other situation obtains (type III), then the burden is on me to approach the would-be fence builders and be prepared to offer a price to compensate them for not building the fence. In the first setting (type I) the ability of those who wish to bargain with me is constrained by their income and wealth position. In the latter setting (type III) it is my income and wealth position which constrains my ability to impose my tastes on the fence builder. The incidence of transaction costs is central to the matter of environmental economics and has a profound effect on the definition of the "ideal outcome." If I have a right protected by a property rule (type I) and the fence builders cannot proceed without my consent – and I do not give it – then no fence gets built, and an observer would say that the two parties attempted to reach an agreement but could not. Therefore the outcome (no fence) would appear to be ideal. On the other hand, if there is the other property rule (type III) and I am unable to muster sufficient resources to prevent the fence from being built, then the observer would note that an attempt at bargaining had been made and conclude that since the fence was actually built, that must represent the ideal outcome. The structure of entitlements leads to alternative notions of the ideal outcome.[2] Thus, it is the structure of entitlements which defines the nature of the bargaining process between two or more parties in environmental disputes, and hence defines the "optimal" outcome: under one configuration a fence seems optimal, under another no fence seems optimal. While a fence may not seem a compelling environmental problem, the logic of the story holds whether one is concerned with air or water pollution, the siting of locally unwanted facilities, or toxic waste problems.

Now consider the liability rules. Under a type II entitlement an individual may undertake actions which may interfere with me but that individual must be prepared to compensate me; I am protected not by a property rule, as before, but by a liability rule. Under the type III property rule protecting the other party the burden was on me to buy off the other individual, and my ability was constrained by my income. Now I must be compensated for the other's actions, and my income is no longer a constraint on the bargain. It will be necessary to engage an independent assessor (the public sector, perhaps) to arrive at "fair" compensation, but the new structure of entitlements has shifted the situation considerably in my favor. Now if a fence is threatened which would block my view, the burden is not on me to buy out the fence builder, nor is the burden on the fence builder to seek my prior approval via bargaining. Instead, the fence builder proceeds, and a third party decides on a level of just compensation for having blocked my view. If the fence builder cannot (or does not) pay the compensation, the fence comes down.

Under a type IV entitlement, actions taken by another party (Alpha) which interfere with me may be stopped by me, but I must pay compensation; Alpha is protected by a liability rule. Just as in the previous case, the burden of proof places differential constraints on the bargaining process. Under a property rule protecting me (type I) no fence could be built without my consent, and thus the income of the fence builder imposed a constraint on the ability of that party to bargain with me. Under a type IV entitlement I can still retain my view of the lake if I can afford to compensate the would-be fence builder, the amount to be set by a disinterested assessor.

The final category of entitlements concerns those considered inalienable. That is, the previous cases were situations in which collective decisions must be taken regarding who is to own something, the nature of that ownership (a property rule or a liability rule), and what price is to be paid if it is used, taken, or destroyed. But there is an additional burden for society and that is in prescribing the preconditions for a sale – including the prevention of some sales.[3] In the discussion at hand, inalienability could become relevant when significant third-party effects arise. That is, even though an upstream and a downstream firm may agree on the value of the river for the dumping of waste, all those potentially affected by its use as a sewer are not represented in the transaction. I mentioned a similar third-party problem in the previous chapter where it was seen that the Audubon Society had agreed to lease oil pumping rights. To assure representation of third parties would imply transaction costs so great that the reasonable solution may sometimes be an inalienability rule which simply precludes the two-party transaction.

Another type of inalienable entitlement is relevant when third-party impacts may be minimal, but unambiguous monetization is impossible. Here the issue is not one of transaction costs but of our inability to evaluate the full nature of the transaction. That is, if we assume transaction costs to be zero, but recognize the importance of a future stream of benefits from the preservation of a unique environmental resource, we may still have great difficulty in reckoning all of these

Table 3.1 Alternative entitlement rules

Rule I (property rule)	Alpha may not interfere with Beta without Beta's consent Beta is protected by a property rule
Rule II (liability rule)	Alpha may interfere with Beta but must compensate Beta Beta is protected by a liability rule
Rule III (property rule)	Alpha may interfere with Beta and can only be stopped if Beta buys off Alpha Alpha is protected by a property rule
Rule IV (liability rule)	Beta may stop Alpha from interfering but must compensate Alpha Alpha is protected by a liability rule
Rule V (inalienability rule)	Alpha may not interfere with Beta under any circumstances, and no compensation is required Beta is protected by inalienability

possible benefits. If the action is characterized by irreversibilities, and if we are not certain of our benefit measures for such things into the future, the inalienability rule may be preferred.[4]

The various forms of entitlements are listed in table 3.1. We can reach several conclusions from the five-part distinction among entitlements. One important issue relates to why some matters might best be covered by property rules while others are properly the domain of liability rules. The obvious answer pertains to the implied transaction costs of the two alternative entitlements. Under a property rule it is necessary for the parties to negotiate prior to the action and to arrive at some bargain. Under a liability rule it is understood that actions with interfering aspects are going to occur, and compensation for the inconvenience follows the action.

For the property rule to be effective, it must be possible for the parties to the interference to meet before the fact and to negotiate a bargain. When many individuals have an interest in the situation – say in the case of public (collective) goods – this prior agreement will usually be impossible. Thus, a liability rule would be more practical in that the interfering party could proceed, but with the knowledge that a subsequent payment would be necessary. Environmental legislation such as the 1972 amendments to the Federal Water Pollution Control Act (PL92-500) modified the structure of entitlements for pollution emissions into streams, lakes, and rivers by changing it from a type III (property rule) to either a type I (property rule) or a type III (liability rule) entitlement, or an inalienable entitlement for toxic substances.

The National Pollution Discharge Elimination System required the issuance of permits for effluent discharges, with a graduated fee paid by the dumping party. This requirement is neither an effluent tax so often advocated in the economics literature, nor compensation in the sense implied in the above discussion of the liability rules. Yet, the new law does represent a shift from the former situation in which discharges enjoyed a type III entitlement.

It is also important to recognize that the tendencies for interference will differ between the two types of entitlements. Since the property rule requires a prior arrangement, we might assume that if my lake view is protected by a liability rule my neighbor will have a greater incentive to build a fence in my line of sight than if I am protected by a property rule. Even when we assume that the required compensation from the neighbor under a liability rule exactly matches the bargained price under a property rule, under the latter entitlement the neighbor must approach me first and begin the (possibly) tedious bargaining process. The level of transaction costs for the neighbor is much greater under a property rule than under a liability rule; hence we might expect interference to be greater under the latter. This difference in transaction costs arises since, under the liability rule, it is I (the "injured" party) who must initiate action which will result in compensation; I must actively initiate the compensation process, even though I did not initiate the action for which compensation is to be paid. Under an entitlement by which I am protected not by a liability rule but by a property rule, the active party must initiate the action to seek my approval.

Another matter concerns entitlements in use and transfer compared with entitlements in litigation. For example, an owner of a piece of land is protected by a property rule in use and transfer of that land, but by a liability rule in the case of condemnation through eminent domain. But if a neighbor persisted in dumping garbage on that individual's land, there might be injunctive relief from the courts which validates and enforces the individual protection by a property rule in litigation.

The distinction between a liability rule and a property rule can be very helpful in understanding a critical element in the famous cattle–corn conflict developed by Coase (1960). In his analysis – and in much of the literature which followed – one can conclude that the assignment of property rights between the corn farmer and the cattle rancher is immaterial with respect to resource allocation. If the cattle rancher is "liable" (in Coase's terminology), then the rancher proceeds to add steers, knowing that damages will be assessed and must be paid to the corn farmer; these damages would need to be arrived at by an independent assessor acting with the force of law. The corn farmer is protected by a liability rule (type II). However, if the corn farmer is "liable" (in Coase's terminology), then the farmer must approach the rancher and pay *not to have steers added*. The rancher is protected by a property rule (type III). If the corn farmer is protected by a type I property rule (a case not discussed by Coase or others), then the rancher would need to approach the corn farmer and arrange an *a priori* bargain; of course, this type of entitlement prevails in most places where ranchers rent forage from others. That is, this entitlement represents what we understand to be the rights inherent in normal market processes.

The interesting issue here is the mixing of types of entitlements when Coase and others say, in one case, that the rancher is "liable" and in the other that the corn farmer is "liable." Under the latter situation, we have the curious circumstance that the corn farmer must pay the rancher not to add steers which will graze the farmer's land; if expressed in terms of my paying someone not to drive his car across my yard the novelty of it is more obvious. Coase also had a tendency to focus on externalities between producers, where both parties were able to pass on the difference in costs to consumers of their products. But if we move from a world of idealized producer–producer conflicts to one of producer–consumer conflicts – or of consumer–consumer conflicts – then the situation becomes more complex.[5] No longer are the parties to the interference indifferent as to whether their receipts come from the corn or cattle market or from their neighbor. Under this new situation, income becomes a constraint on behavior and the resulting bargain. In the producer–producer situation, income is not a constraint since both are merely trying to maximize net revenue. But when the situation involves shifting property rules and liability rules between producers and consumers, or between two consumers, not only do income effects become important, but also current endowments and entitlements dominate the outcome. If the paper manufacturers have a type II entitlement, then those who favor oxygen in the rivers and pine scent in the air must pay to attain these amenities. On the other hand, if those who favor amenities have a type I entitlement, then it is the paper manufacturers who must incur the costs. Depending upon the structure of entitlements, environmental resources can be utilized either by producers to lower the cost of manufactured goods or by consumers to enhance the quality of life. Under one form of entitlement, consumers must pay to return the natural resources to their natural state, while under the other form of entitlement it is the producers (and ultimately the consumers of their products) who must pay to alter the natural environment. In one case there is the willingness to pay for something now held by someone else (the right to dump by producers, or the right to a cleaner environment by consumers); in the other case there is the reservation price necessary to induce one to sell that which is currently protected by a property rule.

Finally, a treatment of entitlements and externalities is not complete without discussing the concept of interference. If odors from a cattle feed lot pollute a residential neighborhood we can think of the odor as an interference with the happiness of those on whom the smell is imposed. On the other hand, if the feed lot is precluded from its polluting activities, the owner of the feed lot would define that injunction as interference.[6] To the economist the obvious answer is to balance, on efficiency grounds, the interference (harm). But this prescription will not always provide a reliable decision aid. If we undertake a benefit–cost assessment for the purpose of determining the greater harm, we may introduce a market/monetary bias which seriously discounts nonmarket/nonmonetary aspects of the situation. A billboard or an apartment building which blocks a scenic vista has monetary attributes which will be weighted against the "mere" pleasure of a beautiful sunrise; the fetid air which attends the economic activity generated by a kraft-process paper mill is not likely to receive the same weight in the decision process as the jobs that may be jeopardized by a strict air quality policy. It is one thing to say that, in a perfectly certain world, the decision is to be made by balancing the harm, but where uncertainty enters and where important yet nonmonetary effects are relevant, a serious bias can be introduced into the outcome. As many others have noted, the production of goods often tends to be favored over the preservation of amenities (Mishan, 1971, 1974).

My point here is that any particular status quo can be defined in legal terms as consisting of a structure of actual rights and presumptive rights. Actual rights have correlated with them a duty on the part of others to recognize those rights, while presumptive rights support no correlated duty but simply reflect the ability of a party to act *as if* there were an actual right present. Fee simple ownership of land bestows the right to construct certain types of buildings on that land, and for non-owners to exercise their duty to enter that land or building only at the prior agreement of the rights holder. To have a right that is protected by a property rule is to be protected against unwanted (and proscribed) incursions of either a physical or an economic nature. To have a right that is protected by a liability rule is to rest assured that, even if an untoward act occurs against your interests, the party committing that act is liable for damages. Fee simple ownership of land is a right protected by a property rule. In certain instances that same right is protected by a liability rule; this would be the case if errant chemicals ruined your garden and the guilty party were made to pay damages. The essence of actual rights is a correlated duty exercised *ex ante* (when a property rule is in place) or *ex post* (when a liability rule is in place). What we have then is a situation where the duty bearer is compelled to recognize a set of actual rights.

Instances of actual rights and correlated duties are best thought of as situations where the law is reasonably clear, although that does not imply that it deals adequately with new situations. The law can be clear about my not trespassing on your land, but quite unclear about my chemicals drifting to your land and causing harm. That is, I "trespassed" on your land in both instances – once physically and once by allowing my actions elsewhere to harm you. Externalities are found precisely in this gray area of the law, and instead of a clear institutional setting of rights and duties we are more likely to find ourselves in the domain of presumptive rights on the part of the perpetrator and no rights on the part of the victim. The terminology used here for this situation is *privilege* and *no rights*. Recall that privilege is the legal setting in which Beta is free to impose costs on Alpha without any regard to the latter's interests. We say that Beta has privilege, while Alpha has no rights. Externalities are precisely those instances in which the victim has no rights and the party imposing the unwanted costs has privilege – or presumptive rights. Of course not all externality situations are exactly so clear cut. Families that knowingly move into the immediate vicinity of a major airport cannot really be considered innocent and helpless victims of aircraft noise. For one thing, houses can be purchased in such neighborhoods at a discount over comparable housing in the absence of noise. And, as Coase reminded us, many externalities are reciprocal in the sense that stopping the unwanted costs to Alpha will entail forcing unwanted costs on Beta. The solution to the airport-noise problem is to tax the airlines for the marginal damage caused by each flight (which then creates an incentive for airlines to seek quieter engines), but not to compensate the "victims" of noise (since they have already been compensated through reduced housing prices). Of course if an airport comes into an established residential area then the case for compensation would be more compelling since residents will suffer an asset loss. But if airports seek remote locations, only to be subsequently surrounded by business and residences soon to claim "damages" from noise, neither efficiency nor equity is served by compensation flowing to the "victims" who knowingly *went to the nuisance* (in legal parlance).

For the most part, the interference we call an *externality* arises in situations in which one party has privilege and the other party has no rights. In the case of acid rain the coal-burning utilities have privilege and those with forest or agricultural lands – or those who care about the quality of northern lakes – have no rights. We can elaborate upon a point made earlier to the effect that *property rights indicate which costs must be considered by the various decision-making units in a society.* In the early days of the Industrial Revolution workers had no property in their labor power, and so it was cheap for early capitalists to ignore the costs to those workers suffering injury in the workplace; it was, of course, not unnoticed as an inconvenience to the families of the injured workers, but the workers had no rights, and the capitalists had privilege (Bromley, 1989a).

We should not assume from this that the privilege–no right correlate is the only one in which costs are imposed on ungrateful victims. A binding labor contract is an instance where the rights–duties correlate holds and yet those with duty may still be bearing some large unwanted costs. The essence of protection by right and privilege – and the more specific protection by property rules, liability rules, or inalienability rules – is that one can disregard certain costs. Property arrangements define which of these costs might legally be ignored, and property legitimizes those costs that are then visited on others. It is the confrontation between those causing such costs and those on whom they fall that is at the heart of the conflict over social arrangements in general – and environmental resources in particular. When people complain about "government interference" what they are really saying is that some costs which they were formerly able to ignore must now be internalized. One man's government interference is another's government protection (Samuels, 1971).

3   ON THE NATURE OF INTERDEPENDENCE

The primary purpose of the previous section has been to demonstrate that the property rights concept is much richer than has traditionally been recognized; there is more to the matter than merely knowing whether Alpha or Beta is "liable." Indeed, both parties can be protected by three types of entitlements. But economic analysis of interdependent activity would also benefit from a more detailed understanding of some of the important considerations which define the various types of interdependence. Not only is it important to recognize that inter-dependence is pervasive, but also it is critical to know whether the

Table 3.2 Some policy-relevant attributes of interdependence

	Nature of impact	Frequency of impact	Third-party effects	Transaction costs	Unique damage function	Irreversibilities
Cattle–corn	Irritating	Intermittent	None	Low–high	Yes	No
Railroad–wheat	Irritating	Intermittent	None	High	Yes	No
Confectioner–doctor	Irritating	Constant	None	Low	Yes	No
Fence–view	Irritating	Constant	None	Low	Maybe	No
Water pollution	Irritating	Constant	None	Low–high	Maybe	No
Crowded beach	Irritating	Intermittent	Yes	High	No	No
Blocked view	Irritating	Constant	Yes	High	No	Maybe
Chemicals	Physiological Ecological	Constant	Yes	High	No	Yes
Destruction of open space	Irritating Ecological	Constant	Yes	High	No	Maybe
Filling wetland	Ecological	Constant	Yes	High	No	Yes

interference is potentially damaging to human health or ecological integrity, whether there are significant third-party effects, and whether there is an empirically ascertainable damage function. A better understanding of these attributes of human interdependence would seem to be helpful in making a determination as to which type of entitlement – a property rule, a liability rule, or an inalienability rule – might be adopted. In what follows I offer a suggestive taxonomy of attributes which would seem helpful in gaining a more accurate and complete understanding of interdependence. This understanding should then make it easier to suggest the appropriate policy instruments for dealing with the various types of interference.

One of the important attributes of human interference pertains to the manner in which that interference affects the recipient: Is it merely irritating to another party? Does it pose a danger to human health? Or does it threaten ecological integrity? Another attribute is whether the interference is constant or intermittent. Yet another pertains to whether or not third parties are significant. In many of the examples of the traditional literature, third-party effects are not very important. The dispute between the cattle rancher and the corn farmer is of little moment to others, as is the case in the Coase discussion of the doctor and the confectioner, and in Buchanan and Stubblebine's fence-building example. Related to the importance of third parties is the level of transaction costs necessary to resolve the interdependence. And it would even be useful to consider distinctions among various categories of transaction costs, with the usual breakdown being information costs, contracting costs, and policing costs.

The argument for taxes on effluent discharges presumes the ability to estimate a unique damage function, and indeed it is sometimes possible to determine the relationship between discharges and offsite costs. However, it is not often possible to estimate such a damage function with any reliability, particularly when the damages are nonmonetary. This problem is related to the issue of whether or not there are irreversibilities implied by the interference. When wetlands are destroyed, when unique wildlife habitat is covered with houses, when a Hell's Canyon is flooded, or when a species is eliminated, we extend the impact of our actions to all generations yet unborn. Many of the usual examples do not account for the irreversible nature of some interdependences.

To highlight the differences between those externality cases which we ordinarily use as classroom illustrations and those instances of interdependence which may be more typical, I have displayed the foregoing attributes for two sets of externality situations in table 3.2.

In the upper portion of the table are five rather standard examples, while in the lower portion are listed five ways in which the actions of one individual (or group) are detrimental to others.

The traditional examples (upper portion) would seem to hold little implication for human health or ecological integrity and are usually of the sort which merely inconvenience another party; usually we can attach a monetary figure to the damages experienced by the recipient. Third-party aspects are generally assumed unimportant (the nature of the examples makes this a quite reasonable assumption), and transaction costs are usually not very significant. Finally, irreversibilities are not considered relevant. But in the lower portion of the table we see that the attributes are quite different for the instances listed. Human health and/or ecological concerns are relevant, third-party effects are significant, transaction costs are high, there is no unique damage function, and irreversibilities may be important. Our conclusions from this depend upon our view of which attributes are most important. But it seems clear that a realistic environmental policy can only be derived from a more accurate understanding of the complex nature of externalities. Our conventional analysis has been extremely useful in many respects, but simplicity must give way to more complex analysis if we are to have any impact on policy makers. We cannot continue to build stylized models of externalities from which we derive "optimal" policy prescriptions and then denounce politicians for failing to adopt our suggestions.

4   POLICY IMPLICATIONS

Economic analysis of environmental problems – and hence the basis for our policy prescriptions – would be much enhanced if we began to introduce greater reality and complexity into our analytical approach. Such complexity would come in two areas. The first would be a greater recognition of the variety of entitlements which define the parties to an interdependent situation. The second would be an admission that each interdependent situation can be characterized by a variety of attributes. Once these two dimensions are given greater resolution, policy prescriptions more appropriate to each type of interference might result. For example, when certain actions precipitate irreversible effects upon unique environmental resources, an inalienability entitlement is most appropriate for keeping options open. If the action is not irreversible, yet a great many individuals are potentially affected, a liability rule may be more appropriate. If only a few parties are involved in the interference, perhaps a property rule is appropriate. But the provision of good advice from economists will depend upon a more careful understanding of the nature of the interdependence. Buchanan and Tullock (1975) have lamented the apparent disregard for the economist's policy prescription (an effluent tax) in water pollution control, and many others have echoed this concern. Yet, the world rarely conforms to our idealized two-party models.[7]

Indeed, our models often seem quite ill suited to a world in which transaction costs are high, public goods (bads) abound, irreversibilities are often central, and income effects are important derivatives of whether producers or consumers have the entitlement to the valuable services offered by the natural environment. If consumption-related uses must bid away environmental services from producers, then there will be a different mix of, say, clean water and paper products than if the producers must bid resources away from those who prefer pure water: in the first instance a type III property rule obtains, whereas in the latter instance it is a type I property rule. In the former case the income of consumers constrains the bid price, while in the latter case only the competitive nature of the producing industry prevents much of the increased costs of doing business (in the form of now paying for something which was formerly free) from being passed on to the purchaser of the product. To the extent that the former price was artificially low, reflecting non-payment by the producer for a valuable input, then overall resource allocation is improved. But we must remember that the neat neutrality of the Coasian world is an artifact of an idealized producer–producer interdependence. The essence of interdependence is the ability, and the presumed right, of Alpha to impose unwanted costs on Beta. Alpha can build a fence and block Beta's view; Alpha can put carcinogenic compounds in the food Beta eats; Alpha can dump pulp mill effluent into the river from which Beta drinks; Alpha can construct an apartment in the line of Beta's view of the sunset; or Alpha can sell land to a developer who will then destroy its natural character – all acts which adversely affect Beta.

Thus, the logical question for policy formulation becomes the following: Is Beta's interest worthy of protection from this interference? One would not wish to attempt an answer to this question in isolation from the various policy instruments available; an absolute yes/no answer is not what the economist should provide. What analysis can provide is a way of viewing the advantages and disadvantages of various policy instruments available for protecting Beta's interests. Of course one policy is to do nothing, thereby allowing the current situation (most probably a type III property rule) to prevail. But the job of the economist would be to assist in the assessment of possible shifts in entitlements in the particular conflict under consideration.

As indicated previously, there are at least four entitlement options which would affect Alpha's ability to impose costs on Beta. These are (1) protect Beta with a property rule which requires prior consent for Alpha to act in an interfering manner – the type I property rule; (2) protect Beta with a liability rule which permits Alpha to proceed with the cost-imposing behavior but then requires compensation to be paid to Beta based on an independent assessment of those costs – the type II liability rule; (3) protect Beta with a liability rule which would allow Beta to stop Alpha from the cost-imposing act but would require Beta to compensate Alpha for the cessation – a type IV liability rule which really protects Alpha rather than Beta; and (4) protect Beta with an inalienability rule whereby Alpha is no longer allowed to impose costs on Beta, and the cessation requires no compensation to Alpha.

How do we decide which of the four possible entitlements to choose? It seems that the obvious place to start is by inquiring into the nature of the imposed costs. If Alpha is imposing costs on Beta which are detrimental to human health or to long-run ecological integrity (which might then show up as detrimental to human health), the inalienability rule would seem most appropriate. The analyst's job is to ascertain, perhaps in conjunction with other scientists, the extent to which any particular act by Alpha is, in fact, of such a serious nature that inalienability is relevant. An interesting aspect of environmental quality problems is that we are slowly learning – through improved ecological knowledge – that certain actions have a far different implication than formerly thought. The example of wetlands draws a distinction between the preservation of such areas and general open space – say, land that is in agriculture or natural vegetation. At one time it was thought that wetlands were just waste areas. First, changing tastes and preference resulted in their consideration as interesting places to view. Then, we began to understand their role in the overall ecology of a lake or estuary. As a result of this progress in knowledge, acts to drain a wetland have changed from completely costless in a social sense, to slightly injurious to local aesthetics, to potentially serious in an ecological sense. As indicated earlier the inalienability rule will most probably find increasing relevance as we attempt to deal more realistically with acts with uncertain future impacts.

It is when we move away from those acts which have serious physiological or ecological impacts that we encounter more scope for alternative policy instruments. That is, some interdependences were seen (in table 3.2) to be more of an irritant than a direct threat to public health and safety. Many examples of water quality problems are those where turbidity is high, or some odor is present making it undesirable for swimming. Another situation would occur when Alpha dumps effluent in a river which then requires purification by Beta before it can be used by the latter. In each instance the poor water quality interferes with others, but usually is not thought to constitute a health problem. The same may apply to instances of blocked views and open space (say, farmland in an urbanizing area) which is being subdivided. The move to a new form of entitlement would need to be predicated upon an assessment of the impacts upon several performance indicators. That is, a move from the current (presumptive) entitlement by Alpha to any of the other four entitlements might be assessed with respect to at least the following four performance indicators: (1) the value of goods and services gained and forgone under each of the four possibilities in moving from the current situation; (2) an indication of those who gain and those who lose under the alternative entitlement structures; (3) an assessment of the administrative feasibility of each of the four options; and (4) an assessment of the enforceability of each of the four.

This form of broad-gauged benefit–cost analysis would not seek to end up by stating which policy instrument (including the one of doing nothing) is the putatively optimal one. Each policy instrument will have its advantages and disadvantages with respect to various social objectives, and with respect to different actors. Some forms of entitlements may favor production services over consumption activities. Others may be neutral with respect to that view, but favor one group of producers over another, or one type of consumer over another. But perhaps the real benefit from this more thoroughgoing analysis will be a better understanding of the real complexity of interdependent situations. In contrast with much predictive work in which the reality of our assumptions may be less important than the accuracy of our estimates, prescriptive economics demands that our models be an accurate reflection of reality. That implies greater complexity of the sort under discussion here.

NOTES

1   A subject of great interest to John R. Commons in *The Legal Foundations of Capitalism* (1968).
2   A point made by Mishan (1974).
3   See Arthur Okun (1975) for a good discussion of this.

4   This matter is closely related to the notion of a safe minimum standard of conservation whereby, in the presence of uncertainty and irreversibilities, we give the benefit of the doubt to preservation (over development) in the hope of minimizing our maximum possible losses. See Ciriacy-Wantrup (1963).

5   Mishan (1974), Randall (1972, 1974), and Baker (1975) have noticed this and discuss it in varying detail.

6   This is what Coase and others mean by "harm."

7   This will be elaborated upon in chapter 5.

4
Property Rights and Externalities

The right of property includes then, the freedom of acquiring
by contract. The right of each to what he has produced,
implies a right to what has been produced by others, if
obtained by their free consent; since the producers must
either have given it from good will, or exchanged it for what
they esteemed an equivalent, and to prevent them from doing
so would be to infringe their right of property in the product
of their own industry.

John Stuart Mill, Book II, Chapter II,
Principles of Political Economy

1 THE EXTERNALITY PROBLEM

The general recognition of a divergence between private costs and social
costs can be attributed to Adam Smith in the *Wealth of Nations*, although
it was Alfred Marshall (1890) and A.C. Pigou (1912, 1920) who gave the
concept specificity.[1] In essence we are interested in instances where
the actions of one party (Alpha) result in unwanted costs being visited
on another party (Beta). In this context, social costs are those falling
beyond the boundary of the decision-making unit that is responsible
for those costs (Bromley, 1989a). This notion of costs going *beyond*
the decision unit that creates them explains the origin of the term
*external*ities. There is clear agreement among economists up to this point.

In a world where a multitude of decision units go about their business
of producing or consuming, it hardly requires elaboration to understand

This is a modified version of a chapter from my *Natural Resource Economics: Policy
Problems and Contemporary Analysis* (1986a). I am grateful to Kluwer Academic
Publishers for permission to use some of that material here.

that there are a multitude of ways in which these units make decisions that hold implications for others. It is the very nature of human interaction that what we do influences the actions that others might take – and the costs that they must bear. The theory of externalities is concerned with this immense domain in which unwanted costs are visited on others. When the economist attempts to employ externality theory in the service of public policy a number of very critical issues intervene. And it is here that economists begin to quibble.

Before turning to these matters it would seem appropriate to discuss, in an introductory manner, the policy problems and the current issues in contemporary analysis. These brief remarks are intended to outline the theoretical turf I intend to cover, and to suggest the relevance of those conceptual issues for the role that economists might play in the policy-formulation process.

Atomization and Externalities

Although not listed in order of importance, I start with an implicit problem in externality theory and policy that may be one of the most troubling. Economic theory and conventional folk wisdom are in agreement that the world works best when individuals possess the widest possible range of choice in their daily task of making a living. Again going back to Adam Smith, who was formulating his conceptual model at a time in history when the Crown and the state held inordinate control over the individual, we see the celebration of individual initiative, individual choice, individual control of economic resources, and individual responsibility for actions taken. Economic theory and political thought are melded into a tribute to the individual, whether voting in the polling booth or in the market place.

This individualization of the world – its atomization really – is argued to be the very best means for individuals to be made better off and, by simple aggregation, for the collection of all individuals (call it society) to be better off. Now, if externalities arise at the boundary of decision units, and if theory and policy celebrate and sanctify atomization, then theory and policy would seem to advocate the maximization of decision units and, *ipso facto*, the number of boundaries across which costs might travel. Bluntly put, atomization ensures potential externalities. The interesting question in this regard then has to do with the policy response to these ubiquitous external costs. One obvious response is that all the atomistic decision units begin to bargain over those costs that now transcend their respective boundaries. A whole new domain

of commodity relations is opened up – only now in terms of discommodities rather than in terms of commodities. But how is this new
market to arise? Will it not require an infrastructure not unlike that
now in place for commodities? Will not some entity be required to
define and protect property rights? Will there not be a need for
information and research when two bargainers in dispute cannot reach
agreement? And will not third parties have some interest in the
bargained outcome even though they are not present at the bargaining
table? What sort of entity might be called upon to establish this new
market in discommodities?

The dilemma is seen to be that the very result of extreme atomization
is to seek assistance from that force in society that is often viewed as the
enemy; the state. Those who celebrate atomization in the most exuberant
terms find themselves proceeding down a path that is logically contrary
to what they seem to desire. Another dilemma of extreme atomization
appears if yet a different externality solution is offered. While this latter
solution does not raise the specter of the state, there are anticompetitive
implications that would seem to be uncomfortable for those who
advocate atomization. Essentially, one of the preferred solutions to
externalities is to internalize them by combining the number of decision
units over which unwanted costs are visited. If the pulp mill discharges
liquors that impose costs on the downstream brewery and cheese
factory, then the proffered solution is simply to unify their ownership and
management so that the quantity of liquors being dumped by the pulp mill
subsidiary will be what is best for the aggregate of the three. Ignoring,
for the moment, the fact that there may be fishermen who would not
be part of this new unified firm and thus who may continue to have
unwanted costs visited on them, the idea of one or two firms in major
river basins, each with several hundred subsidiaries, is not a thought
to be considered favorably by those who believe in atomistic competition.

So, perhaps *the* fundamental theoretical and policy issue in the domain
of externalities is how to reconcile these seeming contradictions between
the idea – in both theory and popular political wisdom – of extreme
atomization and the abundance of opportunities thus created for the
rise of externalities, and the need to address those externalities with
collective action (the state) or with anticompetitive firm consolidation.

Liability

A second issue in externality theory and policy concerns the matter
of the liability for unwanted costs. Economists have disputed this issue

incessantly since Coase's article on social costs. The issue as put by Coase was that property rights are as much a factor of production as are labor and raw materials. Firms could buy and sell rights to visit external costs on others and, if the market for rights was well functioning, the ultimate outcome in terms of goods and services was said to be identical regardless of who held the initial rights. In the classic case of Alpha's cattle wandering into Beta's cornfield, if the rancher was liable for damages then Beta would be reimbursed for the corn eaten and would be indifferent whether the corn was sold on the market or eaten by Alpha's cattle directly and then "bought" *ex post* by Alpha for (presumably) the market price. If liability ran the other way then Beta would pay the rancher to keep cattle away from the corn and the rancher (Alpha) would take this new income and make other feeding arrangements. Lost in all of the interest in Coase's quaint examples is the fact that he mixed up quite different forms of legal entitlements, all under the name of liability. The presentation in chapters 2 and 3 should make this point clear.

Subsequent literature has pointed out that the very assumptions necessary to render the Coase neutrality conclusion true are the same assumptions that would deny the existence of externalities in the first instance. That is, in the absence of transaction costs, and assuming away income (wealth) effects among disputants, the assignment of liability would not matter for resource allocation for the simple reason that there would be no externalities to bargain away. I shall return to this matter in more detail in sections 3 and 4.

Incentives and Sanctions

A third major issue in externality theory and policy concerns the distinction between taxes, subsidies, and standards for dealing with environmental pollution. Early on, economists argued that either taxes or subsidies would result in the same level of pollution abatement. That was soon refuted (Kamien, Schwartz, and Dolbear, 1966) and now there is widespread recognition of the important distinction between emissions per firm and the number of emitting firms. Specifically, subsidies encourage more firms to enter an industry and, while emissions per firm might be reduced compared with the status quo, there would be more firms and so total loadings might be greater than originally. Another aspect of subsidies is that the regulatory agency may leave itself open to extortion in that firms may threaten to pollute more so as to collect a subsidy not to.

The other aspect of this issue concerns the role of standards. Essentially, economists are united in their preference for effluent charges as opposed to discharge quotas (or standards). In spite of this near unanimity in the profession, politicians and industry overwhelmingly prefer standards. We shall explore the probable causes for this divergence below.

Transaction Costs

Let it be noted, and in the clearest possible language, that *in a world without transaction costs there could be no externalities*. What do I mean by transaction costs, and how do they contribute to the presence of externalities? The acronym ICE is a convenient way to remember the three types of transaction costs – information costs, contracting costs, and enforcement costs. Any transaction requires knowledge about the opportunities for exchange, the nature of the items to be exchanged, and the willingness of the participants to engage in a bargaining process. This information is not costless and the lack of information can prevent certain exchanges from ever occurring. Efforts to acquire information fall on individual decision units and the incidence of information costs is an important policy issue. Once willing bargainers locate one another they can get down to the serious business of striking a deal. However, this is also a costly process, perhaps in terms of the time involved. Finally, once a bargain is struck, there are certain enforcement costs that must be incurred. Although these costs can be covered by the state, it is also possible that the individual participants must pay these costs.

To see that transaction costs are necessary for externalities, we must consider the important distinction between physical interference being transmitted from Alpha to Beta and the existence of an externality, and we must develop a careful definition of what exactly constitutes an externality. Most economists agree that an externality has two aspects. First, there is the fact that a decision unit's utility or production function contains real variables whose values are chosen by others. Second, the decision unit responsible for choosing the value of those real variables does not compensate the recipients by an amount equal to the marginal cost of its actions. In the case of positive externalities the responsible decision unit does not receive compensation for the beneficial effects made available to the recipient. We now must differentiate this situation from the case where physical interdependence exists but is *not* an externality.

The distinction is to be found in the fact that there is an economically appropriate level of physical interference among atomistic decision units, and when those directly involved in this interference – as perpetrators and as victims – have bargained out the preferred level, we must conclude that the externality has been resolved, even though the physical interdependence is still present. Notice that the externality no longer exists, *by definition*, since the parties have bargained away all possible gains from trade. We shall encounter this matter again in the following section where we talk of Pareto-relevant and Pareto-irrelevant externalities.

Hence we see that the absence of transaction costs – the costs of information, the costs of contracting, and the costs of enforcement – implies that all interdependent decision units have costlessly bargained away all *relevant* physical interactions and by definition there can be no externalities. This does *not* mean that some physical interdependences would not remain; it simply means that our notion of an externality could not exist.

We see, therefore, that transaction costs are essential ingredients in any conception of externalities. As will be seen later, Dahlman considers externalities to be nothing other than manifestations of nonzero transaction costs.

The Status Quo

A fifth issue pertinent to externalities concerns the policy response to the presence of uncompensated costs falling on victims. Imagine a situation in which the status quo structure of property rights allows Alpha to discharge large quantities of smoke containing certain chemicals that, when combined with atmospheric moisture, produce acids that allegedly cause damage to crops, forests, and buildings owned by other decision units (Beta). The nature of scientific knowledge means that we cannot be absolutely certain that the emissions from Alpha's factory are uniquely responsible for damaging Beta's crops. Alpha, and those in similar lines of work, will marshal political support for the position that we do not yet know enough about cause and effect to be absolutely certain about the alleged link between emissions and crop damage and so more research is required. This strategy ensures that Beta will continue to bear unwanted costs while the search for a definitive answer goes on.

Alternatively the policy response could be to force Alpha to cease all emissions immediately, thereby imposing a different type of cost.

This would surely be the preferred action on the part of the recipients of Alpha's emissions since it would liberate them from the damages, or so they think. If the situation is truly one of pure uncertainty then both parties have a reason to be concerned about the policy outcome; fairness requires that costs not be imposed in a cavalier manner. Economic efficiency demands as much.

And yet the status quo means that one party is able to continue to impose unwanted costs on another while the (possibly) lengthy search proceeds for a definitive answer. Some would argue that this is as it should be – after all, they might argue, Alpha has the presumptive right (privilege) to continue with its discharges until its fault is clearly established. The victims (Beta) would probably respond that, while the legal doctrine of presumed innocence is fine in the courtroom, it is positively pernicious when the preponderance of the evidence points to a link between Alpha's emissions and Beta's damages.

Many environmental externalities are characterized by precisely this situation. New chemicals and new processes seem to hold some responsibility for environmental problems; DDT, 2,4,5-T, Kepone, Aldicarb, and PCBs come immediately to mind. Yet the status quo is permissive of continued use until definitive causality is established. That this situation puts the burden of proof on the victims – and the bulk of the transaction costs as well – is not lost on those who seek relief. Externality theory has not yet developed a meaningful way of handling this matter of presumptive rights, uncertainty, and the incidence of costs. It is possible that the reason for this lacuna is the simple fact that these matters are not theoretical ones at all, but ethical. We shall return to this theme later.

The Margin

The sixth externality issue to be explored concerns what we consider to be the marginal expenditure in production and consumption decisions. An example from the automobile industry will illustrate the general issue. A few years back we were told that the auto industry opposed putting stouter bumpers on cars because it would add something like $50 to the price of a $7,000 automobile. At the time there was general recognition that as much as $1,000 of a car's purchase price is attributable to model changes – by which is meant styling modification. It might seem both efficient and fair to reconsider stouter bumpers at $50 against the last $50 spent on model changes. Would consumers prefer cars with $950 of embodied model changes and a stouter bumper, or would they choose cars with the present bumpers (evidently ineffective since they are said to collapse in a 5 miles per hour collision)?

This issue finds policy relevance in the externalities associated with the strip mining of coal. In the mid-1970s there was considerable interest in restoring land that had been strip mined for coal to approximately its original condition. Predictably enough the arguments offered against reclamation by mining interests were in terms of the high cost of doing so – a classic response that applies to any regulatory discussion. First we must recall that the presence of externalities means that certain costs beyond the boundary of the responsible firm are not being compensated for. In this instance, these costs are in the form of downstream sedimentation, altered natural vegetation, and the aesthetic insult of large areas of stripped land.

Simply put, the consumers of coal are not paying for the full social costs of producing that particular commodity. If coal were priced correctly it would be somewhat more expensive, the use of coal would fall somewhat as cheaper alternatives found more favor, and there would be less environmental damage (and fewer offsite costs). But the real economic issue concerns how we consider the costs of producing coal. If restoring the land after the coal is removed is considered to be a legitimate cost of producing coal then it is logically impossible to assert that "reclamation costs too much." When reclamation expenses are a part of production costs then the *marginal decision* becomes one of whether or not to dig up another hectare of land so as to produce yet another unit of coal. This is as it should be. This approach also coincides with coal-mining policy in Europe for many years now. An important issue in externality theory and policy, then, is one of creating an institutional environment – a property rights regime – that recognizes the true marginality of various actions by decision units.

Efficiency

Another central issue in externality theory and policy concerns the way in which existing institutional arrangements influence our concept of economic efficiency. Several times in the preceding discussion I have mentioned the status quo, and presumptive rights. The firm that emits sulfur dioxide is considered to have a presumptive right (or privilege) to continue its discharges until enough evidence is accumulated to mobilize politicians to alter the institutional arrangements. And, as we just saw, as long as the institutional environment is permissive of coal mining without reclamation, it will appear that reclamation is not "economically efficient."

Markets and market processes operate within an institutional structure that defines rights and duties, obligations and opportunities. Because of this, the prevailing institutional structure defines what it is that will be considered efficient (Bromley, 1989a). Recall that for every structure of resource endowments – and institutions define and specify resource endowments – there is a Pareto-efficient outcome. Change the institutional environment and there will be a new efficient solution. Since institutions define markets, and since markets indicate to the economist what is considered to be efficient, institutions define what we consider to be efficient outcomes. But economists usually prefer to consider institutions as exogenous parameters and to search for efficient outcomes within a fixed institutional environment.

Unfortunately, the bulk of what happens in externality policy concerns the necessary restructuring of institutional arrangements (property rights). This poses a unique analytical challenge to the economist. After all, welfare economics and its applied analogue benefit–cost analysis, are analytical devices for considering gains and losses from *within* an existing institutional (resource endowments) environment. These are tools for measuring gains and losses of actions within the prevailing rules of the game. But institutional change is to change the rules. We face some difficult questions in this regard.

Summary

To summarize so far, externality theory and policy is defined by at least seven issues that make it still, after a number of years, one of the least coherent and most contentious areas of economic analysis. Theory and popular wisdom favor a large number of atomistic producers and consumers, yet this very atomization is itself responsible for many of the externalities requiring resolution. The literature still contains a number of references to the refuted Coase conclusion about the allocative neutrality of rights assignments. There is puzzlement over why, in the face of near unanimity among economists in their preference for emission charges on pollutants, most policy is still one of mandated emission standards or quotas. Transaction costs are said by some to be the *raison d'être* of externalities, and yet the literature is not of one voice with regard to the important role to be played by such costs, and to the differential incidence of transaction costs under different institutional structures.

Much of externality policy is dominated by uncertainty over cause and effect. In the face of that uncertainty, some suggest that policy responses are stifled so as to empower current emittors to continue to shift abatement costs to victims, while at the same time sounding high-minded by calling for more research and study of the matter. The policy response is further distorted by the failure of economists to illustrate the pernicious nature of how externality disputes get framed; this is the matter of marginality – do reclamation costs, for instance, become a recognized part of the costs of producing coal, or does the industry continue to oppose reclamation because it is "too expensive?" It is this institutional environment that defines what is a cost, who shall bear unwanted costs, and how we compute what we consider to be the efficient outcome. This dimension is often not well understood.

In the remainder of the chapter I shall develop the theory of externalities in a way that will allow explicit recognition of these issues, and possibly some general agreement as to their importance.

2   TYPES OF EXTERNALITIES

The newcomer to the study of externalities is sure to be overwhelmed by the number of ways that we refer to them – technical, technological, political, pecuniary, ownership, potentially relevant, Pareto-irrelevant, depletable, undepletable, marginal, inframarginal, Pareto-relevant, positive, negative. Small wonder that there is confusion. This complexity can be improved by considering externalities in one of four distinct – but not mutually exclusive – categories. Before turning to that, note that two broad categories of externalities can be clarified straightaway. The actions of Alpha can impose either costs or benefits on Beta. While this visitation is usually considered to be unintentional on the part of Alpha, in the sense that it is incidental to Alpha's main activities, the ultimate impact on others (here characterized as Beta) can be either beneficial or detrimental.[2]

If I like flowers and decorate my yard in a bright profusion of colors I am visiting positive externalities on other garden lovers and they receive those benefits without paying me. These are positive externalities. If, on the other hand, I paint my house pink with large purple dots, chances are that I will be imposing negative externalities on others. While externalities can be either harmful or beneficial, the bulk of the environmental externalities that we deal with are of the harmful kind.

Externalities as Types of Interdependence

Beginning with Viner's classic article on the nature of cost curves, economists have drawn a distinction between pecuniary externalities and technological externalities. Pecuniary externalities are transmitted through the pricing system (hence pecuniary), while technological externalities are real-valued physical effects transmitted from Alpha to Beta – smoke, toxic chemicals, noise, odor, traffic congestion. When a large retailer moves into a small community and puts downward pressure on the prices of certain commodities that had heretofore been somewhat sheltered from intense competition, the economic environment of the old-line retailers is substantially altered. To the extent that they must now lower their prices and experience revenue losses, the older retailers suffer pecuniary externalities. They are pecuniary because they are transmitted through the price system, and they are external because another decision unit has altered the economic environment of the existing firms. However, the very fact that these effects are transmitted through the price system suggests that they should not be referred to as externalities. The term externalities implies, after all, that there is a problem requiring a solution. With pecuniary externalities we may conclude that the market is doing its job of promoting competitive behavior and therefore one may logically inquire as to why we even use the term externality.

It is the class of technological externalities that captures the interest of the economist and the politician in natural resource matters. Here we are dealing with non-price-transmitted (hence physical) interdependence among independent economic decision units. A third dimension of this distinction was added over twenty years ago by Buchanan (1962). Buchanan, being a good Paretian *and* a good Wicksellian, pointed out that whenever we have political action with less than unanimous consent then the choice set of decision units has been altered without their agreement or compensation. He argued that this too is an externality. We therefore have three general classes of externalities based on their origin – pecuniary (which some dispute as externalities at all), technological, and political.

Externalities as Types of Market Failures

In his seminal article "The Anatomy of Market Failure," Francis Bator (1958) introduced the profession to three conditions that would cause individualistic wealth-maximizing behavior to result in outcomes that were less than socially optimal. Because of the close association among economists between externalities and market failure, Bator's analysis warrants mention here. Specifically, Bator found three general reasons why normal market processes might not result in the best of all possible worlds; he classified these as ownership problems, technical problems, and public-goods problems.

An ownership problem arises when all the relevant variables to a production or consumption outcome are not owned and traded in markets. The classic honey bee–apple orchard problem comes to mind. The apiarist benefits from pollen collected far and wide but the ownership of that pollen is too difficult to ascertain and so proper remuneration of the owners never occurs; the apiarist is free riding off apple orchardists and others. As another example, my neighbor invests in time and materials to construct Purple Martin bird houses so that the bugs in his vegetable garden are controlled without the use of chemicals. My garden abuts his and I too benefit from the appetite of the bug-killers that his investment attracted in the first place. Moreover, by eating some of my bugs, his birds may be satiated and do a less-than-satisfactory job on his bugs. These are ownership problems and they lead to a less than optimal investment in bird houses, beehives, apple orchards, and broccoli. These suboptimalities are surely not of the nature or magnitude that would induce the well-meaning economist to lie awake nights. But neither are they irrelevant.

In one of the celebrated ownership externality cases, apple trees were harmed by a rust infestation that used red cedar trees as an intermediate host (Buchanan, 1972; Samuels, 1971, 1972). Apple orchardists managed to convince the Virginia legislature to pass a law that would empower the state – on a petition of at least ten affected orchardists – to destroy without compensation red cedar trees serving as hosts for the rust in the vicinity of the affected orchardists. Some landowners owned the red cedar trees, and other landowners owned the apple trees. But no-one owned the spores that travelled from cedar trees to do their thing to the apple trees. Bator's analysis would suggest that the bulk of classic externalities are indeed ownership failures – the difficulty or impossibility of establishing control over phenomena that affect other decision units.

A second class of market failure arises because of technical problems, by which Bator principally meant lumpiness. Economic theory is most adept at treating mobility and divisibilities; when things such as dams, electric power lines, and highways come in discrete chunks then the continuity that we like in theory does not exist. As a result, conventional theory as a prescriptive norm becomes less relevant. Since technical problems are not much present in externality matters we shall have little more to say about this type of market failure.

The third type of market failure, and one of considerable significance to externality theory and policy, is what Bator called "publicness" – public goods, or bads in the case of negative externalities. The matter of publicness is well understood by economists and we need little elaboration here; particularly since it will appear again very shortly under another name.

Externalities as Policy Prescriptions

In a 1962 article, Buchanan and Stubblebine develop a classification scheme for externalities that emphasizes the policy prescriptions to be drawn from the nature of their existence. These authors presented three general categories of technological externalities: (1) marginal or inframarginal; (2) Pareto relevant or Pareto irrelevant; and (3) potentially relevant and irrelevant. Buchanan and Stubblebine were concerned with externalities in consumption and I will continue that focus here. These authors represented an externality as existing when the utility of Alpha is dependent not only on the activities chosen by Alpha, but on an activity whose level is chosen by another individual (Beta). Formally, Alpha's utility function would be represented by

$$U_A = f(X_1, X_2, \ldots, X_n, Z) \tag{4.1}$$

A marginal externality is said to exist when the partial derivative of Alpha's utility function with respect to Beta's activity is nonzero. That is

$$f_Z^A \neq 0 \tag{4.2}$$

Assume that the variation in Z is evaluated with respect to a set of equilibrium values for the Xs optimally adjusted to the given value of Z.

An inframarginal externality is said to exist when condition (4.1) is present, and

$$f_Z^A = 0 \tag{4.3}$$

and

$$\int_0^Z f_Z^A dZ < 0 \tag{4.4}$$

The essence of inframarginality is that while the incremental effects of Beta on Alpha (through Z in the utility function) are zero (condition (4.3)), the total effect is negative (condition (4.4)). We can imagine a situation in which a high-rise building blocks a scenic view; regardless of the height of the building, once it reaches a certain height, the damage to Alpha will not be any greater if the building becomes taller.

I am concerned with the relevance of externalities since policy should be directed toward those interdependences that cause economic inefficiencies. Buchanan and Stubblebine define an externality as potentially relevant when the activity generates any desire on the part of the externally affected party (Alpha) to undertake actions with respect to the imposing party (Beta) to halt the unwanted effects. Such actions may include payments, threats, agreements, or "going to the legislature." When an externality exists (condition (4.1)) yet there is no desire on the part of Alpha to correct it, then, by definition, it is irrelevant. Formally, a potentially relevant marginal externality is said to exist when

$$f_Z^A \Big|_{Z = \bar{Z}} \neq 0 \qquad (4.5)$$

where $\bar{Z}$ is an equilibrium level of Z.

Buchanan and Stubblebine suggest that the mere desire to alter the behavior of the imposing party (Beta) does not imply the ability to accomplish this change. They define a Pareto-relevant externality as one in which the extent of the activity can be altered so that the victim (Alpha) can be made better off without the imposing party (Beta) being made worse off. That is, there are mutual gains from trade. We see, therefore, that a marginal externality can be potentially relevant (since the victim may seek for it to be eliminated) but still be Pareto irrelevant (since it is impossible for both parties to gain from an adjustment of the status quo). When the economy is at a Pareto-optimal point we can only conclude that all remaining externalities are Pareto irrelevant, even though there are surely many that remain potentially relevant. That is, there will remain physical interference between two or more parties even though that interference is not said to constitute a deviation from efficiency.

This situation obviously implies that the costs of the status quo fall on the victim. If those costs are insignificant then we have what Buchanan and Stubblebine would call an irrelevant externality. If, however, those costs are important to the victim then we have a potentially relevant externality. However, unless the party responsible for imposing those unwanted costs on Alpha will be made no worse off by eliminating those costs, then theory dismisses the costs as *Pareto irrelevant.* While as theorists we may find certain satisfaction in this elegance, the victims of externalities may be excused if they are somewhat less sanguine.

Externalities as Experienced by the Victims

The final way in which we find externalities grouped is in terms of how the unwanted costs ultimately affect the victims, and also how the bearing of those costs by one victim influences the costs available to injure others. In essence we are here dealing with the obverse of public goods; that is, our concern here is with the nature of the incidence of public "bads." The pure case of a public bad is represented by smog or haze in which case the "consumption" by one victim does not reduce the quantity of the smog or haze available for others to consume. In this example the victims, in the course of experiencing the costs of not being able to see a scenic mountain range, do not really use up (or diminish) any of the externality. That is, they do not consume it. This type of externality has been labeled "undepletable' by Baumol and Oates (1975). Consider the externalities associated with urban airport noise. A given number of landings and takeoffs will generate a total decible level for a twenty-four-hour period. If no-one is around to hear the racket there can be no externality. When one person comes within earshot of the airport, a potentially relevant externality can be said to exist, although we would probably suggest that it is Pareto irrelevant. However, when the second individual comes within earshot of the noise there is no reduction in the noise level remaining for the first individual; there is no rivalry in the consumption of the externality. It is a *pure public bad.*

As against undepletable externalities there are depletable externalities wherein the very act of being victimized by unwanted costs reduces the amount available to harm others. Consider the situation in which a farmer contracts with an aerial spraying company to spread a certain insecticide on his/her fields. If the wind comes up and scatters that spray onto a neighbor's beehives then the externality is depletable to the extent that insecticide on Alpha's bees is unavailable to drift and to kill another's bees. The distinction between depletable and undepletable externalities was used by Baumol and Oates to motivate a discussion about differences in policy as regards the two classes of external costs. While that policy conclusion has been questioned by Freeman (1984), the power of the distinction for heuristic purposes seems to remain intact.

Summary

The complexity of the literature on externalities is seen to lie, in part at least, in the plethora of overlapping conceptions, and in the different purposes for classifying the phenomena. The remainder of our concerns with externalities will be confined to negative externalities of the technological variety. While I shall return to the distinction between depletable and undepletable externalities, the bulk of our time will be devoted to the theory and policy of externalities as informed by the treatment of them as potentially relevant, irrelevant, inframarginal, Pareto relevant, and Pareto irrelevant.

3   AN EXTERNALITY MODEL

There have appeared over the years a very large number of externality models, each designed to illustrate different theoretical or policy conclusions. Some of the better known models are those developed by Baumol (1972), Baumol and Oates (1975), Marchand and Russell (1973), Buchanan and Stubblebine (1962), Randall (1972), and Freeman (1984). It would be impossible in the space available to present each of these, nor is a simple synthesis possible. To anticipate the treatment in the following sections we require a model that allows us to illustrate several issues: (1) transaction costs; (2) the effects of alternative status quo property rights structures (institutional arrangements); and (3) the cost incidence of alternative outcomes to externality solutions. The model used here follows the approach taken by Burrows (1980).

Zero Transaction Costs

We shall consider several cases, moving from the most abstract to the most realistic. Case I is characterized by the most severe assumptions in that transaction costs are non-existent. Imagine an externality situation in which Alpha is a firm that imposes unwanted – and uncompensated – costs on Beta, a firm in a separate industry. Alpha has an opportunity to abate the pollutant rather than dumping it on Beta, but to do so would be quite expensive to Alpha – better (cheaper) merely to dump it. Alpha has, of course, a supply curve of abatement; this is a schedule that shows the level of abatement undertaken by Alpha at various prices. I label this MAC in figure 4.1. It should be noted that

Alpha's supply curve for abatement is also a demand curve for discharging effluents into the waterway. Beta also has a schedule, but this is in terms of costs incurred by being downstream from Alpha. I shall call it the demand for abatement on the part of Beta; this is shown as MPC in figure 4.1. Note that MPC is also a supply curve for pollution.

If we start with an assumed property regime that is permissive of the discharges on the part of Alpha – that is, a legal structure that gives Alpha presumptive rights – then Beta would initially be willing to pay as much as R to be spared the first unit of pollutants. As we move to the left toward increased abatement we see that at level E_1 Beta would be willing to pay as much as MJ to Alpha for reduced emissions, but that Alpha would only require KJ to be willing to supply that level of abatement. If we move beyond E_2 to emissions level E_3 we see that here Beta would be willing to pay only GF for Alpha to undertake that level of abatement, yet Alpha would require HF. Hence, emissions at E_2 would be the equilibrium outcome starting from E_n and the presumptive rights protecting Alpha. At this equilibrium level Alpha's willingness to undertake abatement for a payment of VW exactly matches Beta's willingness to pay for abatement.

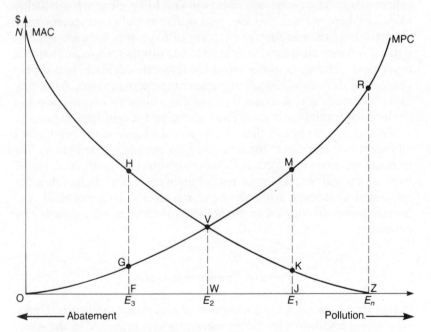

Figure 4.1 Efficient abatement with zero transaction costs.

Once we reach emissions level E_2, Beta has had to pay WVRZ to Alpha, of which WVZ has been spent by Alpha on abatement. The remainder, VRZ, represents rents accruing to Alpha because of Beta's ignorance of the exact amount necessary to bribe Alpha. Of course, in a world of zero transaction costs we know that perfect information is costless and so Beta would only pay Alpha the amount VWZ – which is the exact minimum that Alpha would require.

Now consider the alternative property rights structure in which it is Beta who is protected by presumptive rights. In this case we start at the origin with zero discharges (and full abatement by Alpha). Here, however, Alpha has a significant incentive to convince Beta to permit some discharges. At the outset Alpha could afford to pay as much as ON to Beta to be permitted to discharge the first unit of effluent. Using the same logic as above the two parties would ultimately settle on an emissions level of E_2.

Notice that in a world of zero transaction costs the equilibrium level of emissions is indeed the same regardless of the status quo structure of rights. When Alpha is protected in the status quo it is Beta who must buy abatement at level E_2. When Beta is protected in the status quo it is Alpha who must buy discharges at level E_2. When Coase and others assume away income effects it should be clear what is being said. For here we see that the two different rights structures have different implications for the direction of payments between the two parties. To assume away income effects is simply to assume that this movement of funds does not affect the respective demand and supply curves that define the bargaining space of the protagonists. Assuming away income effects does not mean that the ultimate income position of the two disputants is indifferent to the status quo legal structure.

We should also notice that in this world of zero transaction costs all Pareto-relevant externalities would have been bargained away. The ultimate level of emissions at E_2 has exhausted all gains from trade. Here Beta is still bearing unwanted pollution costs, and Alpha is bearing unwanted abatement costs. As indicated earlier, in a world of zero transaction costs there can be no Pareto-relevant externalities, by definition.

Positive Transaction Costs

In case II we now relax the assumption of zero transaction costs. Under an assumed institutional structure where Alpha is protected by the status quo it is Beta that is harmed and so Beta will seek relief. Under the alternative legal structure it is Alpha who will desire to be allowed to discharge pollutants. Once transaction costs are no longer assumed to be zero, the efforts of either party will require time and financial resources. Recall that it is the party *not* protected by the extant legal structure who must initiate the action to deal with the other party. Information and contracting are expensive, and these costs are, for the most part, borne by the party that is vulnerable to unwanted costs in the status quo.

Under the status quo protection of Alpha it is Beta who must pay the costs. In terms of figure 4.1 we must then recognize that Beta's net willingness to offer payments to Alpha will be diminished to the extent that the transaction costs have fallen on Beta. This new net bid curve is labeled BNB (for Beta's net bid) in figure 4.2. If E_n again represents the status quo emissions level when Alpha is protected by presumptive rights, then Beta's new net bid is R' rather than R. Notice that this has the effect of shifting the ultimate equilibrium level of emissions to the right compared with the solution with zero transaction costs (E_2). Beta must experience an increased pollution load. At this

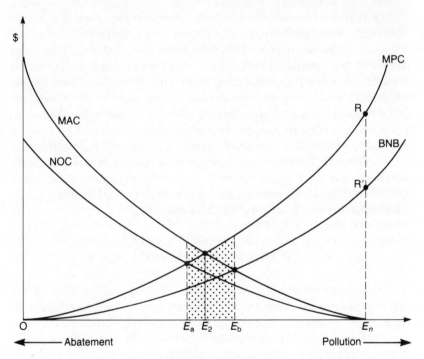

Figure 4.2 Efficient abatement with positive transaction costs.

level Beta still has a willingness to pay along MPC, but a reduced ability to buy out Alpha because of the transaction costs that must be incurred. The shaded area represents the residual costs that Beta must bear because of the presence of transaction costs.

Now consider the opposite situation in which it is Beta who is protected by presumptive rights, and it is Alpha who must incur expenses to bargain with Beta over the possibility of emissions. Using the same logic, the incidence of these transaction costs on Alpha will reduce the ability to offer payments to Beta to be allowed to discharge effluents. We thus derive a new net offer curve (NOC) in figure 4.2. The equilibrium level of pollution under this new assumed status quo (E_a) is seen to be restricted beyond the original equilibrium level when transaction costs were assumed not to exist. The shaded area here indicates the excess costs borne by Alpha because of these bargaining costs. The economically efficient level of an externality is seen to be dependent upon the status quo institutional setup, since it is this structure that both liberates and constrains decision units. Moreover, the structure is responsible for a different burden of transaction costs to the several parties to a dispute.

The real world is obviously much more complex than the simple two-party issue explored here. For one thing there may be many members of the two parties (Alpha and Beta) discussed here. With large numbers we encounter important third-party effects that merit consideration. But the central conclusion to be drawn from these simple models is that the still-widespread notion that externalities are indifferent to the status quo property structure is untenable. Nor does it seem reasonable to assume zero transaction costs, and no income effects. If transaction costs are zero there are no Pareto-relevant externalities to consider. But since transaction costs are obviously nonzero, and since income effects are surely important, externality theory and policy is dominated by the institutional realities often overlooked in much writing on the subject.

4 TOWARD EXTERNALITY POLICY

The essence of externalities is that costs are imposed on others via a physical interdependence that links nominally independent decision units. I say "nominally" for the reason that as long as the two decision units are linked in this manner they are not really independent units. Not only are there unwanted costs visited on recipients of externalities, there are no contracts between the linked parties to cover these effects.

What is it that allows certain costs to transgress nominal boundaries of decision units and to persist in the face of opposition by the victim? It is the prevailing structure of property rights that gives an emittor a presumptive right to continue such activity until challenged by the affected party. Factories have always spewed smoke and dumped their liquid garbage in rivers; farmers have been applying chemicals to control weeds and insects for the past forty years; new buildings have been blocking the view from older buildings as long as there have been cities.

While we have elegant models with which to derive the optimal level of externalities, it remains obvious that any optimality position we might derive is an artifact of the structure of entitlements taken for granted when the analysis is done. There is, after all, a Pareto-optimal allocation of resources for every possible structure of resource endowments, where such endowments include the extant property arrangements. To recognize this, and to discuss its implications, is not to abandon objectivity. It is, however, to address the question of institutional arrangements and so to raise fundamental questions about the conventional wisdom of externality theory and policy.

To understand the incidence of unwanted costs, and the relationship to efficiency analysis, we must first understand the prevailing structure of entitlements (institutions), and we must be capable of viewing that structure in a conceptually useful way. This is necessary for the simple reason that it is the institutional structure that allows certain unwanted costs to remain uncompensated. That is, the status quo rights structure allows the perpetrator of unwanted costs to decline to enter into a contract with the victim(s), at which time some would place that particular externality in the category of Pareto irrelevant. After that definitional *coup de grâce*, the economist could announce, with some apparent satisfaction, that we had a Pareto-optimal outcome. Policy makers, however, are not much smitten by the notions of Pareto optimality and Pareto irrelevance. They see trees devastated by acid deposition, they see fish killed by Kepone, they see warnings not to eat whitefish, lake trout, and coho salmon from the Great Lakes and they ask – at the insistence of a subset of their constituents – why, if things are optimal to the economist, are these events going on? For the economists to hide behind Pareto irrelevancy is to invite the most complete disbelief – not to mention scorn.

The economist who wishes to say useful things about externalities is faced with several difficulties. Our models are most rigorous when concerned with incremental change within a constant institutional setup. Welfare theory – the *explicitly* normative branch of our science – offers direction for judging bargains struck by individual decision makers.

The insights from much of this literature have been important in developing a coherent body of thought. However, one senses that economists and those responsible for externality policy are, after all of this impressive progress, still failing to communicate. It would seem that as theorists we need to work harder to rationalize our own constructs, as well as to connect them more closely with the world of public policy.

The obvious place to start would seem to be with the explicit policy conclusions derived from externality models – specifically the conclusion of Pareto irrelevancy. Of course everyone, not just economists, should be interested in gaining efficiency. But it remains true that some economists have a tendency to advocate efficiency to an extreme that ensures their isolation from the everyday policy struggle that is concerned with reconciling unwanted joint costs. The quest of economics as a social science has been unremittingly toward the idea of an objective value-free discipline. The result of that search for truth has been to strip externality theory of any ethical content.

As theory that is as it should be; as policy science it leaves us with a sterile message. Pareto irrelevancy as a theoretical justification to excuse us from the policy arena will continue to plague economists. Until we admit that externalities are about unwanted costs borne by members of a political system, and until we incorporate this reality into our theory, I fear that we shall remain isolated. A larger measure of the problem may be that economists have yet to come to grips with the relationship between the state and markets. The consistent liberal (in the European meaning of that term) economist starts with the notion that the state should set up the conditions for atomistic choice and then step aside and let consensual bargainers get on with the business of maximizing aggregate satisfaction. The minimal state – when new conditions require any modification of the prevailing institutional structure – would follow Pareto–Wicksellian dictates by compensating those who were harmed by the change. This would prevent the state from willy-nilly shifting economic advantage among the polity.

That this sanctifies the status quo should be obvious. In practice it means that all manner of offensive or dangerous activity, just because it is in existence, must be bought off by those who seek relief. Such economic theology is innocent of the Constitutional distinction between eminent domain (which is compensable) and exercise of the police power (which is not). The tyranny of the status quo in externality policy, justified by the concept of Pareto irrelevancy, is a serious matter. Such a view of the world subjugates the political process to the market – a breathtaking convolution of reality. It also confuses the very essence of welfare economics, specifically that for any particular institutional structure there is a Pareto-efficient allocation of resources against which any number of externality situations might be judged Pareto irrelevant. Because it is the institutional structure defining property rights that indicates which costs must be reckoned by atomistic agents, we find ourselves using welfare theory inside this very institutional structure to disregard certain unwanted costs as irrelevant.

It should be clear, therefore, that the concept of government intervention is thus stripped of any analytical – though not emotional – content. Just when did government intervene? When the prevailing market processes were first established? Or only when those currently protected by presumed rights see that they might be forced to internalize costs hitherto shifted to others? Alpha's intervention is Beta's relief.

One persistent puzzle in externality theory and policy concerns why we continue to see primary reliance upon pollution standards and quotas in the face of near unanimity among economists favoring effluent taxes? In this economists are opposed by both politicians and the industries currently imposing unwanted costs. Surely perceptions of the potential administrative costs of a system of effluent charges figure in shaping this particular policy outcome. But another measure of blame may go to economists for failing to show that we understand the politics of unwanted costs. One might speculate that we see here the familiar ambivalence of business to real market processes. By that I mean the observation that those in business celebrate the metaphor of the market – but most especially when it is serving them well. When conditions turn less favorable it is not so easy to agree with market outcomes; indeed it is then that any number of erstwhile market apologists seek government relief. Consistency in such matters may be too much for us to expect.

The economist can regain currency in the political economy of externalities if we would focus the policy debate in a way that highlights the efficiency and distributional aspects of unwanted costs. That is, it should fall to us to frame the issues in a way that allows the policy process to reach of its own accord those solutions that we would consider both equitable and avoiding the most egregious inefficiencies. As Dahlman (1979) reminds us, workable policy prescriptions must be derived from comparison of the status quo with an attainable concept of the desideratum. To the extent that our usual view of the ideal world assumes away transaction costs and welfare (income) effects – conditions that preclude the existence of Pareto-relevant externalities in the first instance – then the policy goal can never be achieved.

But an alternative model that admits of the presence of transaction costs, income effects, and the very real fact of cost incidence on unwilling parties provides a feasible starting point from which to undertake an analysis of externalities and their resolution. The very fact that environmental control is still regarded as the *marginal* cost of a polluting commodity (coal, electricity produced with coal, paper, many products containing chemicals) indicates that we have not been successful in correctly framing the issues. Until we convince those in charge of environmental policy that the full marginal social cost of offending products is not being paid by consumers then we have failed in our educational mission.

Yet another educational job is to be found in the matter of the cost incidence of the status quo while the search for decisive information continues. As indicated earlier, those benefiting from the current structure of institutional arrangements will continue to press for more research – all the while shifting costs to others. Those now bearing unwanted costs might be excused for growing impatient while the search goes on for the perfect data. The burden of transaction costs falls mainly on those currently not protected by rights. Economists would do well to study externalities from this perspective.

It seems reasonable to suppose that externalities will persist, and in fact become a more important element of economic life. Population density and certain technologies almost guarantee as much. There is yet another factor. One aspect of technology is the growth of knowledge that allows us to establish with greater precision causality of certain events hitherto blamed on mother nature. As medical science advances we find out that certain outcomes were contributed to by all manner of human artifacts. These soon result in efforts to resolve the matter; such efforts being aimed at the legislative or judicial branches of government. While acts of God are not policy variables, actions taken by other individuals or groups clearly are. One ramification of science's reducing the unexplained variation in the world around us is to bring ever more conflicts up for mediation. You feel differently about unwanted costs that are an inexplicable part of life than you do about unwanted costs visited on you by a neighbor – or some distant corporation. Economists will continue to have an important role to play in the domain of externality policy. That role will be enhanced to the extent that we understand the legal aspects of rights and duties, privileges and no rights, and inalienability. It will also be enhanced to the extent that we appreciate statutory and case law in matters of nuisance, tort, and property law.

NOTES

1 Recall, from the previous chapter, that it is more correct to regard such problems as a conflict of private or individual interests.
2 It is also necessary to point out that many externalities are not quite as innocent as this statement would suggest. When a steel mill or a chemical factory undertakes to manufacture its primary product, there is no doubt in the minds of the engineers that certain by-products of this manufacturing process will cause disposal problems. Hence, while we may conclude that pollutants are indeed *incidental* to the main business of the factory, they are far from *unintended* (Schmid, 1987).

5

Property Rights,
Missing Markets,
and Environmental
Uncertainty

> It is a partnership in all science; a partnership in all art; a
> partnership in every virtue, and in all perfection. As the ends
> of such a partnership cannot be obtained in many
> generations, it becomes a partnership not only between those
> living, but between those who are living, those who are dead,
> and those who are to be born.
>
> Edmund Burke,
> on the contract between generations, from
> *Reflections on the Revolution in France*

1 INTRODUCTION

While property rights are now recognized to play an important role
in environmental policy, several issues remain in which the significance
of this role has not been fully recognized. One will often hear economists
insist that the government merely needs to establish private property
rights and then allow bargaining among competing interests over those
rights. It is claimed that, regardless of the initial assignment of rights,
economic efficiency will result from the ensuing bargaining. In practical
terms this would suggest that owners of factories and those who fish
in polluted rivers should be able to negotiate over the efficient level

An earlier version of this chapter appeared in the *Journal of Environmental Economics
and Management*, 17, 181–94, September 1989. I am grateful to the journal for
permission to include it here.

of dead fish. Ignored in such optimistic prescriptions, as seen in chapter 4, is that transaction costs may well preclude the necessary bargaining. We may have a Pareto-irrelevant externality simply on the basis of high transaction costs that render the status quo "efficient." The interference leading to the externality is rendered irrelevant in a policy sense solely on the basis of the transaction costs that preclude negotiations between affected parties. In that case, some are not above claiming that what exists must therefore be "optimal."[1] Hence if the status quo is one of massive fish kills from industrial pollution, and those who fish are unable to offer enough to the factories to reduce their pollution emissions, then it must be optimal as it stands.

But of course this outcome, as Coase himself recognized, cannot stand close scrutiny.[2] In their early survey of property rights issues, Furubotn and Pejovich note that:

> different property rights assignments lead to different penalty reward structures and, hence, decide the choices that are open to decision makers . . . "property rights" tend to influence incentives and behavior. . . . A central point . . . is that property rights do not refer to relations between men and things but, rather, *to the sanctioned behavioral relations among men that arise from the existence of things and pertain to their use.* Property rights assignments specify the norms of behavior with respect to things that each and every person must observe in his interactions with other persons, or bear the cost of nonobservance. The prevailing system of property rights in the community can be described, then, as the set of economic and social relations defining the position of each individual with respect to the utilization of scarce resources. (Furubotn and Pejovich, 1972, pp. 1138–9)

If one were to believe the full allocative neutrality of property rights assignments, efficiency would obtain regardless of who had a *right* and who had a correlated *duty*. With the assumption of zero transaction costs, and in the absence of income effects, mutually beneficial exchange was sure to result in efficiency. But of course transaction costs are never zero. It is, after all, high transaction costs that explain intertemporal externalities. If there were but a way to negotiate with the unborn at low cost, then we might safely assume that the interests of the future could be reflected in contemporary policy choices of significance for future generations. In the absence of a market through which the bids of the future might be entered, the present stands uniquely empowered to pass on the endowment that *we* decide is appropriate for the future.[3]

I have suggested, in chapter 3, that entitlements in environmental policy can be regarded as rights protected by *property rules, liability rules*, or *inalienability rules*. When the present stands able to act without regard to the interests of the future then the present has *privilege* and the future has *no rights*. That is, if the present generation is able to ignore the costs it is imposing on future generations then a *de facto* legal situation of *privilege* and *no right* exists. Under this status quo entitlement it will often seem to be inefficient to require that abatement expenditures be undertaken. But when property rights are understood to be a policy variable, and when entitlements are modified to one of *right* for the future as against a *duty* for the present, then the economist has three policy instruments to consider: (1) mandated abatement; (2) full compensation for future damages; or (3) an annuity that, in all likelihood, will exactly indemnify the future for the costs we impose on it.

That is, if we regard those living in the future to have a *right* not to have their interests disregarded, and correspondingly those living now to have a *duty* not to interfere with those interests, then the analysis takes on a new dimension. First, how shall the present deal with the right of the future not to bear unwanted costs? A *right* protected by a *property rule* requires that the two parties arrange an exchange agreement *ex ante*. This would entail those who will live in the future negotiating with those of us living in the present; a difficult feat indeed. That leaves only the *liability rule* or the *inalienability rule* as a means of protecting the *right* of future generations. An inalienability rule would require specific control (or abatement) of all future damages. Current policy for addressing hazardous materials is an example of protecting the *right* of the future (and acting on the *duty* of the present) by an inalienability rule. Essentially, we are admitting that no bargain is possible and ameliorative action today is appropriate. Where the presumed *right* of the future to be free of possible harm is complicated by uncertainty – as is the more realistic case – we can explore the probable cause of political action that seems to countermand the expected utility postulates. I shall suggest that this political response to uncertainty over future damages is the *inalienability rule* at work.

But not all environmental policy need be addressed through the inalienability rule; there are instances in which it ought to be quite acceptable to protect the future's *right* through a *liability rule*. In this chapter I shall illustrate how a fuller consideration of the rules defining entitlements can suggest novel policy instruments.

2   THE INTERTEMPORAL PROBLEM: MISSING MARKETS

Consider the familiar situation in which the present generation takes an action of known and certain costs – such action precluding, ten years hence, known and certain damages to those living at that time. While the assumption of certainty here is unrealistic, it will simplify the story and help to focus attention on the pertinent analytical issue. Economists involved in environmental policy confront such matters repeatedly. One example might be the control of SO_2 to reduce future damages from acid deposition to lakes and forests. Another might be efforts taken today to improve the otherwise unsafe storage of hazardous materials. Abstracting from the uncertainty of these policy choices, the problem is seen to be one in which the current generation has the ability to take unilateral actions of potential harm or benefit to the future; it is often said that *the present stands as a dictator over the future*.

There are several dimensions of intertemporal externality problems. The first concerns the intertemporal *asymmetry* of the choice problem. I stress the notion of asymmetry to emphasize that, unlike many externality problems, there are few actions that the victims (those living in the future) can take to ameliorate the detrimental effects of our actions today. These are situations of *asymmetrical externalities* in which only the present generation is able to act so as to relieve the future of unwanted costs. The second aspect concerns a *missing market*; the present generation is faced with the choice of spending funds today that will have the effect of reducing (or eliminating) future damages. Because the future is not able to have its interests represented in this matter, I suggest that we regard this as an instance of a missing market. It is not a situation of *market failure* since, quite clearly, there is no market present. If by a market we mean a structured opportunity for two or more agents to exchange ownership of future benefit streams, then there is no market in situations of intertemporal externalities. It bears keeping in mind that regardless of the actions taken by the present to provide for the interests of future generations – as those now living perceive and define those interests – the existence of a market still requires the willful coming together of two consenting agents to exchange for mutual gain.[4]

In the face of intertemporal asymmetries and the related fact that markets are not capable of operating, how is the policy choice likely to be cast? Assume that the present generation, by expending $300 today, could preclude the visitation of $450 of damages on citizens ten years from now. If the choice problem were assessed in the conventional manner, one would compute the present value of the future damages and offer that as a comparison with the required expenditure of $300 today. At an assumed discount rate of 8 percent, the present value of $450 ten years hence is $208. The economist would regard a present cost of $300 as against a present-valued loss of $208 and be hard pressed to suggest that intertemporal efficiency is served by spending $300 today to avert future damages whose present value is but $208. That is, there seems scant reason to support the idea that the status quo can be fairly characterized as one of "market failure." Only when the present-valued losses exceed $300 is there a prima facie case for market failure. Alternatively, technological change might reduce the necessary control cost from $300 to, say, $200, at which time it would indeed appear that there is now a market failure. That is, now the present-valued costs ($200) are less than the present-valued benefits ($208) and hence the status quo is not efficient.

Lacking technological change to reduce necessary costs of abatement, and unless damages increase, the policy analyst might be inclined to suggest that it is efficient for the present generation to ignore the costs imposed on the future. Others could be expected to argue that the analyst's logic is suspect, and to advocate the expenditure of $300 now to avoid future losses of $450. In the course of that debate, the moral poverty of discounting would be a major item of discussion; indeed, at a discount rate of zero the calculation would suggest that spending $300 today to avoid $450 in damages ten years hence is the right thing to do. Those concerned with pollution damages in the future would probably carry the day and there would soon be a law requiring the expenditure of $300 to avoid present-valued damages of $208. The economist will not be amused.

Recognizing that this is an instance of a missing market, it will be necessary to take yet one more step to see the essential feature of the choice problem. The economic analysis has implicitly assumed that the present generation has a right to impose costs on the future and can only be denied that right if it is more efficient to do otherwise. The politician, on the other hand, may doubt that the present generation has the right to impose costs on the future. More significantly, others might well argue that the present generation has a *duty* not to impose unwanted costs on the future. The economist, if sufficiently enamored of Coase, will be inclined to suggest that entitlements are (1) analytically irrelevant; or (2) acceptable and therefore beyond question; or (3) the proper domain of the politician. The politician is sure that entitlements are everything, and will be inclined to argue about which of the parties – the present or the future – has an entitlement that we might call a *right*.

Interestingly, the economist who fails to find a market failure – thus believing the status quo to be efficient – and the politician who demands that $300 be spent now are both wrong. The proper policy stance is not to defend the status quo until there is clear evidence of a market failure (an efficiency loss), nor to demand that control expenditures be immediately undertaken. There is a unique dominant solution to this intertemporal asymmetric externality, one that starts with the realization that property rights dominate the definition of the problem, and so the formulation of the appropriate policy response. This can be established by considering possible policy instruments *from within* alternative entitlement structures.

Under the status quo property rights structure the present generation is free to take whatever actions are regarded as in our best interest. The finding from above that it would be "inefficient" to invest in control (or abatement) measures is a reflection of that presumptive entitlement. The judgment of the appropriate course of action – where appropriate is defined as seeking the policy that is efficient – is made in spite of an entitlement structure that is solicitous of unilateral actions by those of us living in the present, and a missing market in which those living in the future are unable to bid on behalf of their economic interests. Likewise, the political response to mandate an expenditure of $300 is taken within the status quo property structure, but it is a partial (and incomplete) analysis when one considers the more general issue of alternative property arrangements. Traditional economic analysis seems to endorse the status quo property structure until it can be shown to be inefficient; the political response challenges the legitimacy of the status quo property rights but fails to understand the real efficiency issue at stake. Mandating regulatory controls is not in the interest of overall efficiency.

The meaning of efficiency in this decision problem can be considered with the aid of figure 5.1. The line WZ reflects the social opportunity cost of capital and, by assumption, the prevailing social marginal rate of time preference between consumption today ($t = 0$) and consumption ten years from now ($t = 10$). Assume that at $t = 0$ the present generation has $1,800 available that can be allocated for consumption, for investment, or for some combination of the two. We would start at point W by inquiring into the possibilities for using investment funds today that will yield various returns in ten years. The line WZ depicts the return on those funds if invested in a ten-year 8 percent note. For instance, if $300 were invested in $t = 0$ it would yield, after ten years at 8 percent, $648. Notice that WZ defines financial opportunities in a perfect capital market where funds can be loaned and borrowed at the same rate (8 percent). This can be confirmed by noting that $648 has a discounted present value (when $i = 8$ percent) of $300. But there are other profitable uses of the $300 and these are traced out by the intertemporal production possibilities frontier MW. For instance, if the current generation would decide to invest $300 in productive investments (say factory expansion), rather than in a bank note, it would yield approximately $1,080 after ten years; this is a gain of $432 over the return available if that money were invested at the prevailing market rate of 8 percent. Given the assumed discount rate of 8 percent, it can be seen that the efficient point in terms of maximizing the value of consumption over the two periods is found at point R. Here, where the rate of time preference (8 percent) is equal to the rate at which investment today is transformed into consumption in $t = 10$, $400 would be invested. This would leave $1,400 available for consumption in $t = 0$, plus $1,300 available in $t = 10$, for total intertemporal consumption of $2,700. Call this option A.[5]

The choice problem is straightforward, and the status quo property rights regime allows the present generation to ignore the interests of the future. The present generation is, to borrow a Friedmanesque phrase, "free to choose." But the political response will probably be one in which that freedom of choice is soon removed. Specifically, the control option might be required in which case $300 must be spent now, leaving a new intertemporal production possibilities frontier of NM along which discretionary investments can be undertaken by the present generation. After the required expenditure of $300 the present generation would allocate the remaining $1,500 so as to maximize intertemporal consumption benefits. This would lead to point R* on NM, implying productive investments of $180, present consumption of $1,320, and consumption in $t = 10$ of $648. Call this option B.

The economist would be quick to point out that the meddlesome hand of government had forced total intertemporal consumption benefits down from $2,250 to $1,968 – a reduction of $282 simply to save present-valued damages to the future of $208. Another way to look at the issue would be that the present generation was being forced to suffer a reduction in intertemporal consumption of $732 simply to avoid $450 in damages to the future. The gainers (the future) would be willing to pay $450 or less to the present generation, while the present generation would require $732 or more to remain as well off as under option A. The status quo property rights structure produces a situation in which the apparent "freedom" of the present generation to ignore the interests of the future is consistent with efficiency as ordinarily reckoned. Finally, a decision arising from collective action through the political arena appears inefficient if it does anything other than defend the status quo.

There may be a tendency to view this as the familiar problem of sacrificing efficiency for the sake of redistributing income to the future.

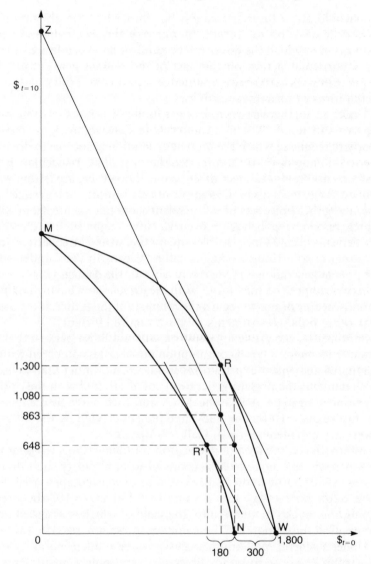

Figure 5.1   Efficiency under two entitlement structures.

But the judgment about efficiency or inefficiency is incomplete. To see this consider a "general equilibrium" analysis. Here one would want to allow institutional arrangements – entitlements – to change and then one would recalculate the efficient solution. That is, imagine that the present generation was not free to choose whether to undertake actions that would abate future damages, but rather had the obligation not to impose costs on the future. Notice that this is far different from a situation in which the government *requires* an expenditure of funds for a particular action on the part of the present generation. That requirement, as seen above, mandated a particular policy *instrument* in the form of abatement activities.

Under an alternative structure of entitlement one has a different policy *objective* in mind. The new policy objective would be to create a property regime in which the present generation is not free to disregard the costs imposed on future generations. The particular policy instruments chosen to meet this objective, however, are left up to the economic agents. This is an example of new institutional arrangements redefining the choice sets of independent economic agents, from within which maximizing behavior occurs. How might such a change in entitlements occur? One possible explanation would be collective action resulting in something we might call a "Clean Air Act" under which the present generation is made responsible for the damages that it would otherwise impose on the future. With the present now having no option about whether or not to regard the interests of the future, it is possible that other policy instruments might be more efficient.

Specifically, the present generation will search for actions that will enhance its intertemporal consumption possibilities compared with the mandated abatement expenditures from before. Rather than investing in abatement, the present generation could proceed with the optimal investment strategy at R along MW, and then agree to compensate the future in $t = 10$ for the \$450 in damages created by the failure to invest in abatement in $t = 0$. Call this option C.

Alternatively, the present generation could invest in a ten-year note at 8 percent and agree to assign this yield at maturity such that the losses (\$450) borne in the future could be exactly compensated. That is, a \$208 note today has a value of \$450 in $t = 10$; the present generation invests in an annuity, the yield of which is assigned to the future. Call this option D. These options are summarized in Table 5.1

Under a general equilibrium analysis, where entitlements are allowed to vary in response to policy objectives, and policy instruments are then chosen by maximizing agents, intertemporal efficiency is served if the present generation pursues option C rather than being forced to adopt option B. Moreover, the future is left as well off as under the mandated control strategy. The new property rights regime does not mean that the present generation has an obligation to improve the wealth position of the future; it means only that the interests of the future must be given protection. Both options C and D protect those

Table 5.1. Intertemporal consumption under different entitlements
($i = 8$ percent)

Entitlement	Option	Present	Future	Aggregate
Privilege for present, no right for future	A (ignore future damages)	2,700	– 450	2,250
Duty for present, right for future	B (control)	1,968	0	1,968
Duty for present, right for future	C (compensation)	2,250	0	2,250
Duty for present, right for future	D (annuity)	2,000	0	2,000

interests, and leave those living in the present better off than if option B had been required by the government. But option C is clearly preferred by the present generation. Does the change in entitlements make the future richer? *Yes*, if the status quo entitlement structure is accepted as the proper one. *No*, if the proper entitlement structure is one in which the present generation is obligated to consider the interests of the future; this entitlement structure merely prevents the present generation from making the future worse off. Notice that the structure of property rights not only determines how decisions are framed and choices made, but also determines how we shall assess the impacts of those choices. If the future is regarded as having no legitimate case to have its losses covered by the present then one might be tempted to view the problem as one of the present generation having to sacrifice present and future income in order to make the future better off. On the other hand, if the future is regarded as having a *right* not to incur losses at the hands of the present, then those now living will be viewed as doing what is correct – giving up ill-gotten income – in order not to impair the well-being of the future.

It is sometimes suggested that the type of intertemporal problem explored here would not arise if the social rate of discount were zero rather than some positive number. To pursue this imagine that the rate of discount were assumed to be zero, a situation in which $1 today is worth exactly $1 ten years from now. In this instance, the intertemporal production possibilities frontier depicting investment and consumption tradeoffs would remain unchanged (MW); after all there are still productive investments in the economy. The mere fact that the government decided to adopt a zero discount rate for the economic evaluation of pollution control would not have any effect on productive investments in the private sphere. However, the line WZ would now rotate around the point W toward the southwest. The general equilibrium efficient solution is option C and so it can be seen that the assumed social rate of discount (by which the $450 of damages gets reduced to $208) is immaterial to the policy choice. Both option C and option D still dominate option B, the only one that could benefit from an assumed zero rate of discount. It is, instead, the new institutional arrangement of a *duty* for the present generation and a *right* for the future that dominates the policy choice. Under either assumption of discount rates, the status quo property regime allows those living in the present to impose unwanted costs on the future. A forced control strategy in the present is inferior to the other entitlement structure regardless of the discount rate.[6]

This issue can be recast in the larger context of intertemporal justice where one expects that the present will take actions *vis-à-vis* the future that reflect, were their respective temporal positions reversed, actions that the future would be inclined to take *vis-à-vis* the present. Rather than casting this as an issue of making those living in the future better off at the expense of those living in the present, the issue is properly seen as one of selecting an institutional structure to mediate intertemporal choice that all participants would agree to from behind a Rawlsian veil of ignorance.[7] There

> no one knows his place in society, his class position or social status; nor does he know his fortune in the distribution of natural assets and abilities, his intelligence and strength, and the like. Nor, again, does anyone know his conception of the good, the particulars of his rational plan of life, or even the special features of his psychology such as his aversion to risk or liability to optimism or pessimism. More than this, I assume that the parties do not know the particular circumstances of their own society. That is, they do not know its economic or political situation, or the level of civilization and culture it has been able to achieve. The persons in the original position have no information as to which generation they belong. (Rawls, 1971, p. 137)

Because the *efficient choice is a function of the presumed institutional (property rights) structure*, the appropriate policy question is one of which institutional structure would be selected if we had no prior basis for knowing which group of citizens would hold precedence in time over the other. It seems reasonable to suppose that unanimous assent would be forthcoming only for a structure of entitlements that bestowed an obligation on the earlier generation not to ignore the economic interests of those to come later. It would seem to strain credulity to suppose that unanimous agreement would be forthcoming for an entitlement structure that gave the early generation complete freedom to do as it pleased with respect to the economic well-being of those living in the future. For what incentive would either group have to vote for such an entitlement structure if they could not be certain that they would be first in time?

In summary, the matter of missing markets and intertemporal environmental problems highlights the central role to be played by the prior specification of property rights, and the particular presumptions that attend those entitlements. Of particular interest is the way in which the impact of alternative property structures is manifest. Specifically, one might expect to find that an entitlement of *privilege* for the present and *no right* for the future leads to dirty air, while an entitlement of *duty* for the present and *right* for the future leads to clean air. Note that this would be the inefficient outcome of moving from option A to option B. In fact, as the illustration shows, the air will be dirty under both the general equilibrium options (C and D) and the question is one of which policy instrument will most efficiently remunerate those living in the future for this fact. Under prevailing technology of pollution abatement, and given the current estimates of damage, dirty air and indemnification of the future is the efficient course to follow.

3 PROPERTY RIGHTS, RISK, AND CHOICES

Until this point we have been concerned with choices under certainty, and my purpose was to illustrate how property regimes influence our assessment of efficiency. I showed that a "general equilibrium" analysis of property rights, in which policy objectives are distinct from policy instruments, would avoid the suboptimization so inherent in partial equilibrium assessments of environmental policy. But the picture is quite clearly complicated by uncertainty. Indeed, much environmental policy is concerned with known costs for the present generation, and with uncertain benefits in the future. How do alternative property regimes alter policy analysis in situations of environmental uncertainty?

Consider the policy problem of air pollution from acid deposition. Here, it is possible to identify at least six different aspects of uncertainty. The first dimension of uncertainty pertains to the identification of the sources of particular pollutants. For instance, what proportion of Canada's damages from acid deposition is attributable to US sources and how much is attributable to Canadian sources? The second type of uncertainty pertains to the conveyance process and hence the ultimate destination of particular emissions. That is, how much of known emissions in the Ohio Valley go northeast toward Canada, and how much moves northwest toward Illinois, Wisconsin, and Minnesota? The third aspect of uncertainty pertains to the actual physical impacts at the point of destination. The fourth aspect of uncertainty concerns the human valuation (or reaction to) the realized impacts at the point of destination of the emissions. The fifth dimension of uncertainty concerns the extent to which a particular policy response will have an impact on emissions, conveyance, ultimate physical impacts, and finally the human reaction (the putative benefits of the policy) to those changes. And the sixth dimension concerns the actual cost level and the incidence of those costs that are the result of the policy response.

These six dimensions of uncertainty concerning the air pollution problem are typical of the uncertainty that plagues policy formulation. This uncertainty creates the opportunity for errors in policy choice and is often used to justify doing nothing until more information is forthcoming. Those favored by the status quo property rights regime will suggest that not enough is known to justify such a "drastic" policy as requiring the elimination (or the reduction) of pollution emissions. These same individuals will also suggest that it is better to continue to fund research to determine whether or not a policy of full (or partial) restriction on emissions would be appropriate. But those bearing costs (or, in the intertemporal problem, those who speak for the future) will argue that to do nothing about current pollution is, in fact, to decide to continue a policy of ignoring costs imposed on unwilling parties. The presumptive right of the status quo – what I call "privilege" – defines a particular decision environment and requires that any action be judged against that benchmark. The burden of proof, and hence the transaction costs, fall on those currently bearing unwanted costs. The existing property rights will make those costs appear to be justified. Invariably the choice is cast as one of acting now or waiting until more (and presumably better) information is available. That this biases action in favor of the status quo ought to be obvious – for it is always easy to protest that we do not yet know enough to be certain that a policy response would improve the situation.[8]

A properly comprehensive analysis of policy choices would include the probabilities attached to alternative outcomes of pursuing a few distinct policy options. For instance, in debates over acid rain policy the options are usually cast in terms of percentage reductions in SO_2 (or NO_x). With that information one may then speculate about the possible impacts on future damages from these alternatives. The concern in such policy is to provide decision makers with an array of choices and to urge adoption of that action with the highest expected value. One complication in this familiar scheme is that public decision makers may not regard losses and gains symmetrically. If that is the case, the existing property regime takes on added importance. That is, the *expected value* decision maker will choose the action that produces the greatest expected payoff, while the decision maker concerned to *minimize maximum regret* will choose the action that promises the smallest expected opportunity loss. Under conventional treatments of risk the expected payoff is simply the obverse of the expected opportunity loss. However, this is a symmetry of theory that may contradict empirical reality. If it does, there is yet another reason why the economist and the politician will approach environmental policy from quite different perspectives.

Specifically, recent developments in the theory of risk analysis provide an opportunity to illustrate the importance of status quo institutional arrangements in problems where uncertainty is present (see Kahneman and Tversky, 1979; Tversky and Kahneman, 1981, 1987). In *prospect theory* one partitions the decision problem into two parts: (1) framing the actions, outcomes, and contingencies; and (2) evaluating the choices to be made. When this is done, the experimental evidence indicates that people do not behave as expected utility theory predicts they will. In an illustration of the "certainty effect," Kahneman and Tversky (1979) found that 80 percent of their respondents preferred a sure gain of 3,000 units to the following choice: a 4,000-unit gain with probability of 0.8 or a zero gain with probability of 0.2. The expected value of the sure thing is 3,000 while the expected value of the gamble is 3,200. Yet the sure thing was the dominant choice. When concerned with losses as opposed to gains they found the opposite effect. That is, a sure loss of 3,000 units was preferred by only 8 percent of the respondents, while the following gamble was preferred by 92 percent: a 4,000-unit loss with probability 0.8, or a zero loss with probability of 0.2. In the positive domain the certainty effect contributes to risk aversion so that a sure gain is taken rather than a larger, but probable, gain. In the negative domain the certainty effect leads to risk-seeking preferences for a probable loss over a smaller – but certain – loss.

This distinction between the positive and negative domains is relevant because, unlike conventional investment analysis, many instances of collective action in environmental policy require that expenditures be undertaken now to protect against probable losses in the future. It is important to understand that *expected payoffs from productive investments differ from expected losses from failure to make defensive investments* – even if the problem is cast in terms of a single generation. Consider the choices studied by Kahneman and Tversky. To keep the problem tractable assume that the policy maker is presented with a fairly simple choice problem:

A   do nothing about acid rain and suffer certain losses in habitat valued at 3,000; or

B   install engineering devices that precipitate out acid precursors.

If action B is taken there are two possible outcomes:

1   there is an 80 percent probability that the devices will not work and we shall lose the cost of the devices plus the habitat for a total loss of 4,000; or

2   there is a 20 percent probability that the devices will work and net losses, after paying for the devices, will be zero.

Here we have a decision problem very much like the one studied by Kahneman and Tversky. The value of the gamble in the Kahneman and Tversky experiment indicated that 92 percent of the respondents preferred option B (control acid rain) to option A (do nothing about acid rain) in spite of the fact that option A (do nothing about acid rain) has the lowest expected value. Moreover, their respondents were risk seeking in the domain of losses in the hopes of hitting the 20 percent chance of no loss at all. In the above choices there is a sure loss if nothing is done, and a fairly high probability of a loss if action is taken.

In another experiment Kahneman and Tversky offered the following choices regarding possible losses:

A   a 45 percent chance of a 6,000-unit loss, and a 55 percent chance of zero loss; or

B   a 90 percent chance of a 3,000-unit loss, and a 10 percent chance of zero loss.

In both instances the value of the gamble is the same (an expected loss of 2,700) and yet their respondents favored option A by 92 percent to 8 percent. If we again imagine this to be an acid rain problem, it is not hard to see that option A (some control strategy that still has only a near 50–50 chance of reducing losses) might be preferred even though its expected value is identical with the do nothing option (B).

Risk aversion and risk seeking have different dimensions when choices involving gains are compared with choices involving losses. Tversky and Kahneman refer to *loss aversion* as the situation in which there is a discrepancy ". . . between the amount of money people are willing to pay for a good and the compensation they demand to give it up" (1987, p. 74).[9] While "loss aversion" may capture what is at work here, I suggest that these differences reflect underlying perceptions regarding entitlements and the presumed rights of the status quo. That is, if one is already in possession of something there is a *presumption* that the individual has an entitlement protected by a property rule.

Public decision makers will often seem to be taking actions that will minimize losses, as opposed to actions that will maximize gains; for this they are often thought to be irrational. Yet recall that rationality speaks to action consistent with preferences, and it may well be that those in a position to make collective decisions are willing to gamble to avoid certain losses but are risk averse in the domain of gains – preferring a certain gain to a probabilistic chance at a much larger gain. The Minimax Regret Decision Criterion from expected utility theory addresses the difference between the payoff from the correct decision and the payoff from the actual decision. Because of the presence of irreversibilities in many choices, and owing to the social stigma of having made "wrong" choices, it is reasonable to suppose that many policy makers – just as with most participants in the Kahneman and Tversky experiments – reject the formal equivalence of the expected value of gains and losses. If so, this fact alone would make policy makers more inclined to adopt a strategy that seems to minimize their maximum regret.

While under conventional assumptions minimizing one's maximum regret seems equivalent to choosing so as to maximize expected benefits, prospect theory suggests otherwise. Perhaps risk-averse choices in the face of certain gains reflect a particular attitude of *property rights* toward the expected gains. If that is so, then decision makers may see no reason to engage in probabilistic games that may enhance those gains but which may also reduce the gains to zero. On the other hand, when decision makers are faced with certain losses unless something is done, they may be quite unwilling to sit idly by without undertaking actions to reduce those certain losses – even recognizing the remote prospect of even greater losses.

The differential perceptions of gains and losses, and the fact that much collective action is concerned with *defensive* actions (pollution control devices, regulation of new drugs, seat-belt laws, laws that prohibit smoking in public places), seem important for how we analyze collective choice situations. But the essential issue here is that the status quo entitlement (property rights) structure will dominate the framing of the choice problem, and also will influence judgments of the "efficiency" of alternative policy options. An entitlement structure that seems to permit individuals to engage in certain behaviors (pollute, use whatever drugs they can afford, smoke wherever they choose) will clearly color the way in which the decision problem is cast and evaluated. Similarly, if politicians perceive an implicit property rights structure in which individuals are thought to have a "right" to something, we should not be surprised to observe actions that display scant interest in taking chances with that perceived right.

4   SUMMARY

The debate over particular environmental policies is usually cast in the metaphor of a "market failure." The Coase theorem is then adduced to suggest that the initial assignment of property rights is irrelevant to the ultimate outcome and hence nothing much can – or should – be done. As long as there is *some* initial assignment, and all interested parties are able to negotiate over those rights, then efficiency will presumably result. With that, substantive consideration of the institutional arrangements that determine the status quo is dismissed and attention turns to direct regulation of the offending activity. The economist looks down on this setting with mixed feelings. On the one hand it seems that, indeed, something is amiss (since there seems to be an externality present), and yet the Coasian finding suggests that nothing should be done since the assignment of rights is held not to matter. On the other hand there is hardly a "market" present and hence how can one show "market failure"? Yet, the public is clamoring for a policy intervention to fix what is perceived to be a serious wrong.

While the idea of a market failure can be helpful to understand certain economic issues, there are times when important conceptual issues can be obscured if problems are approached from the perspective of market failure. If real causes are obscured then we may fail to understand the policy issue at stake, and our advice in the policy arena may be at odds with public perceptions of the problem, and hence of the appropriate solution. In this chapter I have offered a new interpretation of the classical "market failure–government intervention" metaphor that lies at the heart of public policy in general, and environmental policy in particular. I have done this by illustrating how institutional arrangements – property rights – influence the definition of the problem, and so determine the perception of the "optimal" policy response to environmental problems. It was seen that the interests of the future can be protected via a liability rule or an inalienability rule. The inalienability rule requires a control strategy (option B) that may not be in the interest of economic efficiency. Protecting the interests of the future through the mechanism of a right protected by a liability rule was seen to suggest two novel policy instruments – outright compensation (option C) and an annuity (option D). Under option D, where an annuity is purchased in the present, there must be rather precise knowledge of the future costs to be indemnified. Under option C, where the present is obligated to compensate the future, there is more scope of flexibility. But when uncertainty is introduced notice how the residual bearer of risk changes under the two policy instruments. Under the annuity plan (option D) it is the future that bears the risk that damages will exceed the value of the annuity, while the present bears the risk that the future damages will be less than expected.

Under the compensation plan (option C) it is the present that stands fully exposed to the unknown future damages – being required to compensate the future for said damages. Of course the implementation of a compensation scheme is not easy to imagine, unless some "earnest money" is contributed by the present generation; otherwise how can the future exact compensation from those no longer living? The earnest money might be in the form of a tax on polluting activities and dedicated to reducing the magnitude of the national debt that will be inherited by the future. This story about property rights, uncertainty, and efficiency alerts us to the fact that the simple metaphor of *market failure–government intervention* is not only overworked, but inappropriate. It is too simple to assume that government-mandated controls will fix environmental problems – a position that the business community and conservative economists have long held. But neither does it follow that the status quo is therefore appropriate (or optimal). The economist must look beyond the status quo institutional setup to ponder and to analyze – in a "general equilibrium" fashion – the full implications of missing markets in intertemporal externalities. Rather than berating politicians for being irrational (or of favoring "inefficient" policies), the approach suggested here might help us to develop theoretical constructs that explain such behavior. When environmental policy is characterized by uncertainty – as it surely is – then perceptions of the status quo entitlement structure will have an important impact on the willingness of decision makers to expose themselves to charges of having "given away" some perceived "right." While this broader analysis of environmental policy will raise important questions about the meaning of "efficiency" in policy analysis, there are even more fundamental problems on that front. To those we now turn.

NOTES

1   See Demsetz (1967) for a version of this reasoning.
2   The Coase article on social costs (1960) may stand as the paragon of literature that is often cited but rarely read. Given its length, and the detailed legal and historical tone, it may also be that those who cite it started the article but did not finish it. Had they finished it, many of the so-called "conclusions" from Coase would be seen as false. Put somewhat differently, Coase recognized the highly unrealistic nature of the assumptions regarding zero transaction costs and the absence of wealth affects. In the absence of these assumptions, his conclusions about the neutrality of rights assignments cannot stand. Many later writers, who find his *laissez faire* message agreeable, have not been so cautious about the realism of assumptions.
3   See Samuels (1974) for a discussion of the problems with the strict Coasian analysis.
4   One may be understandably troubled by the hypothetical nature of my model. Specifically, I shall reach a conclusion about efficiency without allowing those living in the future to enter a bid, without giving them a chance to express their willingness to pay. My reasoning runs as follows: willingness to pay as an expression of one's interest in particular outcomes is suspect because it is constrained not only by the income of the bidder (as is well recognized), but also by the status quo entitlement structure that indicates *who* must offer payments to have their interests given protection. Individuals have preferences over institutional arrangements, and they have preferences over choices to be made from within those institutional arrangements. Here, the higher-order preference of those living in the future is that they not be in a position of *no right vis-à-vis* the *privilege* of those living in the present. In a sense the future *has* entered a bid, but it is a "bid" over the entitlement structure rather than over resource allocation from within a particular allocation. For more on this see Bromley (1989a).
5   Note that those living in the present are assumed to be living in $t = 10$ and able to consume, even though they are not made to suffer the damages of those not yet born (but who will be alive in $t = 10$). It is as if those living in the present acquire immunity to the damages they will impose on those living in the future.
6   Note that the choice of discount rate could only influence some central controller intent upon finding an efficient allocation based on maximum aggregate present value.

7 This assumes that individuals are not risk seeking.

8 There is growing interest in understanding choice under "ambiguity." Specifically, "There are important psychological differences in the way people experience the uncertainty inherent in gambling devices as compared with those faced in everyday life. In gambling devices, the nature of uncertainty is explicit since there is a well-defined sampling space and sampling procedure. In contrast, when assessing uncertainty in real world tasks, the precision of the gambling analogy can be misleading . . . beliefs about uncertain events are typically loosely held and ill defined. Moreover, feelings of uncertainty are not limited to random influences that affect outcomes from a well-defined process (e.g., the proportions of different colored balls in an urn) but can extend to uncertainty about the underlying data generating process itself. In short, ambiguity or 'uncertainty about uncertainties' is a pervasive element of much real world decision making" (Einhorn and Hogarth, 1987, p. 43).

9 Also see the work by Knetsch and Sinden (1984).

6

The Tragedy of the Commons

> The first man who, having enclosed a piece of ground, bethought himself of saying "This is mine," and found people simple enough to believe him, was the real founder of civil society. From how many crimes, wars, and murders, from how many horrors and misfortunes might not anyone have saved mankind, by pulling up the stakes, or filling up the ditch, and crying to his fellows: "Beware of listening to this imposter, you are undone if you once forget that the fruits of the earth belong to us all, and the earth itself to nobody."
>
> Jean-Jacques Rousseau,
> *Discourse on Inequality*, part II

1 INTRODUCTION

The popular metaphor of the wasted commons has been with us now for two decades, pretending to explain any number of unfortunate circumstances from population growth to over-fishing of the high seas and poverty in the degraded deserts of the tropics.[1] Hence, any discussion of property rights in natural resources must, in some considerable detail, treat the issues inherent in the commons. In undertaking that discussion, it seems most fruitful to turn to that part of the world in which the commons is said to persist even today. The discussion of the so-called "tragedy of the commons" must therefore be concerned with the lands and related natural resources in the developing countries of the tropics, for it is here that one sees the very essence of property regimes that seem to resemble the "commons." In pursuing this discussion of the commons it will be argued that the real *tragedy of the commons* is the process whereby indigenous property rights structures have been undermined and delegitimized. This destruction of local-level authority systems will be seen as the principal cause of natural resource degradation in the tropics. A second dimension of that tragedy is the rather complete failure of the newly independent nation-states to establish the implicit and explicit legal foundations of an economy and society that will guide individual actions toward social betterment. This chapter, therefore, concerns two forms of institutional failure in the tropical agrarian countries following independence from colonialism.

The two aspects of institutional failure that have undermined property relations in natural resources are related, and both lead to the degradation of natural resources and poverty that are of so much concern today. The failure of nation-states to create the institutional preconditions for economic growth and development means that most economic activity is plagued by strategic uncertainty – a situation in which economic actors are precluded from maximization by the ever-changing nature of the "rules of the game." This fluid condition, what Myrdal called the *soft state*, means that the family and the village become the primary unit for economic exchange. In more familiar terms, subsistence production tends to dominate much of agriculture. With the institutional foundations of the economy being ineffective in providing the secure basis of economic calculation over space and time, we also find that social sanctions and conventions regarding land and natural resource use are either absent or contradictory. This situation can be thought of as arising from an *institutional vacuum*, or from *institutional dissonance*. In either case, independent economic agents are, for the most part, left to their own wile and creativity to assure survival. While it can be debilitating enough in an urban setting, the effects in a rural area will be much more profound. This urban–rural difference exists because transaction costs – the costs of gaining information, the costs of contracting with others, and the costs of enforcing contracts – are much higher in sparsely settled rural areas.

Many governments in the developing world, unstable, insecure, and usually preoccupied with maintaining their own legitimacy, view the rural hinterland as either irrelevant or a domain to be plundered for the benefit of the urban classes from whence power and legitimacy flow. The hinterlands are convenient because they can deliver agricultural products to the urban masses, and raw materials with which foreign exchange can be earned. The political and economic autonomy of the rural village is not only deemed to be unnecessary, but positively feared. Destruction of natural resources is the logical outcome of these circumstances, and such practices continue because they serve the interests of the national government. This is the tragedy of the commons that shall concern us here.

The issues are not trivial. First, a good share of the raw materials of such great fiscal importance to the newly independent nation-state originate on lands that are in the public domain, by which I mean nonprivate (nonfreehold) ownership. The plundering of these resources and these lands, usually at the behest and encouragement of the national government, is one tragedy of the commons. The other tragedy refers to the intangible commons, by which I mean the collective good we know as *the legal foundations of the economy*. Colonialism first, and then the new nation-state, both had much to gain by destroying existing institutional arrangements that governed village life. This destruction, and the subsequent failure to replace it with a nation-wide institutional infrastructure that I call the legal foundations of the economy comprise the second tragedy of the commons. The tragedy of this institutional vacuum in the developing countries means that economic activity is restricted in scope and time; poverty is the logical result. This institutional vacuum, and the attendant poverty of people at the village level, then give rise to the tangible tragedy of resource destruction of so much concern. The continued livelihood of approximately three-fourths of the world's population depends upon land and related natural resources that are adversely affected by a situation of institutional disarray. If resource degradation problems are to be solved, they must first be understood, and if we are to understand resource degradation then we must understand human behaviors with respect to those resources. The behaviors that now seem resource threatening are the product of a constellation of rules and conventions. If we are to understand resource degradation then, we must first comprehend the full array of these incentives, sanctions, rights, duties, privileges, and exposures to the actions of others.

2   THE PUBLIC DOMAIN

The so-called Green Revolution promised to put an end to hunger in the developing countries and so development assistance efforts since the early 1970s have focused almost exclusively on private lands under intensive cultivation. This emphasis had strong support from the richer countries who dominate bilateral economic and technical assistance. It was also popular with the major multilateral development agencies for a number of reasons. First, an emphasis on crop agriculture seemed to promise the greatest payoff from limited development resources. Second, such assistance could draw upon the large pool of scientific knowledge in the industrialized world – the majority of which was faced with a bounteous agriculture because of prior scientific progress. Third, crops were a more efficient way (compared with animal production) to produce food from a limited land base, and population pressure was threatening a number of tropical countries. Fourth, cereals comprised the basic wage good of most urban workers in the developing countries and governments could stand or fall over the failure to provide such commodities at affordable prices. Finally, crop agriculture occurs on private lands and the development assistance community has always felt most comfortable when working on projects directed toward private lands. While forestry projects became popular in the latter part of the 1970s, the focus even there has since shifted from projects on public domain lands to projects on farm plots and other privately owned lands.

These development assistance efforts have indeed spurred the production of cereals and other food crops from private lands. Meanwhile, governments and the development community have failed to develop meaningful programs to deal with the natural resource problems on nonprivate lands in the poor nations of the world. While deforestation in Nepal and land clearings in Brazil have received considerable attention in the media, there are millions of people still dependent upon the public domain for the bulk of their sustenance. The swelling urban slums of the capital cities in the tropics attest to the stark life still available to people from rural areas. How bad must it be in the rural hinterland for families to migrate to São Paulo, Mexico City, Calcutta, Karachi, and Khartoum? The increasingly degraded public domain lands, upon which many rural residents must depend, are not trivial in magnitude, nor is the number of people dependent upon them insignificant.

Recent official estimates place the standing forest cover of India at 72 million ha (22 percent of the total land area), but the actual figure is said to be closer to 23 million ha (7 percent). Whichever figure is correct, lands that were formerly forested are part of the public domain of interest here.[2] Degradation over the past century has reduced forest cover from an estimated 40 percent of what was British India (Commander, 1986). Other stories from sub-Saharan Africa tell a similar story. The pastoral/nomadic peoples of sub-Saharan Africa are well-known users of lands at the extensive economic margin. But others are equally dependent upon the public domain. Data from India indicate that for twenty-one (dry tropical) districts over seven states, between 84 and 100 percent of the poor households rely on public domain lands for ". . . food, fuel, fodder, and fibre items" (Jodha, 1986, p. 1172). Between 10 and 24 percent of the richer households in the study areas made use of the public domain for pond silt to enrich their fields and for timber.

This vast public domain in the arid tropics, on which so many individuals must depend – and usually the poorest ones at that – is the subject of a renewed interest among economists and development agencies. Drawing on the writings of biologists such as Hardin (1968) regarding the so-called tragedy of the commons, and the more ideological tracts by conservative commentators (Smith, 1981), one sees increasing belief that the way to solve resource degradation in the arid tropics is to create private property rights in land. While there are instances in which privatization may indeed be the answer, it is not correct to assume that such property regimes provide the widespread salvation promised for them. Specifically, this interest in privatization proceeds from an incomplete understanding of the full gamut of property regimes, from a refusal to acknowledge the obvious destruction of privately owned lands the world over (e.g. soil erosion), and from an unsupported optimism regarding who would ultimately benefit from privatization of the public domain. Indeed, recent research indicates that public domain lands in India have shrunk by 26–63 percent over the past thirty years, and that between 49 and 86 percent of these privatized lands ended up under the control of the better-off segments of society. Moreover, the process of privatization was often the impetus for the destruction of the native vegetation (Jodha, 1986).

Another conviction that warrants reexamination is the belief that only national governments can solve natural resource degradation problems. Individuals with this conviction will observe resource degradation and conclude that the answer lies in nationalization of the natural resource to bring it under more scientific management. They propose to create more government control so as to replace the decision-making authority of the resource users themselves. This fallacy is further compounded by equating government with *central* government, and thus overlooking the potential for various local authority systems and suitable forms of user organizations. Both prescriptions, privatization and nationalization, require careful study. Before getting to that (in chapter 7), it is necessary to understand how the current resource degradation problems in the developing countries have come about. More specifically, what are the institutional conditions that might help to explain the natural resource problems of the public domain in the tropics? But first a few words about the public domain.

By the *public domain* I mean all land *not* held in private ownership (freehold or fee simple) by someone. The public domain includes land administered by national/state/provincial governments, it includes land administered by villages as true common property, and it includes land that is managed by no-one and hence properly called *open access*.

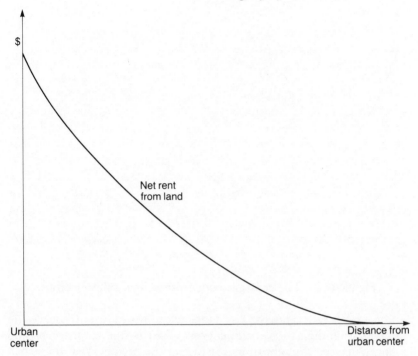

Figure 6.1   The rent gradient from an urban central place.

In economic terms, such lands are at the *extensive economic margin* – by which I mean that the application of labor and capital per unit of land is very low, and the economic returns from such lands are equally low. The concept of the extensive margin is developed in figure 6.1.

Notice that as one moves away from the urban center the profitability of a unit of land diminishes; one can think of this declining profitability as the diminishing ability of a unit of land to earn economic rents. We shall explore in chapter 7 the implications of this concept of the declining rent gradient with respect to alternative property arrangements over land. For now it serves to illustrate what is meant by the *extensive margin*. There are, in a sense, two extensive margins of economic relevance. The first is the rent gradient radiating out from the major urban place in any nation-state (it would look something like figure 6.1), and there is a second rent gradient that locates all spatial economic activity in a nation to that central place. This would resemble figure 6.2.

The concern in this chapter is with the economic environment beyond the major urban center in a developing country. We want to explore what has happened to those rural places as distinct economic entities,

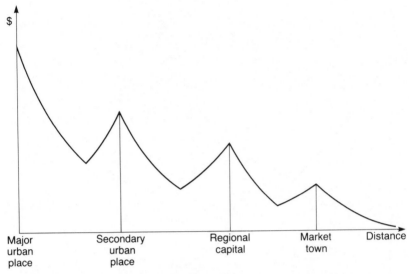

Figure 6.2   The rent gradient from a hierarchy of cities.

and we want to learn what has happened to the natural resources on lands surrounding those rural entities. That is, the rural towns and villages may be thought of as existing at the periphery of the urban center, and hence themselves represent an aspect of economic life at the extensive margin. Then, the rural hinterlands exist at the extensive margin of these rural towns and villages.

I shall start by focusing on these rural towns and villages as an authority system for managing natural resources, and shall illustrate how colonialism and the new post-independence nation-state have destroyed these authority systems.[3] Because of this deterioration in local-level authority, natural resource degradation has been accelerated, and successful project interventions are most unlikely. If we are to have any hope that natural resources are to be managed and protected in the developing countries we must first understand how to revitalize the village as an authority system.

3   THE DECLINE OF THE VILLAGE AS AN AUTHORITY SYSTEM

I start by focusing attention on the village or local community as an authority system, and as the logical center of attention for any program concerned with enhancing the nature and extent of wise use and management of natural resources. I shall argue that the former political and economic cohesion of the village has largely disintegrated and therefore villages have lost their ability to exercise control over the actions of their residents with respect to natural resource use.

Consider first the role of villages in south Asia prior to the complete spread of colonial administration. At that time the village was a territorial concept, not necessarily identified with any particular group of households or families. Still, all households within a specific Cartesian place were of one village. Households had a common and customary obligation to one another in matters both social and economic. While they had other bonds as well – caste, religion, kinship – the principal bond was territorial (the village) (Gupta, 1964). The essence of village life was a structure of authority and control, encompassing both permission and restraint, within which all human endeavor operated. Prevailing status and authority systems left few in doubt as to their domain of choice in a number of private and public affairs. Indeed, one could argue that the very purpose of a village was to serve as a locus of control and cooperation such that the welfare of the group would be enhanced. If villages did not serve this purpose we would not observe them; rather, individuals would live in scattered arrangements with no apparent purpose or pattern. The village, therefore, was an economic and social unit of great significance to the use and management of land and related natural resources. This significance can be understood by considering the relationship of rights in land to the political structure of the Indian village:

> The non-landholding households, customarily as well as socially, were subordinate to the landholding interests. Nevertheless, the village community did enjoy a very efficient system of self-government. The secret of its success lay in the nature of property in land and the various other allied institutions that subsisted in the village. As long as rights in land were governed by rules and customs which prevented the emergence of great disparities in wealth and income and conflicting rights over land within the village, the system of self-government remained efficient. But a change in the institutions of landed property led almost immediately to its decay. (Gupta, 1964, p. 105)

Notice the link between the political structure and the economic structure of the village. In pre-British India:

> land was not considered property in the European sense . . . the legislative introduction of the concept of real property around 1800 was a measure the seriousness and consequences of which are still difficult to gauge precisely. . . . The "King's Portion," the peasant's payment

for protection, was the most important state revenue. In the eighteenth century it amounted to between 30 and 50 percent of the harvest. Often paid in gold, it presupposed at least a rudimentary money economy and markets for agricultural produce. The tax . . . was uncommonly high, and for this reason one ought not to idealize the precolonial period. In practice, the modest profits of the peasants were siphoned off by the state, which used them for paying officials, waging war, and supporting a sumptuous court. It did not reinvest them in land. The situation recalls *ancien regime* Europe. (von Albertini, 1982, p. 27)

The effectiveness of the village as an authority system was dependent upon the exercise of influence and control over actions of members of the community. Part of the role of a village was to mobilize internal resources in its own defense against external forces. In early days those external forces were military in nature. With the rise of the modern nation-state, the military threat was replaced by the ever-present economic buffeting of national policy and political priorities. Prior to colonialism, ruling monarchs/leaders exercised control over the political and economic life of villages. The villages were not only suppliers of necessities for such leaders, but local outposts of control and authority over scattered peoples in the hinterland. The political legitimacy of the ruling entity was secured through the extension of representatives down through the political structure of regional town and, ultimately, rural village.

There was always the need for revenue to support the activities of the ruling class.

The village, usually meaning the headman, was made responsible for collection. This naturally offered ample opportunity to push the burdens off on the weaker and poorer villages or for the old residents to increase the rents levied against settlers on new land. The precolonial village led a largely self-sufficient existence. . . . But it should not be transfigured into some sort of democratic state of nature, ruling itself through the village council, or *panchayat*. The caste system determined the village hierarchy and personal dependency relationships, in which Brahmins and certain peasant castes, for example, farmed their land with workers, some of whom were slaves. Rights and duties were determined by social origin. Tax questions and disputes were settled within the village. The peasants did not own land but did possess highly divergent inheritable usage rights. The one thing they could not do was to sell land and especially not to an outsider. That blocked the possibility that a peasant could lose his land as a result of nonpayment of taxes or indebtedness to a moneylender. Under British rule all that changed. (von Albertini, 1982, p. 28)

During that time the question of who actually owned land was not as important as it was to become later. What was clear, however, was that land could not be alienated. Any villager in need could go off and seek a new allotment of land if taxes or debts became too burdensome. The availability of surplus arable served to relieve population pressure against the land. It was near the mid-eighteenth century that the old relationship between labor and land began to change. Prior to that time the competition had been for scarce labor to cultivate abundant arable; after that time the competition was for scarce land to be cultivated by an abundant and increasing peasantry.

The disintegration of the important role played by villages in India can be traced to the introduction of new land laws, the related intrusion of urban interests into the rural village, the opening up to external trade and markets, and the centralization of revenue and judicial administration leaving the village *panchayats* with little or no formal role. The village structure continued to function much later in south India than it did in the north, primarily because of the greater degree of external influence in the north. Even at that, the village in the northern areas was still viable until the end of the eighteenth century. When the British conquered the Punjab in 1848, villages were still a dominant part of Indian political and economic life (Bhatia, 1964).

The nature of land tenure in pre-colonial India is complex, and it varied by region. In general, however, one may suggest three general classes of land tenure (Desai, 1980).

The Zamindari System

The zamindar, an intermediary between the government and cultivator, retained responsibility for the regular payment of the annual land revenue. This system prevailed in Bengal, Northern Circas (along the Bay of Bengal south of Orissa), and Benares. The British were often confused about whether or not zamindars were, in fact, "owners" of agricultural land.

The Mahalwari and Malguzari Systems

Under the Mahalwari system all the land in the village belonged to the community as a whole. The whole body of co-share holders was jointly and individually responsible for payment of the land revenue to the government. This system prevailed in Punjab, Oudh, and Agra.

Under the Malguzari system, the Malguzars were revenue collectors under the Marathas and they came to be regarded as the proprietors of the land, and as heads of the villages. Here, the settlement officer not only fixed the land revenue to be paid by the Malguzar to the government, but also fixed the rents payable by cultivators to the Malguzars. This system existed in the central provinces.

The Ryotwari System

Here there was individual ownership of land and each individual was responsible for the payment of land revenue to the government. There was no intermediary and the ryot (peasant) owned the land he cultivated. This system prevailed in Bombay, Madras, and Bihar.

To show the variation in land tenures, consider the condition in northern India under the Mughal rulers dating from the sixteenth century:

> The . . . village (mauza) – the primary unit of land revenue – included the arable, the inhabited area, pools, groves, watercourses, forest and wasteland, and had clearly demarcated boundaries. The cultivated land was divided into plots and the average village had about 1,000 bighas (3 bighas = 1 acre) of arable. (Raychaudhuri, 1982, p. 10)

There were two kinds of villages. The ta'alluqa (taluka) villages were each held by a zamindar who paid tribute (or rendered military service instead of paying the land revenue), or a number of villages might be jointly "owned" by a body of zamindars of whom one would engage to pay revenue on behalf of the rest or might form part of a new zamindari acquired through purchase. Raiyati (or ra'iyatu) villages were outside the jurisdiction of tribute-paying zamindars and subject to the standard revenue regulations. That is, "the owners of superior rights in land engaged individually – not jointly through a representative – for the payment of revenue, though there were exceptions to this rule" (Raychaudhuri, 1982, p. 11).

There were also two distinct classes of cultivators. The first was a relatively small group of "owners" with hereditary transferable rights in land (these were described as zamindari ra'iyats, muqaddams, or maliks). The second was a much larger group who tilled the land without any rights (called mazara, asami, or r'aya). These people paid revenue through the "owners." These cultivators did not have, in any sense of the word, secure occupancy rights. After the Muslim period and during the Maratha period (from the middle of the eighteenth century) there was little outside control over the affairs of the village – excepting, of course, the collection of land revenue. Village administration was largely under control of the *panch* or council of leading villagers, including the headman (patil or patel), the kulkarni (village accountant), other village officials, and the leading landholders of the village domain.

> When landholding families died, their lands lapsed to the village and were treated like the waste land of the village. The Patil might convert this land into miras land for himself. Or the village assembly could give it or sell it as miras land. . . . The village assembly was also empowered to give waste land as inam but the government was not prepared to forgo substantial amounts of revenue. If the villagers gave inam lands on a large scale they had jointly to pay the land revenue themselves. (Fukazawa, 1983, p. 179)

Those lands referred to as *miras* implied that superior hereditary rights existed; a *mirasdar* held such rights. Inam lands were held by temples, village servants, and artisans (the village watchman, sweeper, water drawer, cobbler, etc.). They were also held by village officials such as the headman. Both the office and the lands could be sold, though probably not separately. The revenues from these lands compensated the individuals for their services rendered to the village.

Turning elsewhere in Asia, we know a little of pre-colonial Vietnam and here the story is not very different. The ruler of this region resided in Hue, in the Confucian tradition. Authority was exercised through elaborate court ceremony and a council of ministers. These mandarins were at the pinnacle of a hierarchy that reached down into each village. The villages were operationally under the control of landowners and petty merchants. The villages were responsible for taxes to the emperor (mostly in rice), and were required, as well, to provide soldiers and slave labor. As the basic unit of Vietnamese society, the villages were largely free to run their own affairs as long as this did not imply interference with the plans of the emperor.

> One should nonetheless not idealize Vietnamese villages, any more than Indian. Some families, indeed, owned land in addition to that held in common, and notables were co-opted. In practice, the structure was oligarchic. A considerable portion of the peasantry had little or no land, and the notables got their way in matters such as apportionment and collection of taxes, cultivation of common lands, administration of justice, and the provision of soldiers and workers. It should be noted, however, that tradition and the restraints of subsistence farming placed sharp limits on internal village stratification and misuse of power. (von Albertini, 1982, p. 194)

The situation in Egypt differed from many other colonized areas to the extent that pre-colonial rule was ruthless in forcing through modernization. Included in these transformations was the shift to year-round irrigation, the move to cash crops, and social differentiation based on private ownership of land; as elsewhere, these changes tended to atomize the traditional Egyptian village. The *umda* or village sheik was allowed to retain his traditional appointment but he was no longer seen as a representative of the peasants against the government.

> He was simply a village notable, usually a landowner, who had been able to exploit the Egyptian agrarian revolution of the nineteenth century to improve his position. . . . He now registered births, supervised water and canal usage, was responsible for the security of post and telegraph, had some responsibility for law and order, and acted as arbiter in land disputes. . . . Within the context of traditional societies, the umdas were not to be compared in terms of origin with Asiatic village headmen or African village or tribal chiefs. What is striking is that the socioeconomic changes and the individualization process that occurred within the villages in the nineteenth century, when combined with the demands of the colonial administration, had the same effects as elsewhere. (von Albertini, 1982, p. 241)

With the full spread of colonization, much of this political and economic structure – already under stress – was finally destroyed. The essence of colonial administration was to harness the political power of the villages to secure legitimacy for the alien power. It became necessary to undermine existing authority systems responsive to the pre-colonial rulers, and to supplant them with authority systems that would be responsive to the interests and imperatives of the colonial administration. When the British came to India, those areas of permanent settlement (Bengal and Bihar) were originally administered in a way that tax collection was the major change in pre-colonial life. Where the tax contribution was a fixed amount, administrative penetration was less than in other areas where assessment of taxes was regulated directly with the peasants and villages. Here the British did not interfere much with village life and made no attempts to force modernization or westernization.

With the establishment of the office of tax collector in Bengal and Bihar in 1765, the East India Company faced the question of who was to collect the taxes and what was to be done with the zamindars. It was not clear to the British whether zamindars were concessionaires or true landowners. What was clear was that the bulk of the taxes flowed into the pockets of the zamindars and their subofficials. In 1772 the Company took collection into its own hands. Because the Company had no way of knowing how much profit the zamindars were making it decided to auction off the right to be a tax collector for a five-year term. This policy was designed, as well, to protect the peasant farmers against excessive exactions by over-zealous zamindars. But the policy was unsuccessful. City businessmen who often had made their money as moneylenders or as intermediaries for the East India Company outbid the old zamindars. Unlike the zamindars, these new tax collectors had little interest in the long-run viability of peasant agriculture. The entry of this new class of tax collector led to a significant increase in taxes which severely burdened the peasants.

In the southeast of India, and also around Bombay, another system was tried after attempts to auction off collection rights were abandoned. The zamindar was eliminated in favor of direct ownership by the peasant farmer. A tax assessment was levied on the basis of yield relationships, with the expectation being that private ownership would bring the individual peasant prosperity and enable him to invest in improvements. Taxes still remained high, and reductions for bad harvests were only grudgingly conceded. During this period the colonial administrators seemed to want to hold the village together as an administrative unit, and possibly to strengthen it. But by establishing private property and direct assessment they loosened the ties of a society based on caste and customary law and stripped the village headman of his most important function.

> The old idea that rights to the product of the land were determined by social origin and caste status was displaced by the concept of private property, which "mobilizes" the land and permitted it to become a trade good. It heightened rather than reduced inequalities and dependency within the village. Combined with high taxes and rents and a legal system protecting owners, the system encouraged the indebtedness of the renters and ryots and thus imposed a new dependency upon the moneylenders. A real crisis in Indian agriculture was becoming apparent as early as the mid-nineteenth century. (von Albertini, 1982, p. 32)

The individualization of village life, fostered by the privatization of the better village lands, left the peasant increasingly dependent on the market, the remaining village land that had not been appropriated by the village elites, and on the moneylender. Of course moneylenders had been around for millennia. They gave the peasant money for food, seeds, funerals and weddings, and taxes. Interest was high because funds were scarce, and the peasant had little or no collateral to offer. Still, the power of the moneylender was circumscribed; he had to follow village custom and had no recourse to the state or the courts to collect his debts. Indeed, there were usually strict prohibitions against seizure of land for the nonpayment of debt. The moneylender

> could assure himself a portion of the harvest, but could not seize the debtor's land or contest the ryot's hereditary right to his land. The village would not allow transfer of land to outsiders, and according to Hindu law the debt could not build up to more than twice the original principal. With the coming of British tax law and land policy, however, mortgaging became possible and with that, a shift in favor of the moneylender in cases of flagrant insolvency on the part of the debtor. Protection of the village community and customary law largely ceased, since the lender could bring action in British court. The latter, basing its judgment on the common law of contracts, would protect him. In contrast to Indian law, the entire property of the debtor could be seized in service of the debt. Without the protection of the village, moreover, the peasants were often swindled. They signed contracts containing obligations they had not agreed to; false bookkeeping entries were attested to as correct; and oral agreements were no longer, as formerly, valid. . . . Because the local moneylender was very often the local merchant as well, he could easily collect his interest payments at harvest time. Later in the year, however, when the peasant's supplies were used up, he had to buy foodstuffs from this same merchant at higher prices. (von Albertini, 1982, p. 32)

By the time of the Sepoy Rebellion (1857) the sale of land for delinquent taxes had virtually ceased, but the forced sale of land for delinquent debts had become "very frequent" (Bhatia, 1964, p. 98).

> The original owners of land were being rapidly dispossessed of their rights in land by the moneylenders and the landlords and were rapidly being reduced to the position of tenants-at-will. This revolution in the property relations had [a] far-reaching effect on the structure of the agrarian society. The village community lost its authority and gradually disintegrated. The village headman who was previously a representative of the community now became an official of the State or of the landlord. In the past it was the village community which approved the transfer of land from one member of the community to another and allotment of lands to an outsider; no such collective sanction was now needed for effecting transfers. Again, the common rights in the waste-land attached to the village and the functions of constructing and maintaining works of irrigation and distributing water from these were performed by the village community. This right was now taken away from the village community. On the forests and waste-land of the village, the landlord came to have an absolute right in the *zamindari* areas. In the *ryotwari* areas, waste-lands continued to be treated as the joint property of the landowners in the village, each possessing rights in the waste-land

proportionate to the arable land possessed by him. By the middle of the nineteenth century, village communities had lost much of their influence and prestige and were disintegrating. (Bhatia, 1964, pp. 98–9)

It would not be correct to assume that all of these forces leading to the disintegration of the village were the result of colonial rule; many changes were under way prior to colonial intrusion. But of course the subsequent introduction of new land laws and the civil courts sealed the fate of the villages as authority systems.

Moving to southeast Asia, we find similar forces at work in Indonesia. When the Dutch got their colonies back from the British in 1816 they continued the policies of indirect rule that the British had used there (as well as in India), but the results were not encouraging. In 1830 the Dutch introduced forced cultivation under the Culture System. Instead of cash payments the products themselves were required in payment. While the British policy had been to avoid dealing with the traditional authorities by going directly to the peasants, the Culture System implied a reinforcement of the powers of the traditional authorities, the regents, and village chiefs.

> The Culture System was a matter for the entire village, because it had to organize the annual reallocation of land and provide enough for the cash crops, along with seeing to cultivation, seed, tools and harvesting. Although no private property as such had existed earlier, individual and family rights to use land had existed. These rights were now thrown into question by communalization. The village chief was given power, but at the same time became dependent on the colonial administration, which punished or paid him according to the results of the harvest. (von Albertini, 1982, p. 163)

This new structure caused the village chief to be regarded as a source of governmental oppression rather than his previous role as the source of village solidarity and protection.

> The traditional authority structures were slowly eroding. The nobility and the village chiefs were tied increasingly closely to the administration and were losing their representative and protective functions. The village inhabitants, too, were being declassed, losing their rights to participate in decisions and becoming "administered" producers. This change was characteristic under colonial conditions, both in Asia and Africa. (von Albertini, 1982, pp. 163–4)

Between 1890 and 1910 Dutch rule was rather completely solidified throughout the islands. In the early twentieth century the Dutch undertook a number of progressive reforms, and the villages were encouraged to participate directly in these. Villages received their own treasury, and chiefs were told to keep good books. Monthly village meetings were to settle a number of local disputes. In fact:

> What came about from village initiatives and was to be treated as village business was really in practice decided and ordered by the administration. . . . This impatient paternalism would not work without gentle pressure. It achieved positive results in the sense of bettering the public welfare as understood in the West, but it smothered traditional forms of service and decision making, and it encouraged rather than discouraged, as the Dutch had hoped, an attitude of passive acceptance of instructions. (von Albertini, 1982, p. 167)

The Culture System gave way in the late 1800s to a new agrarian law which fostered the symbiosis of sugar plantations and village rice growing. The new law was intended to guarantee native legal claims to the land, and to permit a shift from the Culture System to plantation agriculture under private ownership. Untilled land was declared inalienable state property, and the sale of land to foreigners was forbidden.

> The Javanese villages were drawn into the money economy. The sugar mills paid the villagers substantial amounts in rent and also wages for their labor. . . . The Javanese peasant as a rule did not sink into the landless labor class but remained a property owner within the village community. The latter faced the confrontation with a money economy and production methods dominated by the sugar mills, which initially contracted with the individual peasants, but came to prefer dealing with the village as a whole or, in practice, with the village chief. Village land was thus considered as a unit. The result was the growth of a class of larger holders, often the village chiefs, of quasi-parasitic character. The mills did raise the efficiency of the cultivation, but by organizing it themselves, which undermined peasant initiative. (von Albertini, 1982, p. 169)[4]

A contributing factor to the deteriorating situation was the fact that not only were rice and sugar cropped in rotation, but the peasants working the land also varied, which prevented the development of an independent peasant class. With the growth of sugar plantings and the resulting competition for good arable land, it was necessary to adopt faster growing (but poorer quality) types of rice so that several rice crops might be harvested per year. The increase in population, and the scarcity of land, meant that villagers were forced to terrace new areas and farm poorer land. The ecological implications of this were often severe.

When the French arrived in Vietnam they claimed not to be interested in interfering with the traditional village structures and processes. Yet, they insisted on a major role in public works projects, customs duties, and those activities requiring unified direction and employment of the French. The village headmen became, as in Africa, quasi-civil servants and dependent upon the French for their legitimacy. A head tax was first imposed, followed by a tax on alcohol, salt, and opium. While the opium trade had been sold to the Chinese, the French appropriated it for the state – buying opium wholesale and distributing it through concessionaires. The colonial regime thus had a direct interest in greater opium use. With alcohol, the administration set minimum consumption levels for each region and rewarded village leaders for going above the quota. The French controlled salt, as had the British in India, by confiscating all supplies and selling it to the local population.

Turning to the African continent, we see similar forces at work, with the French being particularly contemptuous of indigenous land-use practices and institutions. In northwest Africa, especially in current-day Algeria, Tunisia, and Morocco the French encountered thinly settled nomadic (or pastoral) peoples in the dry mountainous regions of the hinterland. The French appropriated a portion of the lands unclaimed by the tribes or claimed only on the basis of custom, while the tribes were given firm title to what the French did not want. This process of expropriating land severely restricted tribal territories and thus led to increased crowding of the nomads. The predictable result was overgrazing on those limited areas still accessible to nomadic herders. As with other colonial administrations, the French wanted firm individual land titles, and so a way had to be found to sell land under Muslim law.

> This was particularly true for the *melk* lands, which under Muslim law were private property but held by families, or more accurately, a community of heirs, even if farmed by a single family. But the problem also existed with the *arch* land, which was collective tribal property, with firm and in some cases inheritable usufruct rights. The colons demanded mobilization of the land, meaning that the traditional ordering of land relationships based on Muslim law and custom was to be shattered. At the same time the real property thus created was to be placed under the governance of French law. . . . The result was that [in Algeria, Tunisia, and Morocco] a good part of the best land fell into colon hands, with the natives being reduced to tenants or rural laborers. This development had most serious consequences for a society based on tribes and extended families. (von Albertini, 1982, pp. 266–7)

There was both government and private colonization. The government side of it entailed the establishment of entire new villages in barren areas, but the private colonization was the more important. In 1873 the French sought to break up the collectively owned melk lands by decreeing that individual plots must be established to become the private property of individuals under French law. If only a single collective holder desired individualization, then it was required to occur, regardless of the wishes of the other collective owners. The result was a plundering of tribal properties, and an increase in lawsuits. In the process, Frenchmen, but also urban Algerians and other notables, acquired large estates. French landholdings doubled in the twenty years between 1870 and 1890 – from 800,000 ha to 1.6 million ha. By 1930, 26,153 Europeans owned 2.3 million ha, compared with 7.7 million ha owned by only 617,543 Algerians (von Albertini, 1982, p. 268).

> Problems went beyond the fact that a great part of the best land had ended up in the hands of Europeans and a small class of Algerian land holders, and that the living standard of Muslim and small holders, tenant farmers, and laborers, already close to the subsistence minimum, continued to sink. The individualization of real property and being placed under the *Statut immobilier du droit civil* called for a change in outlook for the Muslims and went far toward dissolving the traditional tribal, village, and family structures. A process of pauperization commenced. (von Albertini, 1982, p. 270)

While the French claim to have been interested in transforming herds-men into sedentary peasants – and one may reasonably ask why[5] – they later admitted that the imposed changes merely shattered the social structure of the herdsmen. Elsewhere, evidence shows that the traditional transhumance had been restricted, meaning that European land sequestration had prevented the hill tribes from wintering their stock in the fertile plains. The partial shift to private ownership even on collective tribal lands had also led to serious social differentiation.

The British in West Africa were not markedly different. They instituted, as in India, "indirect rule." In West Africa this structure had two dimensions: (1) chiefs had their own funds – half of all taxes went to British administration, but the other half remained available for local expenditures on salaries, roads, and festivities; and (2) chiefs retained certain jurisdictional competence and administered justice in the native courts. Indirect rule in Northern Nigeria had some positive effects. Raiding parties and warfare ceased. Slavery and the slave trade were gradually eliminated. On the other hand, the colonial administration was conservative and had some reactionary effects to the extent that a feudal social order was shielded from most modernizing, if disintegrating, influences.

Unfortunately, indirect rule proved more troublesome in southeastern Nigeria. Here, Ibo social structure was based on the village and the clan.

> There were no units of rule of any size. The British had . . . grouped several villages together in a native court and appointed a "warrant chief". . . . But the warrant chiefs they appointed were unpopular, and they and their courts had no legitimacy as natural leaders. Their appointment undermined the democratic system of the villages, with its elders, influential secret societies, and age groupings. The chiefs were supposed to adjudicate disputes according to customary law, but British legal practices were also introduced, such as imprisonment for theft rather than draconian traditional punishments. They were also required to supply porters and laborers. As they were inclined to exploit their positions to their own advantage, they came to be seen as a group of corrupt, particularly hateful, half-educated subaltern officials. (von Albertini, 1982, p. 313)

While indirect rule was indeed conservative, it did have some positive aspects. The British did not treat the traditional social structures, religious ties, and customs with the disregard or scorn typical of many missionaries, or indeed of those within the French administrative service. In the far west – the Gold Coast – cocoa production expanded rapidly because it fitted in well with the traditional economic and social structure. Lots of land "belonged" to the tribes, villages, and clans, but the produce from it went to the individual farming family. Immigrant families "rented" land, cleared the jungle, and planted both foodstuffs and cocoa seedlings, which bore fruit in four to six years. But erosion and a retreat of the forest began. Additionally, more profound changes were under way.

> In the chief cocoa areas food production declined and there was a corresponding rise in imports from neighboring regions or from overseas. . . . It also sometimes happened that . . . there was too little to eat. . . . A social transformation began. There was not only a rapid shift from a subsistence to a money and market economy, but also individualization and social differentiation. Enterprising Africans established large holdings, sometimes purchasing those of Europeans, in one or several locales. The chiefs also engaged in trade or became planters. Labor had to be brought in, and thousands of seasonal laborers came during the following period from the north or from French territories in the cocoa region. (von Albertini, 1982, p. 321)[6]

Moreover,

> The land was also subjected to this individualization process. In the strict legal sense private property in land was not possible, but nevertheless

forms were developed for the acquisition of land that closely approached individual ownership. This phenomenon was more pronounced in the Gold Coast than in Nigeria. Anyone planting seedlings that would bear only after some years wanted a secure title. The administration helped, but found itself on the horns of a dilemma, because it both wished to maintain collective ownership and yet considered making the land individually owned and private property the prerequisite for economic and social progress. Sale of land was thus in practice possible. Still, difficulties occurred with such transfers because of a lack of fixed titles and cadastres. During the interwar period experts critically noted the increase in litigation about land questions, the origin of which was often farmer indebtedness. (von Albertini, 1982, p. 321)

The development of British West Africa in the late nineteenth century and the early twentieth century was primarily based on the expansion of three main crops – palm, cocoa, and peanuts, with rubber and cotton being of secondary importance. As is often the case, European demand fueled the expansion, and British colonial rule provided the supportive economic environment in which productive capacity was able to expand. British indirect rule basically recognized the pre-colonial authority structures and limited itself to supervision and advice to these local entities. The French shattered and largely eliminated the traditional African ruling classes in order to create a centralized hierarchy that reached clear down to the village heads that they installed. The British wished to produce "good Africans," while the French wanted to produce "good Frenchmen" who could speak proper French and aspire to Lyonnaise cuisine.

The Belgians in central Africa followed standard colonial practice by first declaring all noncultivated land to belong to the colonial administration. Likewise, the Germans in Africa declared that all land not subject to well-founded third-party claims – the so-called ownerless land – was Crown land and thus state property which the governor was empowered to sell or rent. The Germans were careful not to interfere with the occupied lands, less out of benevolence or recognition of indigenous rights than because of the sheer abundance of land. The Germans knew full well that so-called "ownerless" land did not exist according to customary law, and that the colonial government would have been able to retain no land whatsoever for plantation companies if the claims of the local population were recognized in their fullest extent.

Portugal, like France, followed the principle of direct rule, believing in the wisdom of dividing the opposition. The Portuguese destroyed the larger African political entities in order to integrate the smaller divisions into the colonial state. The Portuguese also were able to incorporate the traditional elite into their hierarchical system of colonial administration – a feat that solidified their rule. As elsewhere, the authority of these co-opted members of African society no longer derived from their traditional legitimacy, but rested on a diametrically opposed Portuguese conception of legality. The elite were no longer leaders of an African community, but representatives of a hierarchical colonial authority. Through collaboration, the chiefs generally gained in power, but they largely lost their earlier legitimacy and hence authority over their fellow men (von Albertini, 1982). In the central highlands of Angola, cash crops and the spread of perennials soon led to the recognition of land as individual (private) property. Fallow land was no longer returned to the clan but held as family property, and so incipient individualism spread throughout Africa.

In conclusion, we see that the story of colonial administration of village political and economic life was similar – impose European institutional arrangements in order: (1) to encourage the cultivation of those crops of interest to the colonial administration; (2) to provide tax revenues to support that same administration; and (3) to undermine indigenous political structures and processes further to strengthen the position of that colonial administration. These transformations essentially destroyed the village as an autonomous decision-making unit, which was, of course, the very purpose of those imposed institutional changes. Colonialism had both political and economic manifestations, both of which endure in the tangible form of degraded land and related natural resources.

4 THE CONTINUING LEGACY OF COLONIALISM

Natural resource degradation in the developing countries persists, in the main, for two related reasons: (1) unclear institutional arrangements (property rights);[7] and (2) a breakdown in the authority systems that give meaning to those very institutional arrangements. These two situations arise from the historical conditions detailed above. In the absence of an authority system, no convention or entitlement (structure of property rights) has any meaning if an individual or group of individuals chooses to contravene the institution.

The various news media have, of course, emphasized the serious problems of overgrazing and deforestation in the tropics. Often, it will be said that these destructive practices are the logical result of expanding populations. The policy response to this problem will be misdirected, however, if the cause is laid at the feet of population growth. By blaming population growth – and the subsequent land clearing for agriculture and scavenging for fuelwood by the masses – the public focus will be shifted away from the real cause of natural resource destruction in the developing nations. That cause is the ineffective – and often corrupt – governments with little interest in preserving the natural resources of their countries. While population growth is indeed a contributory cause of much deforestation and accelerated soil erosion, it is not the *primary* cause. Until we recognize that governments are largely to blame for the natural resource degradation now so prevalent in the tropics, the proper solutions will evade us.

Governments themselves quite obviously have a vested interest in perpetuating the belief that population growth is to blame for natural resource destruction. If the problem can be blamed on prolific peasants then it is far easier to avoid being held responsible. By allowing population growth to become a convenient scape-goat, governments are then free to posture and protest that they cannot control the rapacious masses. Blaming population growth also helps governments to attract development assistance programs to replant trees that they have been unwilling to protect in the first instance. These reforestation programs often employ large numbers of the poor and unemployed, thereby providing external funds for a potentially serious socioeconomic problem beyond the capacity of many governments to solve. The *major* problem of natural resource degradation in the developing countries can, quite reasonably, be found to rest with governments who claim to be so concerned.

In fairness it must be emphasized that colonialism had left its victims with very serious governance problems. Once colonialism gave way to national independence – largely in the two decades following the Second World War – the imposed systems of authority at the village level were once again in need of modification and realignment with the new imperatives and interests of a national government. These disruptions destroyed, yet again, evolved relationships of power, influence, and authority. During these eras of creation and modification of local-level systems of authority and control over daily life, populations were expanding rapidly, and technology was altering the way in which people used – and interacted with – their natural environment. At the very time when the ability to control individual behavior at the village level was at its lowest, populations were expanding and the pressure on the natural resource base was accelerating. Degradation of natural resources was the predictable outcome. The colonial powers demanded passivity and obedience at the local level. These traits did not serve local administration and imagination in the new age.

There has been a lasting legacy to this process. First, agriculture at the village level is increasingly monetized. In West Africa the younger men in the village have had the opportunity to emigrate to urban or plantation jobs and earn considerably more income than if they remained in the village. Doing so weakens the traditional authority of the village head, and it also results in remittances flowing back into the village. If these men claim village land, as is their right, they will often assign its cultivation to others while they continue to work elsewhere. The rise of an absentee-landlord agriculture not only weakens traditional village bonds, but means a different ratio of labor to land than for traditional agricultural practices in the village. Often such lands are farmed just enough to establish the continuing interest of the absent owner.

Second, there has been an increase in centralized political authority. The forestry code in French West Africa prevents individuals from cutting trees that they might be willing to plant and so there is scant incentive to plant trees. Finally there is the increasingly urbanized policy environment in which governments guarantee cheap food and fuel to acquire the political acquiescence of urban residents. Low crop prices discourage increased food production, and low fuel prices do little to encourage investment in fuelwood plantings.

The new independent nation-states that arose following the Second World War have shown little interest in revitalizing local-level systems of authority. As with previous rulers and colonial administrators, the governments of these nation-states do not relish the thought of local political forces that might challenge the legitimacy and authority of the national government. This means that natural resources have become the "property" of the national governments in acts of outright expropriation when viewed from the perspective of the residents of millions of villages. This expropriation is all the more damaging when national governments lack the rudiments of a natural resource management capability. These new governments are struggling with the problems of governance, economic development, self-sufficiency, and political stability. In this setting, we see natural resource destruction continuing, and even accelerating, with only a very indirect causal link to population growth. In essence, there are three dominant reasons why natural resource degradation continues even today: (1) the intentional policies of governments in need of foreign exchange; (2) well-intended but misspecified policies that were actually established with resource management and protection in mind; and (3) broad economic and agricultural sector policies that cause problems for land use and natural resources.[8]

Intentional Degradation

In many developing countries it is the explicit policy of governments to exploit natural resources for export in order to increase earnings of foreign exchange. The foreign exchange earnings are then used to import manufactured items for industry, or to import consumer goods to satisfy the wants of an urban elite. The problem is one of a local demand for foreign exchange, the use of the natural resource sector to generate that foreign exchange, and the unwillingness of governments to confront the interests of those engaged in this pattern of resource destruction. In addition to the necessary imports that must be paid for with foreign exchange, much foreign assistance consists of loans that must be repaid in specific currencies (dollars, German marks).

Data for twenty-four tropical countries considered by the World Bank to be "low income" reveal that, on average, the two most important export commodities in each of the countries accounted for 64 percent of foreign exchange earnings. Of these twenty-four countries – seventeen of which are in sub-Saharan Africa – coffee and cotton were the primary exports of twelve, with other commodities (e.g. rice, gas, textile fabrics, alcohol, copper, clothing, animals, tea, pearls, ores, fertilizers, and cocoa) being first in the remaining twelve countries. Eleven of the twenty-four countries derived more than 50 percent of their foreign exchange from only one commodity – five of them from the export of coffee and one each from rice, cotton, animals, pearls, ores, and cocoa (World Bank, 1984b; United Nations, 1983).

These twenty-four low-income countries used, on average, 66 percent of their foreign exchange earnings to import just two general classes of imports – manufactures, and machinery and transport equipment; only in three cases did the top two imports show up as something else – in one case it was food, and in two cases it was fuels.

Turning to the thirty-one middle-income countries, a similar picture emerges. Here, these thirty-one countries derived almost 60 percent of their total foreign exchange earnings from two primary commodities; nine of them had petroleum as the first export, while six had coffee as the first export. That is, fifteen countries had only two commodities (petroleum and coffee) as the primary earner of foreign exchange. Only nine other commodities were the major export of these thirty-one countries (iron ore, copper, fruit, rice, fertilizers, sugar, chemicals, clothing, and cotton). Ten of these thirty-one countries had more than 50 percent of their foreign exchange from only one commodity, of which petroleum was the dominant export in five countries, followed by ore, copper, sugar, chemicals, and coffee in the remaining five countries.

As with the twenty-four low-income countries, these thirty-one middle-income countries used, on average, 66 percent of their foreign exchange earnings for the importation of machinery and transport equipment, and for manufactures. In contrast with the low-income countries, the middle-income countries are more serious importers of fuels, with approximately 39 percent showing fuels as either the first or second most important claimant on foreign exchange.

We have the familiar situation of these fifty-five low- and middle-income tropical countries relying on one or two commodities for the vast majority of their foreign income, and using the greater part of that foreign exchange to import manufactures or fuel.

The direct relationship between explicit government policy and natural resources can be illustrated with reference to gum arabic (*Acacia senegal*) in the Sudan. The Sudan has historically accounted for approximately 80 percent of the world's total production of gum; gum exports from the Sudan account for approximately 10 percent of total foreign exchange earnings. These conditions render the Sudan vulnerable to swings in the demand for gum, and in recent years the development of synthetics has posed a serious threat. But an equally serious threat arises from internal management of gum pricing by the state buying organization, the Gum Arabic Company.

When prices are set too high there is an incentive to over-harvest gum by excessive tapping; this is compounded in times of drought when the trees are less hardy. Many of the gum trees are found on lands with uncertain tenures and so these are particularly vulnerable to herders moving through. Conversely, when prices are set too low, farmers will move into other crops and often cut down the gum trees for fuelwood or charcoal – and to make room for other crops. The government can ill afford to lose even 10 percent of its foreign exchange earnings; over the recent past the average annual rate of change in exports has been – 5 percent, while imports have been growing at about 4 percent per annum (World Bank, 1984a). Recently, energy imports have required about 40 percent of total export receipts. Hence gum arabic exports are essential and yet the gum sector is in disarray. A failure to manage this particular resource – rather minor on a global scale, yet of paramount importance to the Sudan – brings added hardship to a country already suffering severe financial and environmental stresses.

This same story could be told about a number of other developing countries. For the non-oil-exporting developing countries in Asia (excluding China), current-account deficits in 1984 averaged 4.1 percent of the export of goods and services. Yet for similar countries in Latin America the percentage was 15.5, and in Africa it was 28.7 percent (IMF, 1984). A sample of ninety developing countries shows that between 1970 and 1983 the ratio of debt to gross national product doubled (from 13.3 to 26.7 percent), that the ratio of debt to exports increased by 20 percent (from 99.4 to 121.4), that the debt service ratio (interest plus amortization divided by the value of exports) increased from 13.5 percent to 20.7 percent, and that total debt outstanding increased almost tenfold (from $68.4 billion to $595.8 billion) (IMF, 1984). For the period between 1965 and 1981, all developing countries taken together increased the value of their exports by a factor of 11 (in constant dollars). Over that same period the low-income Asian countries increased their exports by a factor of 7, while the low-income African group managed to increase the value of their exports by a factor of only 3.5 (World Bank, 1984b).

The export structure of the developing countries is absolutely dominated by the natural resource sector either directly through minerals, timber, petroleum, or fish, or indirectly through the export of agricultural crops whose future production depends upon the wise use of land and water resources. As discussed above, the colonial history of most tropical countries can be understood as a major contributing factor in this particular pattern of resource use. Their early economic development was one of an imposed structure with the explicit intent being to provide the colonizing power with desired raw materials or agricultural products.

This process of intentional government destruction has its insidious side as well. In the Ivory Coast, commercial loggers have long engaged in wanton high-grading of timber stocks, leaving the lesser-valued timber for others to poach and burn so as to provide agricultural plots. As the better stocks have disappeared the value of timber marketings has fallen, putting yet more pressure on the remaining stands so as to sustain export earnings. These practices have – in a familiar pattern – been legislated against, but only indifferently enforced. In fact, since independence the government of the Ivory Coast has pursued an extremely destructive course of action toward its forests so as to earn foreign exchange and tax revenues. As a result

> loggers continue to exploit the remaining forests, more or less uncontrolled, and farmers have followed roads developed for logging operations, establishing cocoa, coffee and food crops, with the

widespread practice of "slash and burn" farming. Such intrusions have also begun in the classified forest reserves and national parks. Government now estimates that this process transforms about 0.4 million ha of unspoiled high forest per year. Were these trends to continue, Ivory Coast could become a net importer of timber before the end of the century. (World Bank, 1985, p. 2)

The World Bank report on this project continues by pointing to a persistent problem in renewable resource management – the problem of showing more interest in the symptoms of problems than in the root cause of those problems. Specifically, we are told that the continued degradation of forests poses scant ecological threat. However, it is reported that the subsequent invasion by land-hungry farmers imposes severe damage on the remaining forest cover, causing increased soil erosion, reduced rainfall, and lower water tables. It is therefore reported that the "Government is becoming more conservation-minded in its approach to forestry in particular, and to natural resources in general" (World Bank, 1985, p. 3).

Unintended Degradation: The Myth of Management

The second class of resource degradation arises from government policies that may actually be formulated with resource protection in mind. As new nation-states emerged following the demise of colonialism, governmental organizations were created reflecting those observed in more industrialized societies. Ministries of agriculture were created, often with a division of forestry or forest management. A few countries elevated forestry to the full status of a ministry. With these organizations in place it was not long until laws were passed, and administrative rules developed, that redefined an individual's rights with respect to the forest. In particular, a number of countries passed laws that prohibited the cutting of fuelwood without providing their residents with any alternative source of energy with which to cook their meals. This evolution of forest management by proclamation created perverse incentives at the local level where it suddenly became a necessity for survival to defy newly imposed rules from distant – and not always trusted – capitals.

In Nepal the government in 1957 nationalized large areas of forest lands that had previously been under the management and control of local village councils or of certain elites. To be sure, many villages had lost their ability to exercise adequate control over many forest-use activities, a point made previously. Still, there remained a residue of local-level responsibility for certain practices in the forests. But with the expropriation of many village forests by the national government the villagers were thus moved to get what they could from these lands before the transition took place. Villagers who had previously operated under certain sets of rights and obligations *vis-à-vis* the local forest suddenly found themselves at the capricious mercy of a distant government (Bromley and Chapagain, 1984). The government of Nepal is now attempting to restore those local-level management systems in the hope of arresting continued resource destruction (Arnold and Campbell, 1986).

We see similar patterns of resource destruction in sub-Saharan Africa where government policies divorce local users from the responsibility for conservation, while at the same time creating negative incentives that discourage villagers from improving resource-use practices (Thomson, 1977). Forestry codes that outlaw the cutting of necessary fuelwood without accompanying programs of supply augmentation simply invite open defiance of the law and are – over the long run – counterproductive. This long-run problem is caused by an attitude of contempt for the national government, the knowledge that certain individuals have bribed their way out of difficulties, and the realization that the national government has no plan to deal with the very real resource shortages at the village level.

General Economic Development Policy

The final way in which destruction of natural resources arises is through economic policies directly related to agricultural (and general economic) development strategies. Specifically, these are national policies directed toward achieving self-sufficiency in certain food crops, and the export of certain cash crops that may be grown under plantation conditions. While not openly directed toward resource extraction, such policies hold important implications for the structure of agriculture and hence its technological aspects. When mechanized agriculture cannot provide jobs for an expanding population, large numbers of individuals in rural areas must leave and move elsewhere. These families are forced from the cultivated lowlands and end up in the swelling urban slums or – more critically – in the uplands, on fragile habitats that can ill afford more human pressure.

Data from the Philippines indicate that (in 1970) approximately 30 percent of the total population of the country resided in the uplands. This represented over 50 percent of the total migrant population in the Philippines – the remainder apparently having gone to urban areas in the lowlands (Cruz, 1984). This marginalization of people occurs in precisely those areas where conventions and rules are the least able to deal with this new resource pressure. In the uplands, resource use has traditionally been guided by custom and local-level institutional structures that were based upon an individual's membership in the village. When migrants invade the uplands not only are indigenous institutions unable to adjust rapidly enough, but more importantly they are not appropriate for the new mix of resource users who have not been raised in that particular ecosystem and who therefore do not understand it.

Here we see derived resource destruction in the tropics that emanates from commercial agricultural policy that may seem quite removed from natural resource integrity. Of course part of this can be found in the heavy use of chemicals in agriculture; that too causes unintended problems for resource integrity. But an equally serious problem – and one that has not received much attention – is that associated with the marginalization of people. In Indonesia we see it in the form of government-organized migration to the outer islands; in Latin America it takes the form of colonization efforts in remote regions. While in other countries these practices may be less obvious, they are still present.

The serious threat for natural resources is that the migrants bring with them an alien institutional structure for guiding resource use, and these patterns of use may fit in quite badly in the new location. If they have the ability to impose their will on the original residents then serious problems can arise in terms of resource use. Even if they fit in with prevailing resource-use patterns, their numbers will be enough to pose a serious threat to the resource base.

5 THE POLICY RESPONSE

These three causes of resource destruction in the developing countries suggest specific directions in which policy reform might be focused. Very often those harvesting timber on a commercial basis are operating with the full blessing of the government, in spite of frequent government protestations to the contrary. The hordes of poor seeking fuelwood are the consequence of past policies that have destroyed local-level institutional arrangements, and of more recent actions that seem to perceive villagers as enemies of the forest rather than as integral parts of it. The posting of forest guards with firearms – and the prevalence of bribes to get relief if apprehended – create an environment in which forests are perceived as outdoor "museums," or as the special preserves of those with money and influence. Finally, the disjointed way in which development policy is removed from general land-use policy almost assures that forested areas will be required to carry the burden of displaced populations from privately held land caught up in the Green Revolution. Where else but to the forest can the landless turn?

Natural resource destruction is occurring in the developing countries for a variety of reasons. But the facile conclusion that "population growth" is the culprit is only partly true. Governments, by definition, are responsible for providing for the needs of their citizens. Such provision must be through the creation of those social and economic conditions that will allow individuals to pursue their individual well-being without destroying the future livelihood of fellow citizens. Many governments have failed to create the social and economic conditions that will assure this condition. Now, to protect their grip on power, they deflect the blame for resource destruction elsewhere. More often than not, it is directed toward the poorest segments of society – the landless, those without political influence – in the hope that we shall fail to recognize the real culprit. A careful analysis of resource destruction in the developing world will reveal, however, that most of it is government inspired, and government caused. A solution will require apprehension of this basic fact.

Is there hope that more responsible resource management regimes might evolve in the developing world? The case for optimism can be made by calling attention to the significant successes of small programs such as the Peace Corps, other nations' volunteer service programs, and the many efforts by national governments to rekindle local-level management regimes. The major development assistance agencies – including the World Bank – are also paying more attention to these aspects of their development programs. The case for pessimism is made, unfortunately, by pointing to the arrogance and elitism of many national governments who continue to see a political threat in the emergence of responsible governance structures at the local level. Perhaps when resource destruction becomes even more serious these governments will understand that revitalized local authority systems are preferable to a squandered natural resource base. In the meantime, expect to see them continue to blame population growth for their own ineptitude and indifference.

The problem, in many instances, is the delegitimization of customary and traditional property rights (institutional arrangements), and government policies that then proceed to favor the private land of certain politically important segments of the population. Let us turn now to that issue.

NOTES

1   The metaphor was defined by Hardin (1968), but earlier authors had written of so-called "common property" problems in the fishery (Gordon, 1954; Scott, 1955).
2   I shall use the term *public domain* here as shorthand for all those lands held in *other than* freehold (fee simple). The conventional view is that approximately one-half of India is uncultivated – and hence public domain land (Bentley, 1984).
3   I use the term "village" in a loose sense to connote units of collective choice over some aspects of economic life. Of course the family, the clan, and the tribe are alternative units of collective choice and so the term "village" should be understood as suggestive.
4   See Geertz (1963) for more on this process.
5   The answer, not far to seek, is that sedentary peoples are always easier for governments to subjugate and control than are nomads. Nomads, by definition, have a rather independent cast of mind that governments find disconcerting and inconvenient.
6   See Polly Hill (1970, pp. 22ff).
7   I prefer to characterize this as an example of *institutional dissonance* in which actors at the village level are faced with several conflicting choice domains – each one predicated upon a different institutional structure pertinent to the village.
8   This idea is more fully developed in Bromley (1986b).

7
Property Rights Problems in the Public Domain

> We abuse land because we regard it as a commodity belonging to us. When we see land as a community to which we belong, we may begin to use it with love and respect.
> Aldo Leopold,
> *A Sand County Almanac*

1 PROPERTY RIGHTS AS POLICY CHOICES

The conventional wisdom is that private property rights are a necessary condition for the generation of economic wealth; in land this means that private ownership of land is a precursor to the realization of an economic surplus. The previous chapter would seem to suggest that the creation of private property rights in the tropics has had some very positive effects on economic productivity of certain lands. However, it also seems fair to note that the process of privatization has had some rather sweeping negative effects on natural resource management. That is, the spread of private land – and the attendant individualization of village life – has undermined traditional collective management regimes over natural resources. The obvious answer, to some, may be that now to solve those management problems we need only convert to private control that land which is left in the public domain. This notion receives support from a recent interest within economics in the so-called "property rights school" of thought best represented by Demsetz (1967), Cheung (1970), Alchian and Demsetz (1973), and Furubotn and Pejovich (1972). This view is reflected in attempts to explain the origins of agriculture (North and Thomas, 1977). The North and Thomas position is that prior to the development of the property rights paradigm there was no theory that could be used to explain the Neolithic Revolution. The property rights paradigm provided them with the foundation to suggest that it was the development of exclusive property rights over land and related natural resources that provided a change in incentives sufficient to encourage the rise of cultivation and domestication. The view is elaborated in the following quote:

> When common property rights over resources exist, there is little incentive for the acquisition of superior technology and learning. In contrast, exclusive property rights which reward the owners provide a direct incentive to improve efficiency and productivity, or, in more fundamental terms, to acquire more knowledge and new techniques. It is this change in incentive that explains the rapid progress made by mankind in the last 10,000 years in contrast to his slow development during the era as a primitive hunter/gatherer. (North and Thomas, 1977, p. 241)

Notice how this position confuses open access regimes (what North and Thomas call "common property rights") with true common property. That is, North and Thomas load the argument in favor of one institutional form – private property rights – by distorting the real essence of common property. We know from chapter 2 that they should have said "when open access over resources exists, there is little incentive for the acquisition of superior technology and learning." Their position is that any property regime other than private (individual) property is "inefficient" and prone to overuse and abuse.[1] It should not surprise us that economics finds considerable comfort in private property. Neoclassical economics is, above all else, a testimony to the wisdom and efficacy of individual atomistic behavior. If property rights are not individualized then it follows, axiomatically, that the nice properties of atomistic choice and maximization will not be met. My task here is rather different from that of many writers on the subject who seem compelled to prove that if only people would behave as in our theory textbooks they would be both happier and richer.

Rather, the current task is to develop a model that offers plausible grounds for the particular property regimes one observes in the tropics – and elsewhere for that matter. This model offers testable hypotheses with respect to the choice of property regimes over land and related natural resources. The analysis begins by addressing the contemporary analogue of early hunter/gatherers – that is, by analyzing those who graze animals and collect food and fiber from the vast tracts of public domain lands in the arid tropics. They are, after all, still *hunters and gatherers* – hunting for forage for their livestock, and for other food and fiber products that are collected and carried back to a home base. Our problem is to compare this ranging activity with that of sedentary agriculture carried on under an institutional regime of private property rights in land.[2]

Consider a village with a fixed population, some of whom must rely on hunting/gathering for sustenance, while the remainder can rely upon cultivated agriculture. In this model labor is the fixed factor of production – the total hours of labor available per unit of time – while land is the variable factor. That is, the fixed labor force will range over an ever-increasing land area in search of food and fiber (or forage for its stock). The only way in which total production of food and fiber can be increased is to range over more land, or to augment the labor force (figure 7.1, curve L_2 or curve L_3). As the necessary distances increase notice that total production increases at a decreasing rate, reflecting the fact that the extra distances being traveled reduce the productivity of the hunter/gatherers. The binding constraint on the production system from hunting/gathering is the spatial distribution of flora and fauna.

Now imagine that we introduce sedentary agriculture into the village economy; the question becomes one of a mix of land uses between cultivation and hunting/gathering. Continuing to hold labor constant and letting land vary we would obtain figure 7.2; the net value of production reflects the net increment to the village over and above the necessary costs of production from the two sectors. Here, assume that the labor force (L^*) of the village is divided so that one portion $(L^* - L_1)$, works in agriculture while the remainder (L_1) works in the hunting/gathering sector. The production function A reflects total net value of production from cultivation, while H/G_1 reflects total net

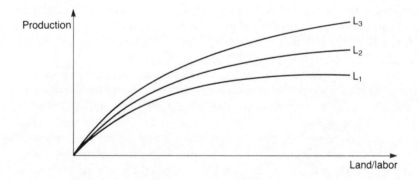

Figure 7.1   **Production from hunting and gathering.**

value of production from hunting/gathering. The function A turns down because good-quality agricultural land at the disposal of the village is in limited supply. Had the relationship been drawn in conventional terms the productivity of workers in the two sectors would cross, indicating the proper allocation of labor between the two. This formulation simply shows the proper land allocation between the two sectors. At point B the net profitability of agriculture falls below that obtainable from hunting and gathering, even though the net profitability of hunting/gathering is barely increasing as more land is combed for sustenance. We assume that the land in the cultivated sector is under private ownership, and that the land on which hunting/gathering occurs is in the public domain.

Those who suggest that privatization of land will bring forth new production have in mind this public domain land beyond point F, the frontier between private land and the public domain. That is, if the land out to F^* could be converted to private ownership then A would shift to A^*, and the incremental net production (P^*) would exceed that now obtainable from the public domain (P). It is said to be the collective management of this public domain land between F and F^* that accounts for its low net production.

The model so far has ignored a consideration that must be reckoned with if we are to obtain a complete picture of the choice over property regimes. That is, I have so far ignored the costs of the particular property regime pertinent for each type of land. On the cultivated private land we know that there must be a system of boundary surveys

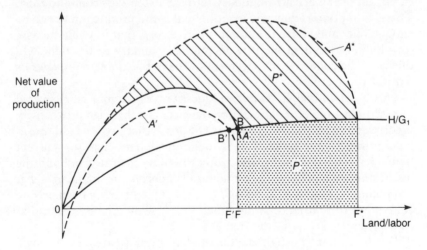

Figure 7.2 The private–public frontier.

to demarcate the various plots of the respective owners. Additionally there must be a process in place to record transfers of plots among new owners; this would include the measurement of said plots, the verification of a clear title to the plot, and the costs of the record-keeping system in which the transaction would be recorded. Add to these official administrative costs those costs associated with the actions of the private owners; foremost here would be the possibility of fencing.

The administration of the public domain is not costless either. There must be meetings among the members of the village to determine the specific locations of use, to discuss rates of harvesting, and so forth. There is a reasonable case to be made that the costs of privatization (fences, measurement, title insurance, record-keeping) are greater than those of the collectively managed public domain of the village. When these hidden costs of land administration and use are incorporated into the model we get a somewhat modified picture. Letting the costs of the public domain be a numeraire, we can depict the differential impact on the net production of the private lands by a reduction in net profit equal in magnitude to the higher infrastructure costs on the private lands. This is shown in figure 7.2 with function A'. Notice that these costs must be paid whether or not there is any production forthcoming from the private lands; A' is negative in the early stages. Also note that this incorporation of differential overhead costs of private land shifts the ideal boundary point to the left (F').

This recognition of differential costs in two different property regimes does not really address the implicit hypothesis of those advocating extension of the private boundary into the extensive economic zone. That assumption is that privatization will *cause* production to rise by enough over and above the administrative costs that it would be wise (profitable) to extend the private/public boundary to the right. On this view the collective management of the public domain *impedes* its natural productivity.

This is, of course, an empirical question that cannot be answered by assertions from economic theory; the mere fact that high productivity is correlated with private land does not prove that private land *causes* high productivity. Indeed, it is maintained here that the current boundary observed in the arid tropics between private land and the public domain represents the economically appropriate boundary – that it is point F' in figure 7.2. Beyond F' the net profitability from private cultivation of that land (along function A') would be less than that enjoyed along H/G_1 in the figure.[3]

To this point the public domain has been treated as a single institutional entity when in fact there are several types of property regimes that must be considered. Indeed, the confusion in the conventional literature over the tragedy of the commons arises from a failure to understand the concept of property, and therefore to fail to understand common property regimes.

2 AN EXPANDED MODEL OF ALTERNATIVE PROPERTY REGIMES

The model of figure 7.2 treats all public-domain land as of a single type, when in fact we know from chapter 2 that there are several types of property regimes over nonprivate land. I will now introduce a model that will help us to assess the more realistic choices from among these alternative property regimes. Before starting, let me note that our understanding will be enhanced if we begin with the recognition that land and related natural resources in the rural sector are characterized by a whole complex of institutional arrangements that will vary across resources and through seasons of the year. In some locations, or at certain times of the year, these resources may be under the control of only one individual, or one household. When this is the case their management resembles that which is pertinent to a variety of individual (or private) resources. However, in other locations, or at other times of the year, the management of some of these resources may transcend the nominal individual or household and involve instead a number of individuals or households. Those unfamiliar with local institutional arrangements will often confuse this situation with an absence of property rights, and will then suggest that the solution is to be found in the establishment of such rights. In point of fact, successful common property regimes are characterized precisely by the existence of individual rights. What changes between different types of property regimes is the *scope* of the primary decision-making unit (Ciriacy-Wantrup and Bishop, 1975; Dasgupta and Heal, 1979; Netting, 1976; Rhoades and Thompson, 1975; Wade, 1987).

The essence of control over resources is that there exist socially recognized and sanctioned rules and conventions that make it clear who is the "owner" of the resource in question; call these owners *decision units*. Each decision unit will have certain interests in the management of the resource, and those interests will find expression in claims made by the decision unit. When various claims are adjudicated and given formal protection we say that rules and conventions are established that bestow entitlements on each decision unit. Entitlements entail a socially recognized structure of *institutional arrangements* that both constrain and liberate individuals in their behaviors with respect to other individuals; as such, institutions are at the core of group management regimes over agricultural resources. It is the institutional arrangements that comprise the binding agreement that transforms the isolation problem of a prisoner's dilemma into a cooperative game.[4] Because *property* represents a secure claim or expectation over a future stream of benefits arising from a thing or a situation (a resource, if you will), we can regard such collective management systems as *common property regimes*. It is this failure to understand property rights that attach to resource decision units that has led to the persistent confusion between *common property resources* and *open access resources*, and therefore to the alleged "inevitability of the tragedy of the commons."

Each property regime has associated with it a particular structure of administrative and transaction costs. Recall from the discussion of figure 7.2 that these costs will include the costs of determining boundaries, of maintaining a set of records (titles, deeds, etc.), of enforcing the particular property regime, and of collective action when the regime is based on nonprivate property rights. The costs are not expected to be the same for each type of property regime. For instance, a private property regime might be expected to have an elaborate record-keeping system indicating boundaries and sales histories for each parcel. A common property regime would not have the need for extensive records on boundaries and sales, but would instead require meetings and discussions where the co-owners decided their strategies for the coming period. In contrast with the more formalized legal system of a private property regime, common property regimes will have different means for resolving disputes among co-owners or aggrieved parties. Finally a state property regime, by definition, will have a government agency that is responsible for decision making and compliance with rules.

It is generally accepted that as the economic value of something is increased then it will be efficacious to undertake steps to assure the protection and wise management of that particular object. One does not undertake to build a $1,000 building to house a piece of equipment whose replacement value is $40. Conversely, a $1,000 building for a $50,000 object is eminently reasonable. Or, we might think about the level of insurance that would be obtained for two objects, one costing $40 to replace, the other costing $50,000 to replace. A responsible party is certainly more inclined to take expensive means to protect the latter investment as opposed to the former.

Let us extend this analogy one step by considering the relative value of land emanating out from the urban center as in figure 6.1. We know from location theory that land at the center of an urban place will be much more valuable than land at the extensive margin. It is not unreasonable to suppose, therefore, that there would be much more willingness to pay to secure the benefit stream arising from land at the urban center than from land at the extensive margin. Those who subscribe to the property rights approach mentioned above would certainly find this hypothesis agreeable. Essentially, societies will undertake to define property rights – *and associated control regimes* – in accordance with the economic value of the objects under consideration. The per-unit costs of such regimes will differ substantially. That is, the administrative costs of 1 acre of prime real estate in central Manhattan will be much higher than will the administrative costs of 1 acre of sagebrush in central Nevada.

I suggest that these differential cost structures for different property regimes can be combined with the rent gradient of figure 6.1 to offer a tentative model of the choice of institutional regimes over land and related natural resources. This is depicted in figure 7.3. Here we see that the administrative costs per unit of privately owned land are high,

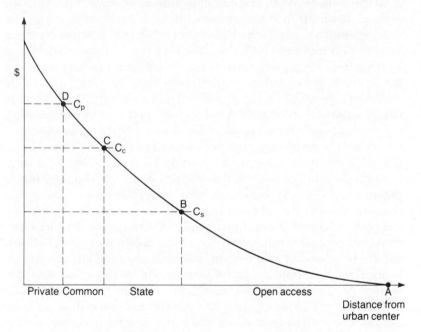

Figure 7.3 **The rent gradient and property regimes.**

the administrative costs for common property land are somewhat lower, and the same costs for state property regimes are lower still. The differences in these costs in the figure are merely suggestive and one should not infer any cardinality. But the figure does suggest to us that there is a plausible reason why land at the extensive margin is under one property regime, while land at the intensive margin is under another.

If we start at the extreme extensive margin (point A) we see that the economic value of the land and its related natural resource is so low as not to justify any property (or management) regime. That is, the per unit cost, even for the fairly economical state administration, exceeds its social value. Such lands (or any natural resource for that matter) would be under a regime of open access in which any use was less harmful than the costs necessary to preclude it. Between points A and B we would find an open access regime over the land and its related natural resources. At point B the economic value of the land as evidenced by the rent gradient is now of sufficient magnitude that some management regime is justified. Here societies will undertake to develop an institutional structure that is adequate to manage the benefit stream from the land and its related natural resources, but there is certainly no incentive to overdo things administratively. Let us call the evolved administrative structure one of *state property*.

As we move closer to the urban center the rent gradient increases as land becomes more valuable. We find that the potential loss of benefits from the rather extensive and "loose" management regime of the state calls for something more elaborate and more attuned to local conditions. Here (beginning at point C) we encounter a group of users organized to administer the natural resource under a common property regime. Finally, as the economic value of the resource increases further (at point D), the private property regime is called into play. Notice that the institutional choice flows from the inherent nature of the land, through the rent gradient, to the property regime of choice. Some in the so-called "property rights school" would have us believe that causality runs in the other direction.

The problem of institutional choice described here has its exact empirical counterpart in every part of the world where institutional choice is possible. Whether in south Asia, sub-Saharan Africa, Switzerland, Australasia, or the western United States we find this pattern. In the rangelands of the western United States small parcels of meadow and irrigated farm land are privately owned, while large expanses of grazing land are owned by the federal government. It is not uncommon in Nevada, for instance, to find a rancher owning

200 acres of good meadow land who then leases grazing rights from the federal government over an area that may reach 5,000 acres in size. The economic unit we know as a western cattle ranch operates under two distinct property regimes.[5] The same pattern is found in Switzerland where valley-bottom land is privately owned and the summer pastures are under a common property regime.

The rent gradient of figure 7.3 should not be taken to suggest that all land and related natural resources at the extensive margin are of low value. I have already indicated that isolated parcels of very productive land occur in the rural hinterland and we should not be surprised to see that these parcels are under a private property regime. We can also elaborate the figure somewhat by understanding that there are different types of state property as well. In India, for example, there are state forestry departments, but also a national revenue department. The forestry departments administer those lands under forest cover (or with some history of forest cover), while the revenue department is concerned with lands of lower quality. In the United States, state property regimes exist under several forms of management. Some land is administered by the Bureau of Land Management (primarily for livestock grazing), some is administered by the Forest Service (primarily for timber production and recreation), some is administered by the National Park Service as national parks (primarily for recreation), and some is administered by the National Park Service as wilderness areas (exclusively for recreation). The administrative costs per acre of these different management regimes certainly vary, and these cost differentials reflect, indirectly, the social value of the asset being managed.

A property regime derives its meaning from the structure of rights that characterizes the relationship of individuals (or, as suggested earlier, primary decision units such as households or kin groups) to one another, and to the object(s) of value. It is the nature of these institutional arrangements that defines the extant property regime over land and related natural resources – whether that regime be one we would call private property, state property, or common property. That is, the institutional arrangements define one individual *vis-à-vis* others – either within the group or outside of the group. I have characterized these relations between two (or more) individuals (or groups) by stating (in chapter 2) that one party has an interest that is protected by a *right* only when all others have a *duty*. Property is a right to a benefit stream that is only as secure as the duty of all others to respect the conditions that protect that stream. There are other situations in which an individual does not have a right to undertake certain actions but instead has only *privilege*. With a right I am protected against the claim of another by their duty. With *privilege* I am free to do as I wish since the other party has *no rights*. Put differently, an individual with privilege is free to ignore the interests or claims of those with no rights.

The difference between a common property regime and an open access regime thus stands on these legal correlates. In a situation of open access I have privilege with respect to use of the resource since no-one else has the legal ability to keep me out; they have no rights. But since I have no ability to prevent them from using the natural resource I have no rights, and they have privilege. It follows, therefore, that an open access situation is one of mutual privilege and no rights. Contrast this with a common property regime in which there are rules defining who is in the resource management group and who is out. That is, some have a right to be in, while others have a duty to stay out. Of those recognized as being in, each has a duty to obey the rules of the group (compliance) and each has the right to expect others also to obey the rules. Here there is mutual duty and rights. It is the rights of the members limiting group size (and hence total use), along with the rights of the members proscribing the use that each will make (the stint), that together constitute property. Hence the term *common property regime*.

The various property regimes described in chapter 2, and elaborated upon here, reflect economic conditions of land and related natural resources and the social "overlay" that reflects how those natural resources are to be used for the benefit of society. Rights and duties, as well as privilege and no rights, define individuals and groups at a particular moment in time. When an individual or a group has the legal ability to alter the status quo structure of legal entitlements then we say that that individual (or group) has *power*, while the party who is put in a new legally binding situation has *exposure*. If a party is not able to change the legal entitlements that define it with respect to others then that party has *no power* and the other party has *immunity*.

When economic conditions change, or when tastes and preferences change, or when a new technique appears on the horizon, then it becomes necessary to reevaluate existing structures of entitlements (institutions) to make sure that they are not counterproductive; if these entitlements change by mutual consent we assume that both parties have been made better off, or at least one of the parties is no worse off. If, however, one party was excluded in the deliberations, or if that party was ignored or overridden, then *power* has been exercised. The discussion in chapter 6 suggests that decision makers at the village level were exposed to the *power* of, first, colonial administrators, and subsequently rulers of newly independent nation-states. The problem now to be faced is whether or not there is a meaningful role for a property regime lying somewhere between individualized private property and nationalized state property.

In chapter 2 I introduced four general types of property regimes: (1) state property regimes; (2) private property regimes; (3) common property regimes; and (4) nonproperty regimes (or open access). Recall that in a state property regime the control rests in the hands of the state. Individuals and groups may be able to make use of the resources, but only at the forbearance of the state. National forests, national parks, and military reservations are examples of state property regimes. The nationalization of Nepal's village forests by the government in 1957 converted a common property regime into a state property regime, though, as seen earlier, the absence of management rendered it more like an open access regime.

In a private property regime the controlling unit is usually thought to be the individual, although of course recall that all corporate property is private property and yet it is administered by a group. It is also essential that we be reminded of the pervasive duties that attend the private control of land and related resources; few owners are entirely free to do as they wish with such assets.

The third regime is the common property regime. Notice that common property represents private property for the group (since all others are excluded from use and decision making), and that individuals have rights (and duties) in a common property regime (Ciriacy-Wantrup and Bishop, 1975).

Finally we have the open access situation in which there is no property. While the aphorism "everybody's property is nobody's property" has gained wide acclaim in the confused literature on the tragedy of the commons, this is logically inconsistent. It can only be said that everybody's *access* is nobody's property. The fallacy of the tragedy of the commons allegory is that by failing to understand property, and thus to see the world as dichotomous between open access (which is bad) and private property (which is claimed to be good), the commentators could leap from the presumption of destruction to the presumption of wise management with one quick sleight of hand.

3 TOWARD IMPROVEMENT OF PROPERTY REGIMES

The recognition of three types of property regimes, and one regime that is not a property regime at all (open access), provides a structure within which to discuss the kind of development assistance that is most likely to succeed in the arid tropics. I will not dwell on the private land resource since that is the subject of most development assistance programs at the current time.

Consider first the open access regime. By definition this is a situation of mutual privilege and no right; no one user has the right (ability) to preclude use by any other party. Here the natural resource is subject to the rule of capture and belongs to no-one until it is in someone's possession. It is not property – that is, it cannot yield an appropriable benefit stream – until it is in the physical possession of the party to take control of it. Whether grazing forage or fuelwood, a resource under an open access regime belongs to the party to first exercise control over it. The investment in (or improvement of) open access regimes must first focus on the institutional dimension. In the absence of that, and if the investment is in the form of a capital asset such as improved tree species or range revegetation, the institutional vacuum assures that use rates will eventually rise to the point of depleting the asset. Hence with open access resources the necessary precondition is to convert them from an open access regime to a common property regime. That is, we need to convert an institutional environment of mutual privilege and no right into one of mutual right and duty. Once the regime is converted to common property for the group – say all the members of the village – then unauthorized use by outsiders will have been brought under control. An example would be if the migration patterns of herders were changed to prevent their use of village lands. The village lands would be converted from an open access regime to one of common property for the members of the village. In the early 1980s a number of nations converted coastal fisheries within 200 miles of their coast from open access fisheries into state property that was then managed under a variety of property regimes. Some nations kept them as state property, while others established regional fishery councils with varying degrees of autonomy. Some of these fisheries became true common property regimes.[6]

Once open access regimes are converted to some form of property regime, it is then possible to address the question of use rates of those within the relevant decision unit – whether regional fishery or a village. A great deal of resource degradation arises from population growth within the relevant decision unit. This use, though exceeding the ability of the renewable resource to sustain its annual yield, cannot be stopped because of the nominal right of every villager to take what he/she needs to survive. The breakdown of most common property regimes arose because of the failure of the decision-making process within the decision group. There is a failure to deal with the obvious reality that, as a village grows, and therefore as the number of rights holders grows apace, the total demands on the resource will ultimately exceed its rate of regeneration. If the village believes that all of this larger population has a right to take what is needed, then it becomes obvious that no villager has a right to anything other than what he/she can capture by being there first. A common property regime for the group becomes an open access regime for the individuals within the group.

To improve the situation requires a reduction in total offtake until the natural resource base can generate sufficient annual yield to meet the needs of the new (lower) harvesting, plus allow for some continued regeneration. The obvious problem is to meet the reduced needs of those deemed to be excessive claimants on the resource base until that regenerative capacity is restored. Alternatively, if it is determined that the resource will never be able to sustain the level of demands to be placed on it, then there must be some capital investment to augment it. But capital investment in the absence of a prior institutional fix will simply assure that the new asset is squandered as the old one was.

The final resource regime on which improvements might be concentrated is the state property regime. The record of management here has been very disappointing (Bromley, 1986b). The appearance of management by the establishment of governmental agencies, and the appearance of a coherent policy by issuance of decrees prohibiting entry to state property, has led to continued degradation of resources under the management of government agencies. If degradation of state lands is to be arrested it will require that current practices of indifferent enforcement be stopped (Thomson, 1977), and that staffing levels and incentives be sufficient to administer and manage that domain which the government has taken unto itself. The record to date is not encouraging.

The final issue to be addressed concerns the *economic feasibility* of investing scarce development resources and time in public-domain lands compared with those lands under private control. It is obvious that, on a per-acre basis, the private lands in the arid tropics are often extremely productive. Would it not make more sense to continue to invest there rather than to invest in the public domain? Or, would it not make more sense to continue to expand the irrigated area so as to convert lands out of the public domain and into the private domain? To answer the question properly requires a number of complex considerations. But, as a brief response, several factors stand out. The conversion of land from the public to the private domain will usually require major investments in irrigation works in the face of a shadow price for foreign debt that is high and rising. Given the dismal record of production from irrigation projects in the arid tropics the burden of expanded irrigation is further compounded (Bromley, 1982; Easter, 1977; Wade, 1987).

Secondly, a few considerations regarding economic feasibility seem in order. Firstly, they must be evaluated keeping in mind that many of the benefits will appear in the rather distant future. Under the conventional practice of discounting future benefits and costs such projects will automatically appear to be less favorable (or less productive) than investments whose benefits appear in the nearer term. That is, most investments imply large immediate expenditures (costs) and then a stream of benefits into the future. Projects with identical net benefits over their respective lifetimes will rank differently depending upon the time stream of benefits received; those with the bulk of their benefits in the future will be discriminated against.

It is incorrect to assume that they are less productive or offer fewer benefits than projects with a different time stream of benefits; we must simply conclude that the *present value of the benefits* is different. If one adheres strictly to conventional benefit–cost protocol then all projects with more distant benefits will be discriminated against. It should be obvious that slavish adherence to an investment criterion that selects only those projects with the highest present-valued net benefits will result in few, if any, resource protection projects winning acceptance. The irony of this cannot be overstated; we fail to take proper care of the livelihood and habitat of future generations because *our* valuation of the benefits is less than that of projects which will take care of the present generation. The fact that we are in a position to dictate the nature of the resource endowment with which they must live has not been lost on philosophers and those concerned with intergenerational ethics. I have discussed this at length in chapter 5.

Secondly, we must remember that benefit–cost analysis is not a dogma but simply an evaluation tool. But being an *evaluation tool* does not also make it an inviolate *decision rule*. It is important to keep these two functions distinct. One can undertake a very conventional (and narrow) benefit–cost evaluation and then employ several decision rules regarding which projects to undertake. Or, one can employ a broader and more inclusive benefit–cost evaluation and then follow a quite restrictive decision-rule regarding which projects to undertake.

Thirdly, the very concept of feasibility is a product of the economic environment within which alternative investment activities are evaluated; the context will dominate the outcome. When an evaluation of the benefits and costs of a project on private lands is undertaken, the benefit stream is largely defined by the existing infrastructure that will allow those investments to appear favorable *vis-à-vis* a public-domain project. Marketing channels, transportation systems, agricultural extension workers, and input supply networks are usually in place and the new project is not "billed" for any of those costs; the benefit–cost analysis will usually include only the direct project costs, allowing the project a free ride on the existing infrastructure. By way of contrast a project on public-domain lands will be less likely to benefit from such infrastructure and hence the project will necessarily reflect all the costs related to its full realization. That this distorts the evaluation process against public-domain endeavors should be obvious.

The maintained hypothesis here is that a broad-gauged evaluation of development assistance efforts directed to natural resources in the public domain would reveal that a number of endeavors are indeed economically feasible. When proper shadow pricing is undertaken on both classes of development assistance projects – that is, those on the private domain and those on the public domain – it is my view that the public-domain projects will prove to be feasible locations for the concentration of institutional development, and technological change. If those lands can be improved in terms of their productivity notice that the curve H/G_1 in figure 7.2 would shift up and suggest that the optimal boundary between private and public land might shift back to the left. Or, in terms of figure 7.3, the rent gradient will shift up and change the efficient boundary point.

I have discussed the feasibility of rehabilitating open access and state property regimes so as to enhance natural resource management. What of the practical side of this? More specifically, is there any hope that villagers living in these natural resource complexes can be relied upon to undertake changes in their use? Can they be trusted to manage natural resources in a reasonable way? I now turn to the results of one study concerned with precisely this question.

4 CAN AUTHORITY AND COLLECTIVE MANAGEMENT REGIMES BE RESTORED?

The dismal record of forest management in many developing countries leads to the obvious question whether or not there are alternative institutional arrangements that offer some promise. That is, the widespread nationalization of forested areas has exceeded the capacity of many governments to implement effective managerial systems and so forests are often national in name only. As an alternative to this system of indifferent management, I suggest that the misunderstood common property regime may actually offer some promise for enhanced forest management. Such common property regimes would entail enfranchising local groups (villages, perhaps) to undertake forest management. Skeptics will respond that it is, after all, local people who engage in practices that often result in overgrazing and the excessive harvest of small timber and fuelwood. Is this not sufficient evidence that local people are indeed the enemies of the forest? My earlier arguments have suggested that local people who rely on the forest for their sustenance are often the victims of policies and forces beyond their control. If there were less interest by governments in commercial timber would there be more land available for fuelwood? If forest departments were less interested in creating European-like forests would there be more scope for people-oriented forests? If agricultural policy had to take account of millions of people pushed onto forested areas would the directions of that policy change? My tentative answer to all three questions is in the affirmative.

Assuming that progress might occur on these three fronts, the pertinent question still remains: how would villagers behave with respect to a local forest? Could they be trusted? One can only offer tentative answers to such questions, but even speculation is useful if we are serious about a reform of land-use policies in the developing countries that will redound to the benefit of their forests. Fortunately, we need not resort to idle speculation; recent research is suggestive of behavioral intentions in the middle hills of Nepal.[7]

My interest here is in the nationalization of all forest lands in Nepal. This action, taken in 1957, upset centuries of traditional forest control by village governance structures; the existing political structure – with its attendant rights and duties – was pushed aside in favor of national forests. Prior to the Private Forest Nationalization Act villagers made use of contiguous forest lands for a variety of products. Although there was no binding legal claim attached to the lands, they were usually considered to be the private domain of the nearby village.

The government was moved to nationalize forest lands for several reasons. First, medical technology had reduced infant mortality and so Nepal's population was suddenly increasing quite rapidly – putting more pressure on local resources. Second, malaria-control programs had made the terai lands (the lower hills and plains) inhabitable and so relatively pristine areas were being cleared for agriculture. And third, there was a new conviction at the center that ultimate resource control should rest with the state rather than with a large number of isolated villagers. As might be expected, nationalization in such a setting was destined to fail for two very obvious reasons: (1) villagers were left with no alternative source of supply for the many products formerly collected on such lands; and (2) the clear inability of the national government to enforce the new institutional arrangement. The new resource management regime was also undermined by the realization on the part of the villagers that local timber was to serve as a revenue source for the state. As mentioned previously, the Nationalization Act increased the rate of forest destruction as villagers hurried to convert affected lands into agricultural uses so as to exempt them from the transfer.

Nationalization shifted the locus of resource concern and management from the village to the national government. When responsibility for control was taken away the village lost something in terms of its own sense of responsibility toward the forest. It is this perception on the part of villagers that was of interest in our research. While we were not able to examine the impact of nationalization on the attitudes of villagers, we did investigate attitudes regarding forest use. To this end, a number of interviews were conducted among households in a Nepal village. The intent was to learn about intended resource-use patterns, and how the expectations of what other villagers would do might influence those use patterns.

This particular experiment follows in the tradition of Marwell and Ames (1981). We asked the heads of 140 households in Belkot Panchayat, Nepal, about their intentions with respect to a willingness to contribute toward the enhancement of a village asset (the forest). It should be clear that we were attempting to measure their behavioral intentions rather than their actual behavior. Each respondent was presented with a hypothetical situation in which they were told that they would receive an amount roughly equivalent to the current average annual tax burden. At the time of our survey (April 1983) this was Rs100. Each respondent was asked to allocate that windfall between a private use (one that would benefit only the household) and a public use (one that would benefit the collectively used village forest, or a community irrigation ditch). Both investment alternatives were said to return 10 percent per year. In addition, the public investment allocation from households would be exactly matched by the national government. It was stressed that all villagers would continue to benefit from the collective resource whether or not they agreed to contribute anything.

The mean investment in the collective good from the Rs100 windfall was Rs49.29, with the remainder going to private investments (Rs50.71). That is, the 140 households split the windfall almost evenly between the collective good and their own private investment. Fifty-one households (36 percent) donated the full amount of the windfall to the collective good, and an additional thirty households (21 percent) donated Rs50. Combined, eighty-one households (57 percent) contributed at least one-half of the windfall to the collective good. Only forty-eight households (34 percent) refused to contribute anything to the collective good.[8]

We asked all 140 respondents to indicate how much of the windfall would constitute a "fair" contribution to the collective good. While one-quarter of the respondents had no opinion on this, the mean of those who responded (105) was Rs61.5. This estimate of a fair contribution exceeds by 25 percent the mean contribution of all 140 households (Rs49.29). Approximately 70 percent of the responding households considered it "fair" to contribute at least Rs50 to the collective good. Two-fifths of the respondents (forty-four) considered it "fair" to donate the entire windfall of Rs100 to the collective good. Only one respondent considered it "fair" to donate nothing to the collective good.[9]

When concerned with renewable natural resources it is possible to contribute to their sustainable yield by refraining from use – or using the resource less intensively than one might otherwise consider. We were concerned about this aspect of contribution to the collective asset. This forbearance may also represent a more reasonable hypothetical situation than did our first group of experiments where we offered an imaginary windfall and asked the respondents to allocate it between their private investment and a collective investment. Respondents were asked to imagine that a nearby forested area had been opened up to the village for the collection of firewood, and that thirty bundles of firewood per year per household could be harvested by villagers on a sustained-yield basis; this quantity of firewood is slightly less than one-third of the annual firewood consumption by village households. The mean quantity of firewood that respondents said they would harvest was twenty-four, with nearly 60 percent of the respondents (eighty-two) indicating that they would harvest less than the sustainable yield of thirty bundles per household. An additional 30 percent of the households (forty-eight) said that they would take exactly thirty bundles; only 10 percent of the respondents indicated that they would take more than thirty. Ninety percent of the households considered it "fair" to harvest at or below the sustainable yield. This intended cutting behavior was unaffected by another aspect of the interview that asked how their behavior would change if they knew that a privileged group in the village was taking more than the sustainable yield.

The question requiring an answer is whether or not effective village-level structures and procedures can be counted upon to restore a sense of management responsibility to local forests and grazing areas in the tropics. For national and regional administrative agencies to relinquish managerial control it will be necessary to have some assurance that natural resources will not be squandered more seriously than at present. Of course one study of intended behavior in a Nepal village will not satisfy everyone – but it may be suggestive. The ultimate question will come down to one of compliance by members of a village with the evolved rules and conventions. That is, will some villagers free ride on the good behavior of others? The idea that free riding is a dominant strategy among people is a venerable one in the economics literature. Would Nepal villagers free ride? Even recognizing the limitations of our survey I am not persuaded that they would. The matter of how much influence the likely actions of others will have on an individual's response is also of interest in a policy sense. We asked the 140 respondents whether or not the likely behavior of others influenced what they would do with respect to their natural resource use, and in each of the experiments approximately 60 percent said that it would not. Thirty-five percent of the households said that they would be influenced by the amount of contribution made by other households in the case of the Rs100 windfall, but when it came to cattle grazing only 19 percent of the respondents said that they cared what others would do. I stress that this independent behavior exists regardless of whether the respondent intends to free ride or to be "a good citizen."

A very frequent response for why the villager intended to act independently of what others would do was that the respondent "could not read others' minds." Many respondents also indicated a strong desire to "make their own decisions." It seems safe to conclude that we found a substantial interest on the part of our respondents to contribute to a collective village asset, and to refrain from exploitive behavior with respect to a village asset. At the same time, a majority indicated that their behavior was not much affected by the likely behavior of others. A clear majority do not free ride, nor would they if they thought that others would. Village resource-use behavior seems to be very much influenced by a sense for the collective well-being. This does not mean that some would not overuse collective resources – especially in the case of grazing. But the magnitude of that overuse is not considered to be large.

The model that guided this investigation links one individual's contribution to a collective good to the anticipated actions of others in the same social unit. Across all our experiments we found that approximately one-third of the respondents considered the likely actions of others to be decisive in their own resource-use decisions. At the same time we found that a majority of the respondents said they would make contributions to the collective good. Hence, while the villagers seem to imply that they do not much care about what others intend to do, we believe it is reasonable to assume that the villagers know what is expected of them, and that others know likewise. Hence while claiming that the actions of others are not generally of concern to them, they may be secure in the knowledge that the resource-use decisions of the others will not be greatly out of line with some accepted norm.[10]

It seems reasonable to suggest the presence of a convention or norm that influences collective resource-use decisions. This norm has evolved over time as the members of a village struggle with the daily task of making a living. The majority care about the collective welfare, a minority will take more than is safe or fair, and both will do so irrespective of what they think others will do. This is not striking unless one believes that all individuals are greedy free riders. But working against this background ethic are two serious threats – one coming from the villagers themselves, and the other from the state. The first is population pressure. The second is the kind of resource policy formulation discussed at the outset: government passing laws and formulating administrative policies that threaten the existence of individual households. Such external influences are critical in the process of pitting villagers against themselves, and of ultimately shifting resource stewardship away from the village. When resource responsibility is taken away from the village, so is the concern for the viability of the resource. It is the "patron syndrome" turned on its head; villagers do not care much for things that the state gives to them, and the same would seem to apply to the things that the state takes away.

The research seems to suggest a residue of concern for collective management of natural resources in a country that has been characterized as one of the most seriously exploited, and where the state has usurped local resource management in name but not in deed. The lessons for the formulation of resource policy would seem to be several. First, the state must not decree what it cannot enforce: to nationalize the forest in name and yet to leave it unmanaged and unadministered is probably worse than having done nothing. Second, supply-side policies that restrict local resource access must be matched by innovative policy on both the supply side (in the form of providing alternative supplies) and on the demand side (in the form of helping to develop techniques and institutions that will dampen the need for the threatened resource).

5 SUMMARY

The recognition of property arrangements as policy instruments would seem to offer some hope that ideological fervor may give way to careful consideration of the social utility of alternative property regimes. Those who see thoroughgoing wisdom and efficiency in private property regimes fail to understand that different ecological circumstances – and vastly different cultural contexts – must be dominant factors in the choice of institutional arrangements. The nomadic pastoralists of Africa are not mobile because they prefer wandering; rather they wander because their economic system demands it. To think that one "solves" some problem by forcing them to be sedentary and by creating private property regimes over fixed Cartesian space is to confuse cause and effect. The only certain outcome is that their economic system would be destroyed under some ideological campaign to "civilize" them by forcing them to adopt an ecologically unsound – and culturally inappropriate – property regime.

The institutional boundary between private property regimes, common property regimes, and state property regimes is the very essence of blending socioeconomic interests with ecological imperatives. Wise natural resource management consists in finding that blend which will assure human survival and also avoid ecological degradation. It is not inevitable that common property regimes will be over-exploited, any more than it is inevitable that private property regimes will be wisely managed in the interest of the long run. The policy problem is to eschew ideological conviction in deference to careful analysis.

NOTES

1 The North and Thomas account of the origins of agriculture has been challenged on logical and historical grounds elsewhere (Runge and Bromley, 1979).

2 Parts of the following two sections appeared in an earlier form in *World Development*, 17 (6), 867–77, June 1989. I am grateful to the journal for permission to reproduce parts of that material here.

3 The presence of irrigation is one obvious way in which the optimal boundary can be adjusted in the arid tropics. However, in the absence of irrigation the presumption must be that the village has located the efficient boundary between private and public land.

4 The prisoners' dilemma is a situation in which each of the participants has a consistent tendency to defect from an agreement and to seek to better his own situation at the ultimate expense of the others in the group. This tendency to defect means that the aggregate of all participants is less well off than if the individuals had stuck together. See Friedman (1986), Guttman (1978), Schotter (1981), or Shubik (1982).

5   The discussion in chapter 8 regarding the so-called "sagebrush rebellion" suggests that ranchers understand the message of figure 7.3 better than the politicians do. While some politicians hoped to stir deep-seated individualism into support for establishing private property rights over extensive rangelands, the would-be owners – cattle ranchers – were moved by economics rather than by their ideology; privatization was a political dead end.

6   In the United States regional fisheries councils cooperate with the federal government to develop management plans and harvest quotas.

7   Some of the material for this section comes from a paper, co-authored with Devendra Chapagain, appearing in the *American Journal of Agricultural Economics*, 66, 868–73, December 1984. I am grateful to the journal and my co-author for permission to use parts of that work here.

8   We found an interesting relationship between the size of the contribution to the collective good and the caste of the household; since caste is also highly correlated with the size of private land holdings, the contribution to the collective good increased with the size of private holdings. Specifically, low-caste households with less than ½ ha contributed, on average, Rs31.25 as opposed to Rs68.75 for high-caste households owning more than 3 ha.

9   In a slight variation on the above experiment, we attempted to determine how the household heads would respond to a situation of unequal windfalls. Specifically, we told thirty-six respondents that they would be given Rs200 (rather than the original Rs100) and that the other 104 households would be given Rs66. The mean contribution of both groups to the collective good remained almost the same – at slightly under 50 percent of their windfall – a finding consistent with that of Marwell and Ames. Interestingly, the proportion of free riders increased to 40 percent (from 34 percent) among households receiving the small windfall (Rs66) compared with the proportion for a uniform windfall of Rs100 for all households. For the larger windfall (Rs200), free riding went from 34 percent of the households down to 25 percent.

10 The way the problem is framed will often influence the likelihood of cooperation. When the choice problem is framed as a decision on how much to *take* from the collective, research has shown that individuals tend to follow the lead of others in the group (take more if others do; take less if others do). When it is framed as a decision about how much to *give* to the collective, individuals tend to choose contrary to the lead of others (give more if total contributions are small; give less if they are large); that is, they free ride if there's a ride available (Brewer and Kramer, 1986; Fleishman, 1988).

8
Private Property, Public Property, and Social Preferences

Property is the instrument, security is the object, and when some alternative way is forthcoming of providing the latter, it does not appear in practice that any loss of confidence, or freedom or independence is caused by the absence of the former.

R. H. Tawney, *The Acquisitive Society*

1 PROPERTY RIGHTS AS CHOICE DOMAINS

The lawyer is inclined to talk of property in land as a collection of "sticks in a bundle". As such this tends to draw our attention to the fact that ownership is not absolute control. That is, ownership is the right to possess, to use, to manage, to benefit, to be secure, and to alienate. Control, therefore, is the right to disregard the interests of others in the exercise of the above dimensions of ownership. I submit that it is the right to control that is the most interesting in contemporary property issues and conflicts; "ownership" is not in doubt, but full control certainly is. We know that the essence of private rights in land is the ability to exclude others from physical invasion of a definite Cartesian space. What is not so well understood is the transmission of social costs from that same Cartesian space onto the space of others. While ownership is about the congery of rights that go with the landed space, control is about the rights at the boundary of that physical space. Control over land concerns who is entitled by the state to take particular actions without regard to the interests of others.

159

In most contexts the structure of land ownership is decisive in understanding the potential for untoward economic and political influence. This is certainly the case in much of Latin America – and to a lesser extent in Asia. Land ownership in these agrarian societies is a direct entrée to the legislative and administrative processes in which economic advantage is determined. But as societies become more complex, the significance of "ownership" *per se* becomes less compelling than the associated institutional conditions that determine the range of choice open to an owner. *Nominal structure* suggests ownership, while *real structure* suggests control. And it is control over choices that gives rise to social outcomes that are judged to be desirable or perverse. My argument with those who pay exclusive attention to the nominal structure of *ownership* is that this focuses inordinate attention on only one aspect of the entire institutional setup. Before turning to the specifics of my argument, let us pause momentarily to consider the concept of a market, and of exchanges occurring within markets.

The economist is inclined to look to markets as indicators of relative values; and this is certainly true under the appropriate assumptions. But market processes can only reflect relative values within the constraints of the prevailing institutional arrangements (Bromley, 1989a). When we ask about changes in land ownership within the existing institutional setup it should be understood that we are concerned with a fairly limited range of economic values. There are more fundamental matters that call out for analysis.

We start by recalling the Hohfeldian concepts of rights, duties, privileges, and no rights explained in chapter 2. A landowner is said to possess certain rights, while non-owners possess duties with respect to that individual and the thing owned. Property, it must be remembered, is a triad; the owner, the thing owned, and all others. The owner has rights with respect to the thing owned, all others have duty. I shall regard an *explicit rights transfer* as one in which the thing owned is exchanged among willing parties with the rights and duties running with the thing transferred; a new party now enjoys those rights, while the same basic population still has duties. The former owner has moved from a position of having rights to a position of having duty with respect to the particular benefit stream attendant to the object; the new owner now has rights rather than duties. Explicit transfers are thus seen to be the process of shifting the same basic structure of rights and duties among members of the polity. As intimated above, the concentration of rights in the hands of a few individuals is not of immediate concern in a political sense. What matters is the fear that the economic power deriving from this concentration may be put to antisocial uses.

Now consider the correlate of privileges and no rights. Recall that an individual has privilege to the extent that it is possible to shift costs at will to another individual. The exposure of the recipient of those costs is a function of the fact that the individual has no rights. If my neighbor seeks to paint her house some outlandish color there are two options open to me. The first is to buy her house and resell it to someone whose aesthetic tastes match my own. A second option is to offer the neighbor a sum of money to paint the house a somewhat more conventional color. But notice that I have no rights other than to enter into market transactions – both of which might be quite expensive. If I buy the house we would record that as an explicit transfer. If I offer the owner a bribe to discourage her strange tastes we get the same outcome (a different color house) but no explicit transfer. Similarly, if I decide that a neighborhood restriction on house colors would be cheaper to effect than a side-payment to the owner then I might pursue a new institutional arrangement through city hall. Again, if I am successful we might obtain the same outcome (a different color house) yet without any transfer having been recorded. That is, without a change in *ownership* (or what I call nominal structure).

But, I would submit that a change in entitlements of greater social import has occurred, and this change is not captured by conventional accounting. If I am able to exercise Hohfeldian "power" to change the legal standing of the neighboring homeowner then I have brought about a change in the uses to which land can be put. Should we not record this as an important event in the "ownership" of land? This process of modifying the degree of control to be exercised by "owners of record" over land is what I mean by *implicit rights transfers*.

I suggest that many interesting economic questions in land are to be found in the domain of *implicit* rather than *explicit rights transfers*. I earlier suggested that property is a triad – the owner, the thing owned, and all others. There is no property in a one-person world; there is only property when there is a duty holder (a right regarder). What is it that such duty conveys to an owner? One essential aspect is the presence of security over future values. Tawney suggests as much when he says: "Property is the instrument, security is the object, and when some alternative way is forthcoming of providing the latter, it does not appear in practice that any loss of confidence, or freedom or independence is caused by the absence of the former" (Tawney, 1948, pp. 73–4). Put somewhat differently, it is real structure as opposed to nominal structure that gives meaning to one's claim to a benefit stream.

The economic core of property is security of exchange value; how else does one explain the almost fanatical interest – codified in the US

Constitution – in eminent domain as opposed to the exercise of police power? The economics of property in land is really concern for futurity. The social problem in land is to provide enough security to encourage private investment of an improving nature, while at the same time retaining enough collective control to protect others against the spillover effects. Although some will regard the analogy as infelicitous, the state must deal with landowners in much the way that parents deal with children – giving responsibility when it seems warranted, withdrawing it when it is abused. And the contention over property and property rights is concerned precisely with collective notions of what constitutes *abuse* as a basis for redefining domains of choice and control over land use.

The economics of property is a study of the creation and redirection of income and cost streams among members of the polity. Rights give an owner the freedom to exclude others from a certain physical space, and to impose costs on others across the boundary of the land owned. Duty obligates others to agree to be excluded. Land ownership also implies privilege in the form of costs imposed on those with no rights. Economists ought to be concerned about the economic implications of alternative rights–duties configurations, about the economic implications of alternative privilege–no right structures, and about the ways in which different parties can use power to alter the legal position of others in society. This interest in the status quo and in how it becomes modified would bring important insights to bear on what I here call implicit transfers.

An implicit transfer is therefore one in which the legal entitlements that attach to a parcel of land are modified in some way. Traditionally such transfers have been motivated by external costs emanating from a parcel of land. A cattle feedlot may be enjoined from allowing its odors to pervade a residential neighborhood, a wetland owner may be enjoined to prevent the filling of valuable habitat, or the owner of a forested area may be forced to replant trees in the interest of watershed protection to replace those harvested.

As used here, the term *implicit transfer* refers to some form of collective action that alters existing entitlements, such collective action being implemented through the offices of the state. Let us recall, however, that the state acts at the behest of certain entities. It is safe to surmise that those who currently have rights and privileges will view such collective action with distaste, while those currently with duty and no rights will view collective action with more enthusiasm. This simply points up the dilemma faced by the state – to do nothing is to sanction the status quo, to act is to favor those currently seeking relief. The state is damned if it does, and damned if it does not. To those inclined to worry about government "intervention" let me point out, as Warren Samuels and others have done so well, that the state is already involved in the first instance.[1] It is the state, after all, that sanctions and protects the status quo property structure. For the state to do nothing is to protect those who currently have rights and privilege; to enter the fray in some form of collective action to modify institutional arrangements is to act in the interest of those currently bearing unwanted costs.

The economics of property in land is quite properly concerned with the incidence of costs – both cash and otherwise – across members of the polity. Property is, after all, a specific legal sanction for the distribution of certain costs. If I own all the productive agricultural land in Oz, and if I choose not to sell food to someone, then I hold the power to impose the ultimate cost – starvation – on the would-be buyer. Since property defines which costs must be recorded, property also defines what it is that economists consider to be efficient. If some costs are not recorded in the "social books," then it will not appear to be "efficient" to take those costs into account. The matter of pollution control falls into this category. That is, the costs of pollution in the form of forgone benefits do not appear in the economic accounting of firms. Small wonder then that those opposed to pollution control can claim that such regulation is not "efficient."

2   THE INSTRUMENTALITY OF PROPERTY RIGHTS

Several recent legal findings in the United States suggest a new awareness of the instrumental role of property rights in land. Perhaps the most interesting one concerns a Supreme Court decision over the fate of Grand Central Station in New York City.[2] First the facts of the case. The owner of the Station, the Penn Central Transportation Company, was prevented from building a high-rise office building above the existing structure on the grounds that the proposed action would ruin an important (and listed) architectural landmark. That prohibition was, interestingly enough, not regarded as a compensable taking. On these grounds alone traditional thought would have regarded the restriction as an exercise of police power – the uncompensated denial of an activity on the grounds that it would otherwise create a significant public harm.[3]

But Sax suggests that something quite profound was at work here (Sax, 1983). Specifically, he argues that the Supreme Court failed to notice that it was preventing one landowner (Penn Central) from doing what every other adjacent owner had been able to do – construct a high-rise building. Hence, conventional zoning law did not apply. Sax argues that the owner was required by the Court to continue to confer benefits on its neighbors without compensation. The "bad fortune" of having a distinctive landmark, and being the last owner to undertake grandiose plans, worked to Penn Central's distinct disadvantage:

> The owner's situation in *Penn Central* resembles the situation of a landowner who has, up to the present time, refrained from building on his lot, thereby providing his neighbors a scenic amenity. Now he wishes to stop providing that benefit, and to use his property as his neighbors have already used their adjoining tracts. Yet the law requires him to continue bestowing amenity value upon his neighbors even though they have no similar obligation. How can such a result be explained or justified? That is the question Justice Rehnquist raised, and the majority opinion in the case provides no satisfactory answer. (Sax, 1983, p 483)

Sax provides the missing answer. He claims that Penn Central and related cases do not turn on the traditional compensation/no compensation logic dominating property rights cases of the past. Rather, he believes that these cases concern the *allocative role* of property rights in land – an issue close to the heart of the so-called "property rights school" within economics. The difference here, however, is that *private property rights* – the real interest of the hard-core property rights commentators – are being undermined in the interest of a larger collective interest in how individual parcels of land are used. In terms of my concept of implicit transfers, the domain of control is passing from nominal landowners to the larger society which reaps benefits and bears costs of individual decisions over land use. Sax goes on to elaborate, as a legal scholar, on what he means by *allocation*:

> We have endowed individuals and enterprises with property because we assume that the private ownership system will allocate and reallocate the property resources to socially desirable uses. Any such allocational system will, of course, fail from time to time. But when the system regularly fails to allocate property to "correct" uses, we begin to lose faith in the system itself. Just as older systems of property, like feudal tenures, declined as they became nonfunctional, so our own system is declining to the extent it is perceived as a functional failure. Since such failures are becoming increasingly common, the property rights that lead to such failures are increasingly ceasing to be recognized. Thus, the interesting question . . . is not why the owner failed to receive compensation, but why private ownership of Grand Central Station did not lead to the correct allocation, that is, to maintaining the property as an unobstructed, architecturally distinctive railroad station. (Sax, 1983, p. 484)

Of course some might object to Sax's conclusion about the correct outcome by arguing that the market should be relied upon to produce the correct outcome. But that observation simply begs the question of "correct" by asserting that whatever comes from the market is, *ipso facto*, correct. And this is where most debates over individual versus collective interests in land end up – the side favoring markets asserting that market outcomes will be correct unless proven otherwise, and the side suspicious of markets asserting that market outcomes are antisocial. The resolution to this argument is not to be found in economics.

There is another interesting Supreme Court decision, this one concerning the Hawaiian Land Reform Act of 1967 (Hawaii Housing Authority v. Midkiff). This law raises the interesting issue of an *explicit transfer* arising out of reasons that have traditionally been dealt with by means of *implicit transfers*. First the facts. Since the time that Europeans arrived on the Hawaiian Islands, land has been concentrated in the hands of a few chiefs and their descendants. Feudal tenures granted all rights to the chiefs or their deputies; there was no private ownership of land. Beginning in the early 1800s there began repeated, but unsuccessful, efforts to divide these lands among the Crown, the chiefs, and the masses. In the 1960s it was found that while the state and federal governments owned approximately 49 percent of the Islands, another 47 percent was in the hands of only seventy-two private owners. Eighteen landowners, with holdings of over 21,000 acres, owned more than 40 percent of this. On the most urbanized island of Oahu, twenty-two landowners held 73 percent of the fee simple titles (Hawaii Housing Authority, 1984).

The Hawaii legislature concluded that this degree of concentration of land ownership was an impediment to the workings of a land market because it held land prices above some reasonable level; the public tranquility and welfare was said to suffer in consequence. In Honolulu it is quite common for individuals to own homes built on land leased from the major estates. Initially the legislature considered forcing the landowners to sell these leased parcels to the lessees. The landowners objected on the grounds that they would then face a significant tax liability on their immense capital gains. To mollify both lessees and lessors the legislature decided to condemn large tracts of leased residential land and subsequently to transfer those lands to the current lessees. Condemnation made the sales involuntary, thus relieving the owners of the capital gains obligation. A lessee initiates the condemnation proceedings by asking the Hawaii Housing Authority to condemn the leased parcel. The Authority, when a threshold level of lessees has sought such action, will hold hearings. It then acquires, at prices set by trial or by negotiation between lessee and lessor, the former fee owner's "full right, title, and interest" in the land (Hawaii Housing Authority, 1984). Once the Housing Authority acquires title to the land it may sell it to the lessees who initiated the original transfer. To date the entire program has been financed by the ultimate sale to lessees, although the Authority has the ability to issue bonds if it should require operating capital.

The Land Reform Act was challenged on constitutional grounds and ultimately reached the US Supreme Court. The Court found the Act to be consistent with the public use provisions of the Constitution. Conservative commentators considered this decision to be a travesty in that the very "sanctity of private property" was said to be under serious attack. The dilemma is, of course, the interpretation of "public use." The Constitution forbids the taking of landed property – even with compensation – from Alpha for the private use and benefit of Beta. The government may only condemn private land for recognized "public uses" – highways, airports, public parks, and schools. Here the state was taking from Alpha (the large estates) and giving to Beta (the residents now leasing).

What we see here is a gradual transformation in the public perception of what activities comprise legitimate public uses; the Court reflects that changed perception. The land oligopoly in the Hawaii case led the Court to conclude that the usual distinction between the exercise of the police power (which is not compensable) and eminent domain (which is compensable) did not hold in this case. The regulation of oligopoly has long been recognized as a legitimate exercise of the police power. The structure of ownership in Hawaii surely approached oligopoly. Yet the condemnation proceedings and ultimate sale of land to the lessors did compensate the former owners.

We also see here a recognition of important social costs arising from the structure of land ownership and a remedial action that is found to be compatible with Constitutional guarantees against the arbitrary powers of the state. It is an explicit transfer, but the origin is one of social instrumentality of prevailing property entitlements. No longer must a physical structure be erected on a condemned piece of land to justify a collective role in its future use and control.

One might suggest in the Hawaii situation that the former owners received a "fair market" price for their condemned land, and they surely avoided the tax liability that might have been present had they not had some considerable power with the Hawaii legislature. In this way is it possible to conclude that their property (their security) was protected? The Hawaii legislature and the Supreme Court would answer yes. Some economists would prefer to see pervasive markets in operation before reaching any conclusion.

But the central issue for our purposes is not market prices but control over land, the influence over a stream of social benefits and costs that arise from that control over land, and ultimately the instrumentality of private property rights in an increasingly crowded world. It is this ability to impose costs and benefits on disparate parties that is at the heart of the economics of property in land. And it is this very power that is constantly under scrutiny by the state on behalf of cost bearers. The essence of a modern and technologically advanced world is that we now possess a greater potential to interfere with our neighbors. To the extent that ownership of land bestows certain capabilities in this regard then it is essential that we begin to understand the process of implicit transfers. A simple-minded response might be that reduced control for landowners would show up in depressed land prices; that is, we could use market prices to detect state-mandated actions restricting the domain of choice of landowners. Those economists opposed to collective action would cite this as evidence of the "inefficiencies of government intervention." But it does not necessarily follow that implicit transfers are price-depressing. Certain externalities are reciprocal in nature, and being forced to change certain practices that impose costs on others also means that others are constrained to impose costs on me. The relationship between implicit transfers and general land prices is much more subtle than we suppose.

The economics of property in land must first be concerned with an important distinction between ownership and control; it is the latter dimension that defines the ability of the owner to disregard social costs that transcend the nominal boundaries of the firm (Bromley, 1989a). This concern for ownership and control is best understood by considering property entitlements in the Hohfeld sense of rights–duties and privileges–no rights. The neglected domain of implicit transfers is here argued to be of much greater importance than is the more conventional interest in explicit transfers. When implicit transfers occur previous rights and privileges are converted to duties and no rights. How does this process get started? What are the essential aspects? How does an economist begin to understand this process?

These are not idle concerns. It is the process of implicit transfers that is constantly redefining the opportunity sets of landowners. The frequent complaints of landowners that their "freedom" is being restricted is of little help in understanding this important process. Nor should we be surprised to learn that this process of implicit transfers is likely to accelerate. As technology advances, and as population pressure continues to increase densities of urbanized areas, we will find new ways to impose unwanted costs on others. New knowledge also contributes in that it allows us to establish cause and effect with more certainty. In the absence of sophisticated scientific evidence many phenomena were simply accepted as "part of life." Once we possess the ability to establish definite causality, the matter is thrown into the legislative or judicial arenas. The ultimate outcome of that process is surely a further redefinition of the rights and duties that go with land.

3   PROPERTY RIGHTS DISPUTES OVER PUBLIC LANDS

The previous discussion has concerned the instrumentality of private property rights in land and related natural resources in which private land was the object of analysis. I shall now turn to an extension of the instrumentality of private lands, this time by considering land that is now in public ownership. The focus of attention will be on the federal lands in the United States, but especially those federal lands in the western United States. The discussion in chapters 6 and 7 largely concerned land ownership issues in the developing countries, and the contrasts between those situations and that found in the US public domain could not be more pronounced. While most governments in the tropics have pursued policies to extract economic surplus from the public domain, the US government has pursued an explicit policy to protect and manage the public domain.[4] Despite this commitment to manage ment, public-domain programs are not without their critics. Some contend that the administrative agencies are inefficiently managing the public domain. Others, while starting from this perspective, bring a more ideological position to the public domain, arguing that most – if not all – public land should be converted to private property and sold to the highest bidder. In the early, and most zealous, stages of the Reagan Administration (1981–9) these advocates of privatization found a sympathetic ear. From the taunting and self-righteous Secretary of the Interior James Watt down to obscure staff in the White House, privatiza tion was a crusade of religious proportions. Bold assertions were frequently made and the effort took on the air of a determined crusade.[5] But apparently the privatization movement, like many others, tried to accomplish too much too quickly, and died of its own excesses. A student of the political process surrounding the public lands writes:

> On the specific issue of privatizing the public lands, virtually no support emerged beyond the advocacy of a group of committed intellectuals. Although many were economists, they were a clear minority even in their

own profession. Western state and local governments went on record against the idea. Environmental, conservation, and recreation groups – including wilderness advocates, hunters, and off-road vehicle enthusiasts – achieved an unprecedented unity in opposition. Not a single major commodity sector supported privatization: livestock, mining, oil and gas, coal, or timber. (Leman, 1984, p. 113)

In spite of the failure of the privatization movement to gain even modest success, the questions raised in the debate were indeed pertinent. Continuing interest in the role of national governments as owners and managers of environmentally important areas raises the question of how such ownership and control might be assessed in terms of overall performance. This consideration of the public sector as a landlord in natural resource management is long overdue. In a state-capitalist economy, we should certainly pause from time to time to assess the behavior and the performance of both the public and the private sectors. The role of the US government in administering large expanses of timber lands, in managing and leasing millions of acres of grazing lands, and in controlling use of equally large areas of national parks and wilderness areas had gone largely unquestioned until the late 1970s. Then, questions began to be asked about the management objectives of government agencies, about the efficacy of government management practices, and even about the equity of such programs.[6]

The political discussion has tended to focus on two aspects of public sector activity: (1) the balance between what is termed preservation or conservation and those market-oriented activities that result in such tangible outputs as oil, minerals, livestock forage, and timber; and (2) the entrepreneurial agility of those public agencies responsible for managing the federal lands. The first has been referred to as a "need to restore balance" to federal land policies by swinging the pendulum away from conservation and toward production activities. The second often centers on the ostensible need to combat the "waste, fraud, and abuse" that is said to be inevitable in any decision-making organization that is not privately owned.

We should take more than passing interest in both the political discussions described above. Economists with policy experience in Washington, DC, or elsewhere will often confirm that economists are only considered useful in a particular policy debate if they can produce the "correct" numbers to substantiate a forgone conclusion (Nelson, 1987). This preoccupation with economics as outcome rather than process contributed to the rise of benefit–cost analysis as a decision aid in matters of collective choice. It persists today in the form of arguments that the social dividend is diminished by the continued public (federal) administration of much western land in the United States.

In this chapter I shall present a conceptual view of the economics of collective choice over public-land issues. This framework offers a means whereby we might judge the competing view on the public and private interest in the public lands. The framework will be useful to address the accusation that public lands produce an inefficient level of outputs, and that the administration of such lands is inefficient (wasteful) because of bureaucrats intent on maximizing their budgets and the thickness of their office carpeting. The imprecision of language and concepts pertinent to efficiency must be clarified if we are to progress in the dialogue over social benefits of alternative institutional arrangements of the public domain.

4   ON ECONOMIC EFFICIENCY

Outcome Efficiency

I shall start with the notion of outcome efficiency wherein one is interested in securing a total product mix in society that will keep producers and consumers of the various outputs in equilibrium.[7] The idea here simply means that if too much livestock forage is being produced relative to timber then market prices will upset this equilibrium. An output reallocation away from livestock forage and toward timber would increase outcome efficiency. While those critical of current federal lands administration seldom couch their arguments in such terms, they imply as much. Many associated with the privatization movement are not averse to using such arguments to bolster their case. When politicians talk of "balance," they imply that too much of one output is being produced at the expense of another, presumably more valuable, output. While such arguments can be made as simple value judgments,[8] it is more convincing if the argument can be couched in economic terms to give it a patina of scientific objectivity. It is then that we hear that the economy is suffering from too much wilderness and not enough petroleum; or from too many picnic spots and not enough timber. This is an efficiency argument with respect to output mix.

To make such an argument in economic terms requires that the analyst have definitive data on the consumption desires of the citizens for whom he or she claims to speak. Those who celebrate the "magic of the marketplace" will often suggest that the market provides just that information. Overlooked in this confidence is the fact that not all outputs from the public lands are marketable commodities. Nonetheless, those wishing to invoke market norms ask us to imagine that they are so marketed, or to forget about those particular outputs and to concentrate on that subset that contributes to economic "efficiency." Those writing about the alleged inefficiency of federal land administration are vague about the particular usage of that term. At one moment it is quite possible to get the impression that "special interest groups" are having an inordinate influence on the agencies and hence distorting the actual output mix away from some undefined optimum. At another moment we are told that agencies use incorrect benefit–cost procedures so as to justify questionable projects. And then we are told that the prices charged for various outputs do not reflect their true social value. In each instance there must be some norm against which the status quo is to be compared. Though often implicit, rather than explicit, that norm is said to be how the lands would be managed were they under private control.

This preference for private ownership is firmly held if not universally shared, despite widespread evidence that private ownership of natural resources does not guarantee that they will be wisely used. Apparently, some critics of public land management have forgotten the experience of the Dust Bowl years when the prairies were plowed up against the advice of a number of agricultural experts. These lands were not under the ownership or management of allegedly inept public employees but rather were owned and managed by "omniscient" private entrepreneurs. Yet one encounters such statements as:

> Privately owned resources will tend to be owned and controlled by those who are most optimistic about the future. Present wealth in land and renewable resources is the market's expected value of the discounted flow of valuable future products. Optimists, who see higher future values than pessimists do, bid away resources. Future generations *are* represented by entrepreneurs who profit from conserving resources for their expected use. Just as the market ensures efficient allocation to those current consumers with greatest effective demand, so does it ensure optimal allocation to those time periods with expected greatest effective demand. Of course, expectations about the future vary widely and the optimists may be wrong. But that is just the point! If conservation is transforming current assets into future assets, what more reliable and more efficient mechanism for conservation do we have available than the profit motive of these optimistic entrepreneurs operating in the private sector? (Gardner, 1984, p. 171)

Another commentator intent on private ownership of the public domain takes this logic one step further:

private speculators provide the only link that future citizens have with resource decisions in the present. Presently, as voters, future citizens have no clout at all. Politicians, who hurt today's voters to help those of tomorrow harm their election-day prospects. That simply is not a survival trait for politicians. But speculators who correctly forecast price trends can buy today, taking off the current market a resource (development land, for example), and preserving it for the future. Eventually they will gain by selling it when others have begun to recognize the increased scarcity, and the price increases. . . . Further, only the generosity of voters permits preservation, even when the majority knows it is good for the future. With private property, charitable instincts are reinforced by future gains in property values, as both speculators and conservation organizations have realized. (Stroup, 1984, p. 152)

These statements offer the basic economic rationale for turning over federal lands to the private sector. Three assumptions pervade these arguments in favor of private ownership and control of the public domain: (1) no politician cares about conservation; (2) no citizens will push for conservation that will benefit future citizens; and (3) private entrepreneurs – following Adam Smith – will enhance conservation not out of beneficence but out of self-interest. Notice that Stroup helps his case by the phrase "speculators who *correctly* forecast price trends. . . ." Left unsaid in these assertions about the thoroughgoing wonder of private ownership and control of natural resources is what happens if speculators *incorrectly* forecast price trends. More critically, these testimonies to the beneficial social role of speculators seem to miss the fundamental point of modern societies. That essential point is a clear unwillingness to leave important natural resource decisions to the forecasting prowess of private speculators. Gardner, Stroup, and other proponents of private control of the public domain ask us to have faith in the forecasting abilities of private speculators (their words). The general citizenry seems to be saying, "we have seen what speculators give us and we prefer the current setup, thank you." This conclusion is then denounced as irrational and conducive to inefficiency.

But at the heart of the failure of proponents of privatization is their inability to be precise about the several notions of efficiency under consideration; indeed, Gardner's quote immediately above has imbedded in it at least two different ideas of efficiency. Recall that there are at least three components of outcome efficiency that must be recognized and discussed, independent of social welfare implications of production. These components are: (1) technical efficiency; (2) private economic efficiency; and (3) social efficiency.

Technical Efficiency

Imagine a piece of federally controlled western land that provides forage for cattle and for deer. If it is used exclusively for cattle it has a sustained productive capacity of, say, 300 animal unit months (AUMs)[9] annually. On the other hand, if cattle are barred and the land is used exclusively for deer it has a sustained productive capacity of, say, 205 AUMs annually. On the condition that both types of animal could graze the same land, it is not unreasonable to suppose that we might obtain 320 AUMs of cattle forage and 270 AUMs of deer forage on a sustained basis. The complementarity between the two different types of grazing animals results in a greater AUM production (greater carrying capacity) than would be possible under a regime of single use. It is technically inefficient to impose single use on lands that are better suited ecologically for multiple use. There is another aspect of technical efficiency and that is to determine the optimal mix of deer and cattle so as to maximize the aggregate number of AUMs obtained from the lands in question. Hence, technical efficiency is concerned with the physical determinants of ideal output. We could discuss similar phenomena between grazing and watershed protection, timber production and watershed protection, and timber production and grazing. In each instance there is a relationship between the two (or more) outputs that gives rise to a technically efficient level of production. There is no guarantee, however, that technical efficiency will coincide with economic efficiency in either private or public terms.

Private Economic Efficiency

The private case is rather straightforward. The landowner can exercise complete control over the cattle and could select the appropriate number in accordance with market signals. It is not so easy to control deer, and even if the landowner sold hunting access, the deer cannot be prevented from ranging across a number of individual parcels of land. When other uses – such as watershed protection and the provision of amenities – are admitted to the analysis, it quickly becomes obvious that any hope of determining an economically efficient mix between those outputs that pass through markets and those for which no exchange values exist must be abandoned. Those who advocate privatization of the federal lands assume these problems to be minor compared with the alleged "efficiency losses" arising from federal administration.

This willingness to ignore nonmarketed outputs of the federal lands, and then to complain about inefficiency in the administration of such lands, is a common theme among those who would have us believe that proper environmental policy is to be found in privatization. It is indeed ironic, for the accepted view among economists is that the profit-maximizing decisions of a resource user can result in negative externalities.[10] The classic examples, as seen previously, are the smoky factory, the malodorous feedlot, or the paper plant discharging effluent into a river. In the federal administration of western lands, we find an example of the very form of resource decision making that is considered to be the solution to externality problems; namely the "sole owner" who will account for the implications of a number of interrelated actions that, if pursued independently, would carry substantial offsite costs for others. To be sure some commentators did not quite have the public sector in mind when advocating sole ownership of natural resources. But now we are arguing about the precise form of control, not the fact of a single decision maker. A further irony is that these economists seem quite capable of ignoring the possibility of inordinate market power arising from one owner of land in sufficient scope to fully absorb the bulk of the potential offsite costs.

Social Economic Efficiency

Those who frequently celebrate market outcomes make yet another important assumption. That is, they assume that the individual maximizing decisions of independent economic agents will lead to both private and social optima. I would now like to focus attention on an important distinction between private economic efficiency and social economic efficiency, and social welfare optimization. A clear understanding of these distinctions is essential to comprehend the arguments advanced by those opposed to continued federal administration of western lands.

As indicated above, private economic efficiency occurs when independent producers and consumers take market signals – prices – and adjust their production and consumption decisions such that, at the margin, the gain from one more unit of production (or of consumption) is exactly offset by the added costs of that last unit. Here market prices are taken as given and carry great significance based on a theoretical argument. This argument holds that in conditions of thoroughgoing competition among a number of buyers and sellers the social value of inputs and outputs is correctly reflected in their respective market prices. Unfortunately, there are a number of reasons why such prices may not reflect full social value. The presence of uncompensated offsite costs is the classic reason. But there are also problems arising from market power over prices, as well as the inherent indivisibility of certain inputs or outputs. And in environmental problems, of course, the ability to assign ownership to air and fugitive resources (that is, fish) is missing. In these instances, prices as a basis for choice lose their appeal. When this happens, the calculus of the market is suspect. Economists feel most comfortable with those situations in which prices (or value) determine choice, for the obvious reason that such prices appear to be the happy by-product of a number of independent and voluntary exchanges on the part of maximizing producers or consumers. It is assumed that no coercion was involved, and there is thought to be little chance that price manipulation was present.

But what is to be done in those frequent instances where prices are not known? How much is a wetland area really worth to society? What value is to be placed on a magnificent sunset near Mount Rainier? In making difficult choices, two options seem possible. The first is to ignore those outputs for which no market prices exist and to conduct an economic evaluation solely on the basis of market-derived prices. In this approach we let prices determine choices. The second alternative is to make choices based on some other expression of demand, and to let the implicit prices thereby determined become information for future decisions. In this approach we let explicit choices determine prices. In the wetlands example, suppose we knew that such lands, if filled, were capable of earning $750.00 per acre into perpetuity in an agricultural use. If a collective decision is made that enough wetlands have been filled, and that the remainder should be protected, then we are determining the relative value of wetlands to be at least $750.00 per acre each year into perpetuity.

There is a continuing debate among economists concerning this matter of prices determining choices versus choices determining prices (or value). Not unexpectedly, some are disdainful of situations in which political choices are made in the absence of market-revealed demand and prices. And yet, there can be no denial of the fact that a good number of the outputs from the federal lands are not amenable to the assignment of market prices. It should also be recognized that some individuals consider certain amenity resources to be in a class of goods that transcend normal views about commodities. To these individuals the very idea of assigning prices to a sunset, or to a unique hiking experience, is absurd. While as economists we might be inclined to dismiss such protestations as foolish, by doing so we discount an important aspect of social choice. That is, market processes are derivative of the larger social system; they do not supersede that system.

What is meant here by social efficiency is a situation in which the output mix from the federal lands is such that relative social values between any two products are equal to the rate at which one must be sacrificed for the other in production, after recognizing possible external effects (such as watershed protection, amenities, and so on). This formidable practical problem should not detract from its conceptual relevance. Moreover, stating social efficiency in these terms also reminds us of a profound aspect of public-land management: efficiency calculations which ignore nonmarketed outputs (and their values) seriously distort the presumed scientific basis for passing judgment on public-land management. Those who seem devoted to the privatization of the federal lands commit this distortion.

In a sense, the scientific management and public participation (limited though it is) that seems to characterize current federal land management is an attempt to determine technical and social efficiency (Culhane, 1981). To say this is not to argue that it has succeeded. But to those who argue that it has failed, it seems necessary that they provide more evidence than they have produced to date. For critics of public administration of such lands to appeal to the perfectly competitive market as a norm against which to judge the performance of federal land management agencies is certainly not sufficient to make a compelling case against continued public administration.

Social Welfare Considerations

Let us now turn to the social *welfare* implications of production as distinct from social *economic efficiency*. Though there are an infinite number of output combinations from the public lands that will qualify as being socially efficient in an economic sense, only one can qualify as the one to provide the greatest social welfare.[11] The intervening variable is, of course, the importance to be attached to the satisfaction of the various consumers of the several possible outputs from the public lands.

To make the discussion more realistic, assume that Smith is a connoisseur of primitive wilderness, and that Jones sells mining equipment. One economically efficient output bundle will make Smith happy, but Jones sad. Another efficient output bundle will have the opposite effect. We cannot know which of many possible bundles will maximize aggregate welfare for all parties, including Smith and Jones, without knowing which individuals or groups (Smith's hiking companions or the association of mining equipment dealers) ought to be favored. If we assume that a society ought to be structured so that satisfaction between the two individuals (or groups) should be somewhat equal – a difficult empirical undertaking – then only those socially efficient outcomes with rather equal distributional aspects will qualify as candidates for socially optimal results.

This distinction between social efficiency and social optimality is rarely made in economic writings on public policy. Although most economists know better, we habitually equate the two; perhaps because to admit that we do not know what the social welfare function indicates about the relative merits of Smith and Jones would be to admit that economics does not have the definitive answer to collective choice problems.

This extensive discussion of the various types of efficiency and optimality is intended to clarify the extremely complex nature of any analysis of public-land policies. It is, of course, easy to charge that federal agencies are inefficient without specifying the precise nature of that inefficiency. But once the various types of efficiency are recognized, it becomes more difficult to be quite so unequivocal in charging that current practices are inefficient in either a technical sense or in terms of social or economic efficiency (Bromley, 1989a). Neither can it be argued with confidence that the presumed efficiencies of privatization would increase social welfare. While outcome efficiency can be considered a necessary condition for social optimality, it is not sufficient.

5   ON PROCESS EFFICIENCY

Let us now consider the other major class of efficiency pertinent to the management of public lands – process efficiency, or the managerial activities that transform inputs into outputs. Those who celebrate the efficiency of the private sector use as their target the public sector bureaucrat who is said to be driven by the desire for self-aggrandizement through larger offices, budgets, and staffs. It is also said that since these public bureaucrats lack the discipline of the "bottom line," they are slothful in management and not sufficiently aggressive in promoting the interests of the owners. To listen to some of the critics of public administration of such lands would lead one to conclude that the private sector suffers from none of these problems. Yet there is a surprising absence of definitive data on this matter, as opposed to assertion (Nelson, 1981). Nelson addresses three issues in comparing private and public enterprise: (1) administrative parsimony; (2) responsiveness; and (3) innovativeness. These three aspects comprise what I refer to as process efficiency. Nelson summarizes the relevance of modern economics to the debate by stating:

> Even regarding more narrowly defined economic performance criteria, modern welfare economics does not provide very persuasive support for private enterprise . . . standard welfare economics arguments do not propose that private enterprise is better than any other organizational solution; only that if certain assumptions are met, "it can't be beat." But everyone realizes that the real conditions do not meet the assumptions needed. . . . (Nelson, 1981, p. 94)

The argument that private enterprise is more efficient than public enterprise in a process sense is based on stylized facts and wishful thinking on the part of the critics of the public sector. It is, in other words, a value judgment that, with the help of economic terminology, is being passed off as objective science. To quote Nelson again: "Markets and transactions that ignore all but a few dimensions of benefits and costs are cheap compared with those that consider many. In a free enterprise regime the tradeoff is between leaving externalities and imposing a more closely market-transactional structure" (Nelson, 1981, p. 100). Nelson concludes his study with the view that "much of the traditional arguments for private enterprise espoused by economists should be regarded as prejudices and not soundly based on any analytic structure" (Nelson, 1981, p. 109).

6   ON INTERESTS AND RIGHTS

In addition to the need for a more thorough and honest analytical approach to the efficiency aspects of public-land administration, there are two concepts which require careful consideration if we are to understand the ownership disputes over the public lands. The first is the notion of *interests* while the second concerns *rights*. The particular institutional structure that prevails over naturally occurring assets is a conscious collective decision that is predicated upon some assessment of social value. Moreover, that particular structure is concerned to produce benefits in excess of costs. Efforts are made to structure the institutional environment so that individual entrepreneurs can further their own lot and also contribute to the larger social good. In a sense, the entrepreneur possesses a franchise from the rest of us to produce something we need, and for which we are willing to pay. But the private control of certain valuable assets, of course, is not an unmixed blessing. That should be obvious when we think of the deBeers diamond monopoly, feudal estates in the Middle Ages (as well as in many developing countries today), and other instances where private greed leads to socially unacceptable results.

The possibility of socially unacceptable results explains the concerns in the larger society for how valuable assets are controlled. That is why, in western society, private land ownership is far from absolute. The concept of socially unacceptable results also explains why an employer does not have full dictatorial power over laborers. There is a larger social interest in the way that individual firms order their daily business. However, to have an interest in something is far from having a right in something. Rights, as we now know, do not exist in the absence of someone else's duty. That is, rights and duties are obvious correlates. The other set of correlates is that of privilege and no rights.

Prior to the establishment of laws to control access to the rangelands of the western United States ranchers had privilege while all others had no rights. Once the Taylor Grazing Act was passed, ranchers acquired certain duties (as well as a few restricted rights), and the citizenry as a whole obtained rights (and also some duties). Ranchers obtained rights to graze a specified number of livestock during a particular period of time. They also obtained a duty to pay specified grazing fees, and a duty to abide by the conditions of their permit. Citizens in general obtained rights that "their" land (that is, the public's land) would not be destroyed. The duties of the citizenry included the prohibition of interfering with cattle owned by the ranchers. One will hear a great deal about whether those who graze the public lands have privileges or rights, and no-one, certainly not the ranchers, ever talks about their duties. But in formal terms that is precisely what they have. The Taylor Grazing Act converted an open access regime into state property, and then established a government agency (the Bureau of Land Management) to administer those lands.

Turning from rights to interests, it is the notion of *interests* that explains the rationale for public lands in the first instance. In contrast with private lands, the presumption here is that those other than the direct user have an interest in how the asset is used. Thus, the challenge to continued federal administration of the public lands must rest on the premise that *only* the direct user has a legitimate interest in those lands. Put in other terms, those who criticize federal administration of public lands must ignore the interests of third parties (the general citizenry) to sustain a major part of their argument.

It is possible, of course, to argue that the general public's interest in the federal lands will be better protected under a regime of private ownership. This is what the privatization movement apparently hoped to establish by charging that federal administration of these lands is inefficient. But, as indicated previously, this charge not only is poorly substantiated but fails to address the equal concern that efficiency (however measured) may be less crucial than having one's interests protected. The attack against public sector (as opposed to private sector) bureaucrats holds that the former do not have the relentless discipline of profits and losses to keep them alert, vigilant, and agile. All they have, it is said, is a mandate to ensure the long-run viability of the assets in their trust.

Many of us have interests in a number of aspects of public life, but the problem is to determine which interest collective action will move to protect. The rich and the powerful are said to be quite successful in getting their interests protected. In one sense, the privatization movement sought to take control of natural assets out of the arena where it is feared that the rich and powerful may hold inordinate sway. But to throw decision making open to the whims of the market is to cast choice to the fate of forces that many in modern democracies seem unwilling to countenance.

7   SUMMARY

How lands are managed, rather than who owns them, is the key to efficiency. To the extent that they do not recognize this fact, then efficiency is too important to be left to the economists, or to others of a similar mind. (Leman, 1984, p. 117)

The distinction between explicit and implicit transfers points up the fact that much of the interesting policy debate concerns the *control* of land and related natural resources as opposed to its nominal *ownership*. While ownership is not irrelevant, the structure of entitlements that indicates the range of choice open to an owner is of far greater significance. But even recognizing this, we still find disagreements over the performance criteria whereby a particular structure of land ownership and control is to be judged.

The debate between the two views regarding continued federal administration of public lands would be enhanced if the legitimate scope of economic science could be agreed upon. In neither outcome efficiency nor process efficiency is there a scientific standard supporting the contention that federal administration results in the wrong outputs, in the wrong proportions, and at an administrative cost that is above some legitimate norm. All such accusations – and they are usually anecdotal – use as their norm a scientific fiction that is not rich enough to provide guidance with respect to the complex nature of public-land attributes. The existence of goods and services for which demand estimation is still primitive and inexact means that a market test would lead to biased results.

Simply put, those who claim that the wrong output mix emanates from the public lands seem to be basing their conclusions on personal desires rather than on unambiguous economic evidence. Similarly, those who claim that private administration of the federal lands would be more efficient are using a fictional ideal of entrepreneurial agility that is ill suited for the multiple outputs and multiple interests that characterize the public lands. It is my view that there is less dissatisfaction with the federal administration of the public lands than some politicians (and a few economists) would have us believe. Public opinion polls seem to indicate as much. To the extent that there is some concern, I submit that it is largely aided by the writings of a few who use an imprecise definition of efficiency to indict current practices. Irreversible changes in the natural environment are dismissed as a special case, preservation of resources for future generations and indirect users are downplayed as illusory, and multiple use is often confined to the presumed choice between two marketable commodities. But the overriding motivation of much of this literature is an ideological commitment to market processes as opposed to demands and values articulated through alternative means.

There is no divine authority to whom we might appeal for guidance in this matter. The market clearly is a very appropriate mechanism for the allocation of certain goods and services. It is clearly inappropriate for others. On a continuum, markets work best for those commodities and services that are highly divisible, ubiquitous, mobile, self-contained (that is, possess few external effects when produced or consumed), and capable of having clear entitlements (property relations) defined and enforced. At the other extreme we have some goods and services that are indivisible, unique, immobile, carry large external effects in production and consumption, and do not admit of much precision in the establishment of entitlements. Some outputs of the public lands fall at the former end of the continuum, but a good number fall at the latter end.

The abiding interest in privatization was not built upon an analytical base that articulated this continuum and positioned the respective outputs along it. Instead, it appealed to stereotyped notions about blundering bureaucrats, vigilant private entrepreneurs, and assertions that public lands are really a form of welfare for the rich.[12] It could indeed be in the general social interest if The Wilderness Society would purchase the Bob Marshall Wilderness Area, and all of the others for that matter. But that test would require a more careful analysis than we have seen to date. There are some obvious questions to ponder: Why should I have to join The Wilderness Society in order to be sure that a particular area is preserved for the future? Why should I have to pay any private group in order to use a wilderness area? And why should the citizenry as a whole be relieved of the financial and managerial responsibility for the future of these lands?

Wilderness is a small and special aspect of total federal land holdings, and surely the administration of all those lands could be improved. But with what objective in mind? Which of the several efficiencies defined earlier ought to dominate the choice process? Even if the appropriate efficiency measure could be agreed upon, there is no guarantee that social welfare would thereby be maximized. For a natural resource as varied as the public lands, it is virtually impossible to imagine how to recognize an optimal outcome when confronted with it. Getting there would be equally difficult.

I appreciate that this leaves one rather unfilled. The scientific revolution – and the recent rise of decision analysis – encourages confidence that any problem can be fixed by enough thought and analysis. Laurence Tribe has pondered this, and has written of the pressure for results-oriented analysis. He talks of the "ideology" of the policy sciences, and writes:

> the policy sciences' intellectual and social heritage in the classical economics of unfettered contract, consumer sovereignty and perfect markets both brings them within a paradigm of conscious choice guided by values and inclines them, within that paradigm, toward the exaltation of utilitarian and self-interested individualism, efficiency, and maximized production as against distributive ends, procedural and historical principles, and the values (often nonmonetizable, discontinuous, and complex structure) associated with personal rights, public goods, and communitarian and ecological goals. (Tribe, 1972, p. 105)

I suggest that when dealing with the goods and services from the public lands, we are precisely concerned with distributive ends, procedural and historical principles, and the nonmonetizable, discontinuous, and complex values associated with personal rights, public goods, and communitarian and ecological goals. It would seem that the type of analysis that economics could bring to bear on the current and future administration of the public lands would be of great help in determining the degree of efficiency in both a private and a social sense. Our models also can help in determining process efficiency. But we shall require considerable input from the biological sciences in assessing technical efficiency. Furthermore, unless we are prepared to accept the political articulation of the social welfare function, our preoccupation with economic efficiency will distract us from the very issues on the minds of those who make public policy.

A meeting of the minds over the use and management of the public lands is not that elusive. Several states in the west made it clear that they do not wish to assume jurisdiction. And we have yet to see many private parties clamor to take over the control – and the tax liability – of the federal lands. As new scarcities and new tastes and preferences appear, I suspect that future discussions will concentrate on how to make small improvements in the scientific management of the public lands. The process will be slow. It will be cumbersome. But it will also be steady, carefully thought through, and widely discussed in the political arena. While the public sector may disappoint a few for its conservative pace, it will encourage others for precisely that reason.

The nature of real estate still in the public domain is so complex that much of it defies simple classification as a productive asset in the sense of land in the corn belt or in downtown Washington, DC. This is not to say that it is inherently more valuable, only that it is more difficult to be sure of its value. If we are wise enough to admit that we are unsure of its true value to us and to those who will follow, then it seems obvious that the subject of its control needs more public discussion. Just as obviously, the use and control of these lands is too important to be left to private greed.

Those inclined to celebrate market processes are appalled at the thought that outputs from the public lands should be the topic of continued debate, thought, and compromise. To them the answer is simple. Yet it is the essence of government in a modern democratic state that the important decisions remain in the hands of the governed. The continuing political debate over the use and control of the public lands epitomizes this process.

NOTES

1   See, for example, Hughes (1977).
2   The case is Penn Central Transportation Co. v. City of New York 438 U.S. 104 (1978).
3   The equally famous case of Just v. Marinette County is an example of the conventional approach. The Justs were prevented, without compensation, from draining a wetland adjacent to a rather pristine lake. The Wisconsin Supreme Court found that the prohibition on draining was not *to create a public benefit* in the form of improved water quality in the adjacent lake (in which case the prohibition would have been compensable), but was intended *to prevent harm* should the wetlands be drained and thus contribute to the lowering of water quality in the lake. For more on the case see Bromley (1989a).

4   While some revenue is produced from such lands – primarily from timber sales, some mineral leases, and livestock grazing fees – protection and sustained management remain the prime motives.

5   Those favoring privatization of the public lands are best represented by Baden and Stroup (1981), Dowdle (1984), Gardner (1984), Hanke (1982a, b, 1983), Libecap (1981), Stroup (1984), and Stroup and Baden (1982). Several excellent accounts of public-land issues include Brubaker (1984), Clawson (1983), Culhane (1981), Fairfax and Yale (1987), and Francis and Ganzel (1984).

6   Some critics will claim that national parks and wilderness areas are supported by general tax dollars, yet the use of these areas is predominantly by the wealthier segments of US society. See note 12.

7   Parts of the following material are taken from Bromley (1983).

8   President Reagan is rumored to have said something to the effect that "when you have seen one redwood tree you've seen them all."

9   An animal unit month is a measure of grazing capacity; an AUM is the amount of forage normally required per month for one mature cow or five adult sheep.

10   See chapter 4.

11   On the production side I assume efficiency in input application to produce the various outputs – that is, relative marginal productivities of the various inputs are equated to their relative prices. On the output side I assume that consumers of the various products equate the marginal utility of each with its respective price. Finally, I assume that these relative output prices are equal to the rate at which the two outputs can be substituted for each other in production, holding input levels constant.

12   Some critics of continued federal control of the public domain (e.g. Stroup, 1984) appear to take special delight in citing evidence that users of public lands are upper-income citizens, evidently in the hope of enlisting support of "liberals" who are presumed to hold scant sympathy for the rich.

9
Private Property Rights and Presumptive Policy Entitlements

> But one of the first and most leading principles on which the commonwealth and the laws are consecrated, is lest the temporary possessors and life-renters in it, unmindful of what they have received from their ancestors, or of what is due to their posterity, should act as if they were the entire masters.
>
> Edmund Burke,
> *Reflections on the Revolution in France*

1   THE PROBLEM SETTING

The foregoing material has been concerned with the structure of property relations and how that structure is a policy variable in the political arena. When institutional change is contemplated we have seen how the status quo property rights structure gives certain advantages to those currently protected by rights. There is a more subtle dimension that also warrants discussion. One interesting, yet unexplored, aspect concerns the way in which property rights in land can become important in legitimizing other economic policies that directly benefit the owners of those property rights. Specifically, I want to discuss how private land ownership would seem to play an important role in explaining the large benefits that flow to farmers under a variety

An earlier version of this chapter, co-authored with Ian Hodge of the University of Cambridge, England, appeared in the *European Review of Agricultural Economics*, Summer, 1990. I am grateful to my co-author for permission to reproduce parts of that paper here. I also appreciate the willingness of the journal to permit its use.

of agricultural price-support programs. This politically compelling claim on the public purse becomes important in environmental policy precisely because of the externalities associated with much agricultural production.

We know from earlier chapters that under certain (unreasonable) assumptions[1] it will not matter for efficiency which party to externalities has the original property right. Under these assumptions, the government need do no more than be sure that *someone* has clear property rights, and then simply step aside so that atomistic choices might proceed. While seeming to salvage *laissez faire*, adherence to this position simply upholds the dominance of the status quo in economic policy. That is, since it appears not to make any difference on efficiency grounds which party has the property right, there is supposedly little benefit from altering those rights. But of course in the real world it matters very much who has property rights, since a property right gives the legal ability to ignore the wishes of those without such rights. Much of public policy – including agricultural and environmental policy – therefore reduces to political struggles over which parties can enlist the state on their behalf.

With respect to agricultural and rural policy, the property rights in question pertain to land and related natural resources. In the industrialized world these rights – either *de jure* or presumed on the part of the owner – are subject to challenge by those whose interests are in some way adversely affected by a particularly offensive land use. Those who seek a change in practices that *seem to be protected* by some sort of property right will suggest that the political struggle is biased in favor of those who own land. Historically, property rights in land and the associated agricultural production have been strongly upheld in order to meet the economic pressures for greater quantities of food and fiber. North (1984) has argued that sedentary agriculture necessitated a set of exclusive property rights over land, animals, and plants.[2] These traditional property rights remain largely intact – and rarely challenged – today, even though economic conditions and relative scarcities are quite different from those prevailing when modern agriculture first began to develop.[3] Specifically, income elasticities of demand in the industrialized countries for rural amenities such as improved environmental quality (including pleasing landscapes) and viable rural communities are higher than they are for increased food and fiber production. In spite of these changed circumstances, existing property rights in land remain the product of an earlier time when the greatest priority was given to the production of food and fiber.

More significantly for present purposes, contemporary agricultural policy in the industrialized world is largely predicated upon this property rights structure. Today, when agricultural practices give rise to the undesirable side effects we call technological externalities the state is faced with a difficult task. When the agricultural sector (including producers as well as the agricultural business sector which sells chemicals and equipment to producers) resists efforts to alter the prevailing property rights position then a struggle occurs between the presumed right of a landowner to do as he/she wishes, and the right of other members of society to be free from the unwanted effects of agricultural land use.[4] The state will be under pressure to reflect the interests of those adversely affected by the externalities.[5] But, given the apparent sanctity of property rights in land, any negotiations with the agricultural sector will start from a position of political weakness.

When those concerned about the environmental externalities of agriculture are successful in bringing about a change in agricultural practices, negotiations typically result in two possible – but not mutually exclusive – outcomes. Either there will be some form of "regulation" in which specific quantitative goals will be set, or there will be financial inducements from the government to obtain compliance from the agricultural community. Extensive political negotiations will accompany the selection of either policy instrument.

The existing structure of property rights in land implies that the owner (or operator) can – within limits – grow any product in the amounts desired.[6] The fact that farmers produce an abundance of some products in the face of inelastic demand means that agricultural incomes become a political issue as well. Invariably, and with various rationalizations, the public purse is then made available to maintain prices and/or to protect incomes. Notice how the presumed *property rights in land* become translated, through the political process, into *presumptive entitlements in the policy arena*. The modern industrial state has been willing to support incomes for farmers who, for a variety of reasons, have succeeded in resisting virtually all conditions on their producing behavior – whether that behavior results in redundant commodities, in chemical contamination of food and rural water supplies, in accelerated soil erosion, or in rural landscapes cleared to make way for larger machinery. Any change in the status quo production domain of the farmer must inevitably be purchased by the state with bribes, subsidies, or concessions at other places in the policy arena.[7] In short, farmers in the industrialized nations deal with their governments from a position of strength – such strength arising from unquestioned property rights in land, with those property rights then successfully transmitted through the political process into a presumptive entitlement for favored treatment at the hands of policy makers.[8]

We find an example in the financial guidelines for paying compensation to farmers for land-use management agreements in the United Kingdom under the Wildlife and Countryside Act of 1981, such agreements attempting to bring about more favorable treatment of the British landscape. In calculating the payment, an amount is included for the value of any capital grants which the management agreement prevents the farmer from taking up. This clearly implies that farmers have a right to these grants for which they must be compensated if they agree to forgo a claim against that right. A *presumptive entitlement* has been politically created that *compensates farmers for grants that they will no longer be able to acquire by dint of agreeing to treat land in a socially desired manner.* Similar examples could be found in other settings.

Let us recount the argument thus far. The conventional approach in both theory and practice regards land as an input into agricultural production. That land is held by the farmer under some considerable latitude and authority. The use of that land, and the results of that use, are thought to be of scant concern to the state. Only when externalities seem persistent, and of potential serious harm, is a collective role taken by governments. Economists talk of *market failure* and mention several policy instruments such as regulation, or fees/charges. In fact, the few policy initiatives to gain acceptance have been accompanied by bribes and other policy concessions, such inducements being necessary to modify the behavior of a reluctant agricultural sector. The overproduction problem is dealt with by complex programs to support incomes when unwanted commodities accumulate in government storage.

On this evidence I conclude that farmers (and landowners more particularly) in the industrialized nations have been successful in two distinct forms of capitalization. First they have been able to capitalize the value of agricultural programs into their land values. More importantly for our purposes, they have managed to "capitalize" their property rights in land into large, and sometimes embarrassing, agricultural subsidies. Policy options to address these matters seem to have reached a dead-end for the simple reason that the property rights upon which this elaborate and expensive structure rests have never been questioned. That is, economists and policy makers continue to search for ways to induce farmers to grow less of certain redundant commodities, and to employ land uses that are not socially detrimental – if not actually socially beneficial.

I turn now to an alternative model of agricultural property rights and land use that will be seen to suggest novel policy instruments for dealing with the overproduction trap of most agricultural policy. This new perspective will also address the increasing problems associated with a larger collective interest in the quality of the rural environment.

2 AN ALTERNATIVE PROPERTY RIGHTS REGIME

I start with a model that sees land *not* as an input into agriculture for the production of food and fiber but instead regards agriculture as an economic activity that produces a rural milieu and a rural economy of a particular character. This rural milieu would include not only visual attributes, but other environmental quality considerations such as drinking water purity and wildlife habitat. Moreover, I have in mind economic attributes that relate to the continued viability of small rural communities. I shall call these *countryside and community attributes* (CCAs). Such attributes are taken to include the positive contributions that certain forms of agriculture can make both to rural communities and to the nature of rural environments. Thus, rather than modelling the use of land by farmers to produce food and fiber, I posit a model in which there is a *prior* relationship of economic interest – that relationship being one in which society uses farmers to produce a particular vector of CCAs and also to produce food and fiber of a certain quality. This model differs from the standard approach that regards land, labor, capital, and management as the inputs of agriculture, with CCAs as an incidental side effect.

Consider the following. For the full sweep of human history, food and fiber have been the abiding scarce commodities, with the bulk of human energy devoted to their production. Conversely, CCAs were certainly not scarce nor much valued; urban people had not yet come to appreciate the landscape qualities of rural areas, agricultural practices were devoid of modern chemicals and so did not threaten public health, and the economic vitality of rural areas had not become an object of public concern. However, it cannot, in honesty, be said that food and fiber are currently scarce in the industrialized nations under consideration here. Indeed, I note that many agricultural problems in the industrialized world are concerned with an embarrassing abundance of food and fiber. But it is increasingly obvious in the industrialized nations that certain desired CCAs are indeed scarce. Soil erosion, agricultural chemicals in food and rural drinking water, the widespread destruction of landscape to allow the use of ever-larger implements and to gain more land for cropping, and the social concern over the changing character of small rural towns and villages suggest that there is an abiding collective interest in the quality of rural areas that, at the margin, transcends the collective interest in the volume of food and fiber produced.

Some may suggest that CCAs are difficult to quantify. Moreover, it will be said that they defy monetary assignments which will facilitate comparison with market-valued goods and services and that they are therefore of limited significance. But of course this is not true. Most would agree that some rural landscapes are very attractive while others are of little social moment. Moreover, well-recognized techniques exist to estimate monetary values of different types of rural amenities (Anderson and Bishop, 1986; Nash and Bowers, 1988). Perceptions of the value of rural amenities will change over time, but then the relative value of food and fiber changes over time in response to changing tastes and preferences. Beef, once a highly valued product of rural areas, has fallen in consumer esteem as a result of concern for cholesterol. The same might be said of eggs and some dairy products. Cotton, a once-prized rural product, has lost some edge to synthetic fabrics.

The use of this alternative model simply requires that we specify a slightly different objective function and adapt the related specification of production processes that follow therefrom. Agriculture becomes a central input into that production process, for in the absence of agriculture rural areas would become depopulated and the landscape would revert to overgrowth, or grass prairies, or a forested mass that would fail to satisfy the varied environmental conditions that seem to be in demand. I hypothesize that the type of rural area sought by the citizens of the industrialized countries is one containing picturesque farms, a managed landscape, some natural vegetation and wildlife, and thriving small towns. These aspects would be impossible in the absence of agriculture. People residing in rural areas and contributing to its appearance and economic viability are a central part of the sought-after attributes of the countryside.

The objective of the model proposed here would be to provide an understanding of a *particular* physical and economic environment in rural areas, and the appropriate policy instruments could then be chosen accordingly. Recall that under the status quo property rights structure a vector of CCAs arises as a by-product of agriculture. The alternative property rights structure discussed here would imply a very different approach. First, the desired level of CCAs would be determined through collective action at the local level, but with wider oversight if the domain of concern transcended the locality. This might be defined in a plan for a particular area that would specify the constraints over land use required to achieve the desired level of environmental quality. Farmers would then remain free to choose enterprises and methods of production so long as the final result does not violate the plan. Thus it is the collective interest that specifies the level of CCAs that will result from agriculture. Put somewhat differently, the property rights to determine the attributes that shall exist in the rural landscape would now reside not with the farmer but with the collective.

However, the plan is flexible. If a particular farmer should wish to undertake a form of production that would detract from the defined level of CCAs, then it is the farmer who must be willing to pay into the public purse for the right to deviate from the plan. Notice how, with the shift in property rights, the burden of proof has shifted from the general citizenry to the farmer. That is, no longer would individuals, through the state, need to bribe the farmer to adopt a set of agricultural practices that did not violate the interests of the collective. Now the farmer must bribe the state (as a representative of interested parties) to undertake a form of production at variance with the wishes of the collective. When farmers wish to deviate from the accepted plan in order to achieve a greater income, this new income potential offers the source of the payments that would flow to the state. Notice that the payments to deviate from the status quo would flow in the opposite direction from at present.

Some might question the feasibility of this alternative property rights position. Indeed, while conceptually the notion is quite straightforward, it would, in practice, require a considerable administration in terms of specifying the appropriate constraints for various regions of a country, and in terms of assuring compliance. This complexity arises from the characteristics of CCAs, which comprise a range of separate qualities that must be supplied in a variety of combinations, depending upon climatic, topographical, and historical factors. There is no single measure of environmental quality. In some other industries such an alternative property rights specification might simply require that producers do not cause air or water pollution. The vector of elements comprising CCAs renders the determination more difficult, but not impossible. This difference in practice, however, makes no difference to the principle of considering the alternative position suggested here.

3   A MODEL OF ALTERNATIVE PROPERTY RIGHTS

Consider the following model of the change in property rights in land and related natural resources. Under the status quo property rights structure we can envision a demand for increased CCAs; this is shown in figure 9.1 as D. The curve shows the aggregate willingness to pay for increased levels of CCAs. We can also portray a curve that depicts the willingness of farmers to supply greater levels of CCAs. Under the status quo property rights structure, the collective will be able to acquire greater rural amenity only by purchasing it from a reluctant population of farmers. As indicated earlier, this is precisely what has been done over the recent past; the purchase price P represents a combination of payments and policy concessions. The willingness of the agricultural community to supply greater CCAs has carried a price that can be depicted along the curve S. Under these assumptions, the current level of CCAs being provided is CCA in figure 9.1.

When the property rights in land are altered to one in which landowners do not have the automatic right to use land as they wish, several things change accordingly. In figure 9.1 I depict point CCA ~ as some increased level of CCAs specified in a region's agricultural and land-use plan. Thus, CCA ~ becomes the starting point for negotiations under the new property rights structure. S* shows the willingness of the collective to supply less – that is, to accept reductions from CCA ~ , but that this provision of reduced CCAs will require that farmers pay a price. Farmers' willingness to pay to be allowed to produce fewer CCAs is shown by D*.

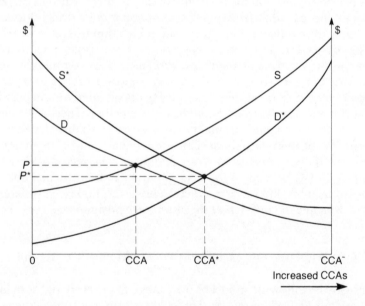

Figure 9.1   **Alternative property rights and "efficiency."**

Why does the demand curve for more CCAs (D) differ from the supply curve for fewer CCAs (S*)? A number of factors contribute to this divergence. Recall that the demand for more CCAs (D) is a collectively articulated demand brought to bear on the state, which is then required to pay farmers to provide more CCAs. The position of D thus depends upon the collective willingness to pay for CCAs. In contrast, S* depends upon the collective willingness to accept compensation for fewer CCAs. It is now well recognized that there is a significant disparity between these two measures of value and that this difference is not just an artifact of the procedures used to value them. Individuals typically demand far greater sums in order to be induced to give up a good than they are prepared to pay to acquire it (Knetsch and Sinden, 1984). Further, the different allocation of property rights will cause a different incidence of transaction costs between the parties involved (Bromley, 1986a, 1989a). With property rights in land (and, indirectly, CCAs) allocated to farmers, the initiative will need to be taken by those who prefer a different bundle of CCAs. This pressure will then compel the state to bear the costs of collecting information, of initiating and negotiating contracts, and of enforcing contracts that have been struck. Conversely, with property rights over CCAs initially allocated to the state, the initiative must be taken by the farmers to seek a reduction in the level of CCAs; they will thus bear the necessary transaction costs under this alternative rights regime.

Also, the status quo property rights structure requires that the collective – taxpayers via the state – pay farmers to produce more CCAs. This means that the size of the public purse is an important factor in how many CCAs can be purchased. This brings us to the difference in figure 9.1 between the supply curve for more CCAs (S) and the demand curve for fewer CCAs (D*). The curve S shows the willingness of farmers to supply increased levels of CCAs. It shows, in other words, what they would require in compensation to forgo the higher level of food and fiber production that fewer CCAs make possible. Under the alternative property rights regime, where CCA ~ is the starting point, the question becomes one of the willingness of farmers to pay to have fewer CCAs (and hence greater production of food and fiber). This willingness to pay is depicted in D*. Here, too, the disparity between willingness to pay and willingness to accept compensation – as well as the incidence of transaction costs – will cause these two curves to diverge.

We see that when the alternative property rights structure introduces a new starting point (CCA ~), the negotiations will proceed along D* and S* towards a new "socially optimal" point of CCA*. This contrasts with the previous "optimal" point of CCA. The switch in property rights has produced a different "optimal" level of CCAs from that prevailing under the status quo property rights regime. It is important to note that neither of the two possible property rights structures – and their respective outcomes – is in any sense "correct." The nature of the status quo structure of property rights is largely a result of historical conditions. However, beyond the consequences for the environment, an equally pressing question concerns the incentives to produce food and fiber, and the persistent problem of rural incomes. The correct outcome – and hence the correct property rights structure – is a function of the *de facto* social welfare function which indicates, in a crude fashion, whose interests shall count (Bromley, 1989a). Under the status quo property rights regime it is rural landowners (especially farmers) whose interests have the sanction of the state. Those concerned to increase the level of CCAs must either purchase it in whatever markets exist or must pressure politicians to pay more attention to their interests. Under the alternative property rights regime it will be the interests of those who place great significance on CCAs who will have protection under the status quo. Then farmers and their allies must pay for – or encourage – the state to give greater weight to their interests. Irrespective of the initial property rights regime there will be an "efficient" outcome. Economic efficiency will not suggest which is the correct property rights structure, for the correct property regime will depend upon one's assessment of whose interests ought to be protected by the state. It should perhaps be noted that in practice, given government and market failures, the actual outcome may not be "efficient" at all.

4   RURAL POLICY AND THE PRODUCTION OF FOOD AND FIBER

The above change in property rights in land would also imply a change in the implicit entitlements in the policy arena. Under the new property regime the nature and scope of agricultural production would, of necessity, be more consistent with a desired constellation of CCAs. The implicit right to pollute rural water supplies, to destroy wildlife habitat, to allow accelerated soil erosion, or to demand public monies to stop these outcomes would no longer exist. The prevailing policy instruments that give financial incentive for farmers to modify their actions would disappear. Rather, agricultural production would be governed by careful consideration of requests for certain environmental changes – land clearance, drainage, building construction, close confinement of large numbers of livestock, increased chemical use – which might threaten important CCAs. This situation would not prevent all growth in agricultural production, nor would it interfere with needed technological change – it would simply realign the relevant incentives. Some production changes have no adverse environmental impact, the use of a new seed variety or of a genetically superior animal strain being examples.

Governments will still have an interest in protecting their citizens from drastic swings in food and fiber supplies (and prices). It will also remain important to insulate farmers from the more serious income swings that can occur in agriculture. It will, in other words, be necessary to ensure that agriculture remains an attractive economic endeavor. But these two policy objectives can be quite consistent with a collective specification of the desired physical and economic attributes in the countryside. Once that desired condition has been determined, agricultural producers are free to produce within those constraints, or to negotiate – and pay for – changes.

It must be anticipated that, without product price increases, farm income levels would be lower under this alternative property rights regime. This would occur because many of the transfers to agriculture, necessary to purchase compliance with collectively determined preferences for certain land uses, would no longer exist. However, over time, the inflated value of agricultural land – now reflecting the capitalization of these transfers – would come down; the resulting net income position of farmers is indeterminant and would vary between them depending upon their asset positions. It is hypothesized that the current incentives to overproduce would be dulled by this change in property rights in land. Thus in some instances output prices may be higher and the political need for price/income supports could diminish as well. There seem to be limited prospects that the political interest in income stabilization in agriculture will disappear. It might be found politically more acceptable to adopt income-smoothing – or even income-supporting – schemes that are not directly linked to agricultural production.

Agricultural producers would come to be regarded as land managers as much as they would be regarded as farmers. There is little reason to suppose that production shortages would result. The price mechanism would continue to suggest which commodities ought to be produced in greater quantities. If food and fiber prices become marginally higher because we are at CCA* rather than CCA in figure 9.1, then this simply represents a tax on consumers of food and fiber for the production of a greater level of CCAs. This differential represents an estimate of the social costs of current agricultural practices; the environmental externalities of the existing agricultural system would have been internalized. There seems to be no reason why this tax need be any greater in total magnitude than the current financial burden placed on citizens of the industrialized nations by current agricultural policies. Indeed, there is some hope that it will be considerably less. More important for efficiency reasons, the tax will be paid as an increment on the price of food and fiber so that those whose demand stimulates the environmental changes would pay the full price. There may be concern that a country's international comparative advantage in traded commodities would be compromised in this process. With the major agricultural producers now dealing with each other on an oligopolistic basis – and with the intervention of the General Agreement on Tariffs and Trade (GATT) – it seems unlikely that any one country would be seriously disadvantaged. This is particularly so if the kinds of property rights changes under discussion here are phased in simultaneously in the industrialized countries.

The alternative property rights regime would also require a restructuring of the agricultural bureaucracy to implement land-use plans and to ensure compliance. It is not clear that the programmatic demands are any greater than those in place under the status quo.

5   SHIFTING PREFERENCES AND SHIFTING ENTITLEMENTS

The proposal under discussion is simply a reflection of new tastes and preferences, and new scarcities relating to the agricultural sector and its use of land and natural resources. However, when institutional changes are considered, those well served by the status quo will protest. Proposals for change will often be met with appeals to presumed "rights" for a certain kind of health care, for a certain education, for a military pension of current magnitude, or for a comfortable retirement. However, none of these appeals can begin to rival the emotional strength and popular allure that farmers can muster with a reference to the property rights in "their" land. Indeed, it is the emotional value of this appeal to property rights in land that has permitted the elaborate and expensive constellation of policy instruments in agriculture. Interestingly, the existing structure of property rights in land is a rather recent historical occurrence. These individual rights arose to serve a particular purpose as Europe was embarking on a major social and economic restructuring in response to new opportunities, new scarcities, and new technological possibilities. Few would suggest that the subsequent institutional changes in land-related property rights failed to accomplish most of what was promised for them. However, neither can many deny that the associated social costs of complete atomization of control over land have become high.

The discussion here has proceeded on the premise that there are two possible starting points for an analysis of property issues in agriculture: one with rather complete property rights allocated to the landowner as at present, and the other with rather complete property rights in land allocated to the state as an agent for others (including future generations). In practice, the level of CCAs will be determined by actions that are subject to a wide range of alternative property rights, some of which can be – and now are – held by the landowner, and some of which can be – and now are – held by the state. Within this range, there is widespread agreement as to where some rights should properly be lodged. For instance, landowners do not now have the right to dump persistent carcinogenic chemicals into watercourses, and they receive no compensation for being denied this opportunity. On the other hand, while the substitution of capital for labor in agriculture may have undesirable impacts on the economic and social life of rural communities, few would deny that farmers should have the right to select their own mix of capital and labor. Between these extremes, the assignment of a whole range of specific property rights will continue to be a divisive issue; examples include those that relate to: (1) allowing soil to erode; (2) draining bogs and marshes; (3) burning crop residues; and (4) applying chemical fertilizers and pesticides.

A general agreement to allocate one particular bundle of rights to the landowner and the other bundle to the state determines a particular *reference point* (Hodge, 1989). This reference point then defines the particular allocation of individual property rights, and hence the level of responsibility which landowners are required to adopt with regard to the wider implications of their choice of land use. There is thus a continuum of possible reference points ranging between the two extremes of allocating all rights to the landowner or allocating all rights to the state. Following from this, there is a range of "optimal" levels of CCAs as illustrated in figure 9.2.

Note that CCA, broadly similar to the same point in figure 9.1, represents the "optimal" level of CCAs arising from the allocation of rights to the landowner. CCA* represents the "optimal" level of CCAs associated with allocating property rights to the state. Between these two extremes lies the continuum of possible reference points. The figure shows a range within which the "optimum" falls. The difference between the upper and lower bounds arises from the possibility of different mechanisms for resolving disputes – private negotiation or state regulation – and consequently a different incidence of transaction costs between landowners, those affected by the various outcomes, and taxpayers. There is a further elaboration to the argument in that the choice of reference point might vary spatially, particularly reflecting local environmental quality. Landowners in attractive environments might be expected to make greater efforts to preserve and to enhance the quality of their local area. This leads us towards policies based on some form of local designation or zoning.

How do shifts in the allocation of property rights come about? Numerous individual rights have been withdrawn in favor of the collective interest – nonsmoking areas in restaurants and hotels, the prohibition of potentially dangerous chemicals, and the protection of certain wild plants and animals. The determinants of such institutional changes are complex and efforts are still under way to explain institutional change. One way to view such institutional changes is to regard them as examples of a *reallocation of economic opportunity* to a different segment of the populace (Bromley, 1989a). Under the

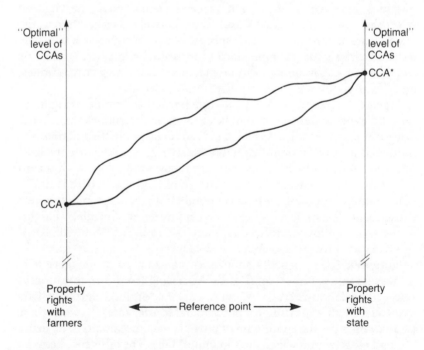

Figure 9.2   **Alternative property rights and "optimal" CCAs.**

status quo property structure it is farmers who are well served. Under an alternative property rights structure it would be another group of citizens that are well served.

Clearly, shifting preferences among the citizenry have a major influence on changes in the allocation of property rights. As demonstrated here, these changing preferences lead to a change in the "optimal" level of environmental quality, but they do not identify the means by which this environmental quality should be achieved. Also, technology is an important determinant. As indicated earlier, new technological possibilities may well trigger latent concerns that had hitherto been irrelevant; chemical pesticides are a case in point. The important issue for the economist is to understand the ways in which shifts in social values and priorities become translated into shifts in property rights.

A further element, less often considered by economists, is the question of fairness. Kahneman et al. (1986) have used survey evidence to indicate the influence of community standards on perceptions of fairness concerning activities in the marketplace. They argue that participants in transactions have an implicit entitlement to the terms of the *reference transaction*, and that firms are entitled to their *reference profit*. The reference transaction represents the widely accepted conditions under which exchanges have taken place, while the reference profit is the firm's profit associated with these conditions. Kahneman et al. emphasize that the reference transaction forms a basis of fairness because it is *normal*, not necessarily because it is *just*. If this notion of reference points is taken with respect to the change in property rights and the associated introduction of controls which limit the actions of farmers, it implies that compensation would be paid in order for the controls to be seen as fair.[9] But changes will often occur in the allocation of property rights in which compensation is not paid. This can occur in either of two possible contexts.

First, and most simply, regulation might constrain activities which are not regarded as "normal." A new chemical process might be banned without compensation because its use is not yet part of standard operating procedures. Second, shifts of presumed property rights for activities regarded as normal may occur only after a long period of struggle between interested parties. A variety of traditional resource uses in the United States are currently the focus of such struggles (Batie, 1984). A first stage in this process is the definition of rights, and perhaps some form of voluntary scheme to encourage landowners to make adjustments to their farming practices (Braden, 1982). This has now been taken further in the United States with the notion of cross-compliance where the right to participate in certain commodity-price-support programs is contingent upon practicing soil conservation. Similar changes are under way in Europe as well, and while they are generally marginal with regard to agricultural and environmental policy, political pressure continues in this direction.

The gradual redefinition of rights in land may be followed by a more fundamental shift of rights, perhaps accompanied by a one-time compensation payment. An example of this is found in the 1947 Town and Country Planning Act in the United Kingdom. This Act transferred the rights to develop land to the state. Development was widely defined to include building, engineering, mining, or other operations in, on, over, or under land, and the making of any material change in the use of any buildings or other land. However, agriculture and forestry were excluded from the definition of development, so that these changes did not have a great impact on the form of agricultural production. The 1947 Act followed a period during which incremental changes had been made in the rights of urban land users. It is perhaps notable, though, that this major legislative change occurred soon after the Second World War, and hence at a time when many aspects of daily life were undergoing fundamental reassessment. Similarly, many of the major successful land reforms in other countries have also been enacted after periods of major upheaval. Such a period often acts both to allow the development of pressures for change and to weaken the resistance of those groups whose presumed "rights" are thereby threatened.

This process of shifting entitlements is consistent with the view of fairness. Constraints are initially introduced over actions where, because of shifting values, social costs are regarded as exceeding private benefits. Where those actions are regarded as normal, compensation will be paid. Once the constraints become regarded as normal – and especially where the level of environmental quality is still regarded as suboptimal – the rationale for compensation becomes weaker and may no longer be accepted.

This type of change can also be applied to the question of policy entitlements. Initial constraints over a farmer's freedom to choose a desired level of production might be accompanied by some form of compensation. But, if the constrained position comes to be regarded as normal, then the bargaining position of the farm lobby becomes weakened and the state will increasingly expect a greater return for agricultural support, possibly in the form of an enhanced physical environment. Alternatively, this might involve some shift in the balance of the agricultural support debate whereby the farm lobby might be willing to make some concessions, perhaps accepting the introduction of production quotas, in return for an assurance that an existing level of support will continue into the future. This represents some degree of attenuation of the underlying property rights position.

6 SUMMARY

Landowners have enjoyed a wide range of actual and presumptive property rights which have undergirded both environmental and agricultural policy. This arrangement automatically places the burden of proof – and of possible compensation – on the state when there is a need: (1) to improve the environmental implications of agriculture; (2) to constrain agricultural output in the face of expensive surpluses; or (3) to modulate swings in agricultural incomes. The location of this burden of proof has been largely ignored in traditional analyses of agricultural policy. Beyond this, the allocation of property rights in land and related natural resources has determined the level of environmental quality which is regarded as "optimal." The presumption of an absolute right to produce food and fiber creates an open-ended agricultural policy in which the state – and its treasury – has become a captive of the sanctity of private rights in land, the political power of farmers, and the technological prowess of modern agriculture. If farmers are on a "technological treadmill," the industrialized state is surely on a "fiscal treadmill."

The generally secure position which landowners enjoy, however, has no immutable legitimacy – though its political legitimacy is another matter. Institutional arrangements are social creations, fashioned to serve collective objectives. The status quo property rights arrangements which serve agriculture so well exist for historical reasons and may not necessarily be appropriate for the future. It is possible to sketch out an alternative property rights position for agriculture in the western world and the ideas in this chapter represent a start on that undertaking. Such a preliminary sketch illuminates several important issues concerning the premises of rural policy in the industrialized nations of the world. It is important to recognize that the current assignment of entitlements in land – and, by extension, in the policy arena – are simply artifacts of previous scarcities and priorities, and of the location of influence in the political process. To assume that these entitlements are necessarily pertinent and socially advantageous to the future is unwarranted. Shifting values and changing perceptions of the role of agriculture will surely bring about at least marginal shifts in property rights and policy entitlements. The analysis undertaken here seeks to inform that discussion.

NOTES

1   Recall that his assumptions require that transaction costs between affected parties be zero, and that there be no income (wealth) effects as a result of changes in property rights.

2   He has even argued that "civilization" and agriculture as we know it required the development of private property (North and Thomas, 1977). This logic – and reading of history – has been questioned elsewhere (Runge and Bromley, 1979).

3   For a discussion of the changing instrumental value of private property rights in urban areas see Sax (1983).

4   I use the term "landowner" throughout even though in many instances the direct land user – the farm operator – may not be the owner. I assume that few tenants use land and related natural resources in a manner that differs significantly from the wishes of the land's owner and so little is lost in the convention followed here.

5   For simplicity I shall speak primarily of those currently affected by externalities, although the state must also represent the concerns of future generations as well.

6   The production of cannabis (marijuana) and other contraband is a notable exception. And some countries do indeed tie supply control into the receipt of income support – dairy products in Canada being one example. Dairy quotas represent an exception to this within the European Community. Some alternative controls limit certain inputs (especially land) without directly limiting the volume of production, such as potatoes in the United Kingdom.

7   I use the term "bribe" to convey the idea that some extraordinary inducement is called for in order to change behavior; illegality is not implied. The concepts of bribes and charges have a long history in environmental economics.

8   When commentators speculate on this phenomenon it is usually said that farmers have political power out of all proportion to their numbers; the blame (or credit, depending) will usually be laid at the feet of "effective lobbying" or "financial clout." These reasons are, unfortunately, circular and beg the ultimate question. My thesis is that this disproportionate influence stems from the social sanctity of private land, the differentiation of food from other commodities in the mind of the public, and a small dose of rural romanticism.

9   In discussions in England and Wales regarding nitrate contamination of water supplies, environmental officials have acknowledged that there should be compensation paid to farmers for reductions in nitrogen applications from a reference point defined as "good agricultural practices." The precise definition of such practices is open for negotiation, but it will certainly be some level of nitrogen applications approaching those now in effect. There is no chance that "good agricultural practices" would imply

a very low level of nitrogen applications such that the chances for contamination of water supplies are nonexistent. That is, the reference point will almost certainly *not* be one of "no pollution" since there would then be no basis to bribe farmers not to pollute drinking water, and a policy change would be difficult in the face of certain agricultural opposition.

10

The Policy Problem:
Ideology, Efficiency, and
Objective Truth Rules

It would be arrogant to suppose that one knew better than
thousands of intelligent and honest economic scholars what
the proper form of argument was. The Received View is
arrogant in this way, laying down legislation for science on
the basis of epistemological convictions held with vehemence
inversely proportional to the amount of evidence that they
work.

Donald McCloskey, 'The Rhetoric of Economics'

1 ON POLICY ANALYSIS AND IDEOLOGY

Our concern so far has been to understand the nature of property
relations, and especially to explore the importance of property relations
in natural resources and environmental policy. To an economist, the
abiding interest in policy analysis is often found in the concept of
economic efficiency. In the current context, that would mean
investigating the efficiency properties of various property rights regimes.
The obvious appeal of efficiency to economists is the presumption that
efficiency is synonymous with objectivity.

Objectivity in policy analysis is said to be important in that the private
wishes and preferences of the analyst are secondary to the dictates of

An earlier version of this chapter has appeared in the *Journal of Environmental Economics
and Management*, 1990. I am grateful for the right to reproduce a slightly modified
version here.

204

dispassionate analytical rigor. That is, regardless of the policy action favored by the analyst, objectivity assures that other analysts may use the same facts at hand to render identical policy advice. In that sense, the essence of policy analysis can be regarded as the search for an *objective truth rule*. Such a rule seems to offer clear and unequivocal guidance regarding what it would be best – in a particular policy setting – to do. When economists become engaged in policy analysis, therefore, we tend to bring to the task a particular objective truth rule. This truth rule is economic efficiency.

Efficiency as an objective truth rule is so much a part of the ideology of economics that few seem to recognize its ideological character. In this particular context, ideology can be thought of in two quite distinct ways. One connotation is as an emotional or propagandistic position held by someone. The *ideologue* is one who engages in a variety of means and tactics in order that the position of others might be altered in specific ways. Indeed, one synonym of ideology is creed, which immediately leads one to such terms as religion, faith, cult, and persuasion. In economics one is thought, on this definition, to be a "market ideologue" or a "collective-action ideologue." This particular dimension of ideology is perhaps foremost in our mind when we strive to avoid subjectivity and the taint of our personal values having an influence on economic analysis. We are taught from an early age that objective (positive) analysis is both the goal of economics and the relentless burden of the good economist. It is said that we must avoid, at all cost, allowing ideology – by which is meant *value judgments* – to color our analysis.

The second facet of ideology receives much less attention from the social scientist. Here I have in mind ideology as an overall view of, or attitude toward, something – a "world view" as it were. On this interpretation, ideology is a shared system of meaning and comprehension. It is a structure within which information is supplied and processed, directions are given, and justification for certain behavior is provided.[1] Of course this dimension can be comprehended under the first meaning of ideology. We can easily understand how a religion represents a shared system of meaning and comprehension, how it supplies and aids its adherents to process that information, how it gives sanction regarding certain behaviors, and how it offers justification for other behaviors.

In this chapter I shall focus on the second – and more subtle – notion of ideology, suggesting that it represents a useful metaphor within which to discuss behaviors and thought processes within a scientific discipline. As such it also provides a convenient basis for addressing policy analysis. Recall that ideology is a shared system of meaning and comprehension, and that it is a set of norms for certain behaviors. To be Kuhnian for a moment, an ideology is a paradigm. Normal science is an ideology in that the recognized body of practitioners hold similar *beliefs* about phenomena and processes that define the accepted domain of enquiry. Indeed the very act of acquiring training in a particular scientific discipline is to understand and accept its ideology in the latter sense. To be "trained" is to be socialized into the paradigm. To talk of the ideology of a scientific discipline is not to imply fervor or propaganda. It is, instead, to recognize that the essence of a discipline is shared beliefs about the meaning of events, about how to process information about those events, and about how to add to the body of systematic concepts that ultimately differentiate one discipline from another.

One abiding truth about a shared belief system is that it appears differently depending upon whether one regards it from within or instead checks it against the external world. A view from within asks just two things of an ideology – is it consistent, and is it coherent? That is, does it meet the test of logical validity, and does it comprehend all of the phenomena to which it claims relevance. An ideology (or a paradigm) is thus rather like a syllogism in logic, in that its validity is determined by a set of rules that have nothing at all to do with its truthfulness. An argument can be valid by the rules of logic and still have no connection with the real world; validity says nothing about truth content. When one moves from internal concerns to external matters attention shifts to the problem of concordance. Concordance is a matter of how closely a model or theory corresponds to the world it purports to explain.

My purpose in this chapter is to explore the ideology of efficiency, both with respect to its consistency and coherence within economics, and with respect to its correspondence to the reality with which it must connect in the policy arena. More particularly, I will discuss an aspect of the ideology of economics with respect to the emergence of *efficiency as an objective truth rule*. Recall that an "objective truth rule" is an accepted behavioral norm that allows the economist to offer up an efficient outcome both as evidence of a "good" thing and – more importantly for the ideology – as proof of the *scientific objectivity* of that particular finding of goodness. I shall maintain here that economic efficiency has no logical claim to objectivity. More fundamentally, if efficiency has no secure claim to objectivity, then its recommendatory value for determining "good" policies is immediately undermined. On this view, efficiency survives as a mere value judgment of the economist who recommends it to policy makers.

I shall further argue that the abandonment of efficiency as a truth rule liberates the economist to focus evaluation and policy analysis on those aspects of collective choice that matter most to those in a position to decide. Finally, I shall propose that we recognize the important distinction between the objectivity of the science and the objectivity of the scientist, a step that increases the scope for economic input into policy analysis.

2   THE EMERGENCE OF EFFICIENCY AS AN OBJECTIVE TRUTH RULE

The Early Positivists

The idea of the scientific objectivity – the ethical neutrality – of economics has its grounding in the methodological writings, dating back to the latter part of the nineteenth century, of Nassau Senior (1836), John Stuart Mill (1967), John Cairnes (1965), and Walter Bagehot (1885). These writers were united in the belief that economics was, to quote John Neville Keynes, "positive as distinguished from ethical or practical, and in its method abstract and deductive" (Keynes, 1917, p. 75). Keynes, building on Comte's positivism, seems to have popularized the now familiar distinction between *positive* and *normative*, the former being synonymous with scientific objectivity, the latter connoting value-laden arguments we know as metaphysics. To state what every economist holds dear, positive economics speaks to what is or what might be, normative economics speaks to what ought to be.[2]

The elder Keynes defined economics as the study of ". . . those human activities that direct themselves towards the creation, appropriation, and accumulation of wealth; and by economic customs and institutions . . . of human society in regard to wealth . . . . *Political economy* or *economics* is a body of doctrine relating to economic phenomena in the above sense . . ." (1917, p. 70). At the time Keynes was writing, political economy and economics were synonymous, and Keynes saw them as providing information as to the probable consequences of given lines of action, but not passing moral judgments or pronouncements about what ought to be done. At the same time, however, he argued that ". . . the greatest value is attached to the practical applications of economic science; and . . . the economist ought . . . to turn his attention to them – not, however, in his character as a pure economist, but rather as a social philosopher, who, because he is an economist, is in possession of the necessary theoretical knowledge . . . . [I]f this distinction is drawn, the social and ethical aspects of practical problems – which may be of vital importance – are less likely to be overlooked or subordinated" (Keynes, 1917, p. 76).

A little over a decade after Keynes's writing, Lionel Robbins published his most influential book entitled *An Essay on the Nature and Significance of Economic Science* (1932). Robbins had been much influenced by the logical positivists of the Vienna Circle and he drew upon their ideas to stress several methodological points that survive today. Of foremost pertinence here, Robbins took from logical positivism the idea that there were only two kinds of propositions that could be countenanced in a science – those that were true by definition (tautologies), called analytical statements, and those that were empirical propositions (called synthetic statements). Propositions that did not fit these two classes were said to be lacking truth content and hence were value laden. It is usually held that since the scientific part of economics consists exclusively of descriptive statements – either tautologies or empirical propositions that can be tested – economics cannot have any ethical entailments, and is therefore value free.

Ends and Means

Unlike Neville Keynes before him, Robbins insisted that economics was the study of the allocation of scarce means among competing ends, such ends being beyond question to the economist. "Being neutral, the argument proceeds, economics does not choose between or pronounce value-judgments on different ends, and it is implied that no value-judgments are involved in recommending 'means' to given 'ends'" (Hutchison 1964, pp. 110–11). To remain objective, economists should not choose between different ends, but must restrict themselves to recommending "means" so as to accomplish given "ends". A close reading of Robbins reveals that he used the word "means" to refer to factors of production or financial resources that could be allocated to alternative employments. That is, Robbins envisioned an economics that was very much like the theory of the firm. Robbins's definition of economics – that it is the study of choice involving scarcity in which conflicting means are considered to reach given ends – is still the most common definition of our discipline. The principal burden of Robbins's work was an attempt to demarcate the scientific part of economics from the value-laden part. He relied upon the distinction between means and ends to effect this demarcation.

The acceptance of Robbins's definition of economics, in which economists are said to study choice among scarce means to accomplish given ends, places a central burden on our ability precisely to differentiate ends from means. To make a clear differentiation between ends and means, however, it is necessary to invoke some external criterion so that the distinction, and the linkage, between the two is placed in context. That is, one cannot distinguish between ends and means without first having a theoretical basis upon which to ground that distinction. At the most abstract level, we might follow Robbins by suggesting that an "end" is something that enters into an individual's utility function, while a "means" would not be found there. This is simply a definition; it fits the positivist idea of an analytical statement – that is, a tautology. But having thus differentiated means from ends what has been accomplished? In one sense, a helpful analytical start has been made; ends are those things that individuals care about, means are mere instruments, of no special notice, for accomplishing desired ends.

On closer inspection, however, it is seen that a criterion external to the investigator is required to determine whether or not something is an argument in the utility function of an individual (or of a group of individuals). It cannot be *our* determination for that is to impose the value system of the investigator into the analysis. While it might be possible to ask all those affected by a particular policy whether there is complete agreement on our analytical distinction between ends and means, this is rarely, if ever, done. Indeed, in most instances the respondents would be hard pressed to make a clear-cut distinction. Hence, the dichotomy upon which Robbins based his edifice of scientific objectivity against the insidious effects of metaphysics is nothing more than a convenient assumption. In a simple world, where the distinction between means and ends may be thought clear, it is necessary to regard the means as simply factors of production or commodities in which there is no intrinsic merit attached to the components of either. This distinction is meaningless, however, in the real world of policy analysis in which there are few – perhaps no – policies that can be assumed to be neutral means without intrinsic value of their own (Hutchison, 1964).

Utility and Ophelimity

Robbins regarded the means–ends distinction as central to the discussion of interpersonal utility comparisons. That is, to discuss ends one must make such comparisons, while to discuss means is to be ethically neutral. The old welfare economics made use of the idea of social utility as a summation of individual utilities so as to discuss the general well-being of the community via something called "material welfare." To these economists, utility was an individual concept, while welfare was an aggregate concept. Utility, on this definition, meant usefulness – rather like the current dictionary definition (Cooter and Rappoport, 1984). Jevons (1970) transformed the term "utility" into a synonym for "desires" or "preferences," a notion that Pareto had referred to as "ophelimity." Prior to Jevons, utility – unlike ophelimity – was not subjective. Once the term "utility" took over both meanings – usefulness and desires – its practical content diminished. When the old welfare economists such as Pigou and Marshall thought of interpersonal comparisons of utility they thought in terms of the general well-being of people, and the usefulness of policies to address their problems. Public programs for the deprived certainly had utility in that they were useful to the needs of the homeless or the ill fed. But to ponder and to ascertain the *desires* of people for public housing programs introduced a serious complication. Hence, the old welfare economists could be concerned with the general usefulness of alternative social states for accomplishing certain social objectives. On this definition of utility, Pigou could argue that the material welfare of the homeless could be increased more than the loss in material welfare of the rich if taxes were raised some small percentage to provide housing for the poor. It is difficult to say that under the current definition of utility.[3]

Building on Jevons's work, Robbins further muddied the distinction between ophelimity and utility (Cooter and Rappoport, 1984). With the assistance of early ordinalists such as Hicks and Allen, he applied the term utility to the notion of desires and preferences, thereby purging from economics any discussion of usefulness. Henceforth economists could talk only of desires, or states of desire. It was then easy to claim that economists could not make interpersonal comparisons of utility since utility now referred to unobservable preferences. Recall that the logical positivists regarded unobservable phenomena to be outside the domain of science. Robbins's admonition about interpersonal comparisons of utility carried the day and thus seemed to undermine any hope for a scientific welfare economics.

Policy Analysis

It was about this time that the formal field of policy analysis was born, bringing with it a renewed interest in the ability to pronounce on what would be "good" public policy. Policy analysis got its start, at least in the United States, with the Flood Control Act of 1933 (amended in 1936) in which it is stated that the government would undertake public works on rivers and harbors if "the benefits to whomsoever they may accrue are in excess of the estimated costs, and if the lives and social security of people are otherwise adversely affected" (Dorfman, 1976, p. 2). At the time of passage it was not immediately obvious what constituted a benefit, while costs were rather better understood as the necessary expenditures to bring about the planned project.

While creating a new branch of applied economics we know as benefit–cost analysis, the legislation also compelled all government agencies to make "explicit estimates of the gains and losses to be expected from their proposals, and to defend the proposals in the light of these estimates" (Dorfman, 1976, p. 3). About this same time the field of welfare economics was greatly influenced by the work of John Hicks (1939) and Nicholas Kaldor (1939). The combined effect of their work was to revive welfare economics in its "new" version via the expedient of a consumer theory based on preferences and the concept of indifference, rather than on utility of the old kind. The key to Kaldor's method was to separate production from distribution, a task that Pigou could not accomplish because of his utilitarianism. To Kaldor, splitting production away from distribution avoided the problem of interpersonal comparisons of utility since production dealt only with outputs per unit of input, and every economist knows that people prefer more to less. This accomplishment tended to reinforce the point that economics was about production (or about efficiency), while distributional matters were for others to worry about.[4] This transition to output, being consistent with Robbins's increasingly accepted concept of the boundaries of economics, tended to reinforce the idea that economics was not about increasing satisfaction of the citizenry directly, but rather about increasing the production of goods and services which – when consumed – gave satisfaction. That is, economics ceased to be about people and their relationships to one another as it had been before, and *began to be about commodities*. Economics came to be about the production of commodities and the "utility" those commodities could impart in consumption. The distribution of income which determined one's ability to acquire commodities and so the relative welfare of members of society from those commodities – or from other sources – may be of concern to the political scientist and the sociologist, but the objective economist had nothing to contribute here. Economic efficiency came to mean the passage of the potential Pareto improvement test.[5]

> Kaldor was thus able to argue that a scientific welfare economics was possible, this being one which analysed situations with a view to establishing whether or not it was possible to make everyone better off. This left the issue of distribution to be settled outside economics, for, he argued, it was "quite impossible to decide on economic grounds what

particular pattern of income distribution maximizes social welfare."
(Backhouse, 1985, p. 302)

Only later would it be realized that one did not know – indeed, one could not know – the *value* of production independent of the distribution of income and the associated price vector that provided the weights to the various physical quantities being produced. That is, the new welfare economics showed the value of an unambiguous Pareto optimum, but in the absence of old-fashioned utilitarianism, economists were unable to say exactly what it was that had been optimized at the Pareto optimum point (Backhouse, 1985). To put it more bluntly, ". . . Pareto optimality is optimal with reference to those value judgements that are consistent with the Pareto principle" (Ng, 1983, p. 30). Put another way, "The Pareto criterion is not a complete preference ordering except in uninteresting societies where all individuals have identical preferences" (Hammond, 1985, p. 424). If a preference ordering is not complete, it cannot be consistent or coherent. Samuelson (1950) soon showed that we cannot even be certain that group A is better off than group B even if A has collectively more of everything. It was beginning to seem that the very essence of economics – that more is preferred to less – was suspect.[6]

The Emergence of Efficiency

The transition from positivism as a behavioral norm for scientific activity, to efficiency as evidence of that objectivity, was aided by those searching for an apparently value-free way to participate in just this type of policy debate. Friedman's confused writings on positivism were instrumental in furthering this transition (Friedman, 1953).[7] For a time it seemed as if the potential compensation test of Kaldor, as modified by Hicks, would offer an escape from the nihilism prescribed by Robbins. But first Scitovsky and later Samuelson would show that it was not to be (see also Chipman and Moore, 1978). Around this time Kenneth Arrow offered his own unique contribution to the evolution of economic thought – and policy analysis – by proving that there was no possible mechanism that would allow us to aggregate over individual choices to arrive at consistent and coherent collective choices. Arrow, in the very first sentence of his famous book, posed the alternatives: "In a capitalist democracy there are essentially two methods by which social choices can be made: voting, typically used to make 'political' decisions, and the market mechanism, typically used to make 'economic' decisions" (Arrow, 1951, p. 1). In the remainder of his book he proceeded to prove that to rely on voting would lead to inconsistent choices.[8] The message, though most probably unintended, was clear – markets are the only way that consistent choices can be made. That is, the essence of markets is efficiency, and therefore analysis that focuses on changes in economic efficiency is said to constitute objective science.

The new welfare economics, after seeming to promise so much, had reached the conclusion that it was not possible to say unambiguously that a new policy was better or worse than the status quo. And Arrow's conclusions represented yet another blow to the idea that economics was, or could be, a policy science. Since it was impossible, on utility grounds, to know what should be done, and since voting would produce inconsistent results, there was only the market to rely upon. Just short of two centuries after Adam Smith's intuitive celebration of the invisible hand, his ideas were confirmed by the best minds in the profession. While no one could say that the market was the best of all possible worlds, future Nobel Prize winners were proving that it was at least as good, if not better, than meddling bureaucrats. Markets at least produced consistent and efficient results. In spite of the findings of Samuelson (1950), Scitovsky (1941), Mishan (1980), Boadway (1974), Chipman and Moore (1978), and others, the Pareto test survives as the last best hope of those who would engage in policy analysis as objective scientists. To abandon the Pareto test is said to cast the economist loose from the alleged objectivity of efficiency analysis. It is, apparently, thought better to stick with a conceptually flawed approach simply because its methodological *bona fides* – scientific objectivity – seem so compelling. That is, because efficiency derives from production, because greater production of goods and services is thought not to imply any value judgments, and because production can be weighted by market prices – which themselves are considered to be neutral – efficiency became synonymous with objective analysis.

Bolstering the Faith

But of course there were still the inconvenient market failures, and the tendency of politicians to want to undertake "inefficient" programs and regulations. In the face of all this public sector activity, there was a real demand for economic advice on what would be best to do. Indeed, it had become quite impossible to follow Neville Keynes's stricture that economists should avoid the policy arena except as social philosophers.[9] It was generally held that economists could do worse than to advise about which courses of action would be efficient.[10] Yet, there were, from time to time, concerns about the applicability of a strict efficiency test for passing judgment on collective action (see Bromley and Bishop, 1977; Mishan, 1975; Sen, 1977; Tribe, 1972). About this time, Arnold Harberger, in a self-admitted tract, felt compelled to reassure the timid, and to bolster the irresolute. Fearing that there was potentially corrosive diffidence among applied economists, Harberger offered the "Three Basic Postulates for Applied Welfare Economics" (1972). There he noted, with some apparent concern,

> In an era when literally thousands of studies involving cost–benefit analysis or other types of applied welfare economics are underway at any given moment, the need for an accepted set of professional standards for this type of study should be obvious . . . while the highway engineer can apply professional standards to such characteristics as thickness of base, load-carrying capacity, drainage characteristics, and the like, characteristics such as scenic beauty are beyond their competence as professional engineers. In the same way, any program or project that is subjected to applied-welfare-economic analysis is likely to have characteristics upon which the economist as such is not professionally qualified to check the opinion of another. These elements – which surely include the income distributional and national-defense aspects of any project or program, and probably its natural-beauty aspects as well – may be exceedingly important . . . but they are not a part of that package of expertise that distinguishes the professional economist from the rest of humanity. And that is why we cannot expect to reach a professional consensus concerning them . . . economists should probably participate more rather than less in the public discussion of such matters, but hopefully in a context that recognizes the extra-professional nature of their intervention. (Harberger, 1972, pp. 3–4).

Had Harberger thought a little more about this statement he would have seen the obvious fallacy. It is clear that landscape design has little to do with the proper engineering of a road. But welfare economists have long known that we cannot separate the way in which income is distributed from the efficiency implications via the potential Pareto improvement test. Harberger introduced a red herring when he equated the distribution of income with the particular shrubbery that is placed along a highway. And then to argue that it is inappropriate for the economist to comment on the former – just as it is for the engineer to comment on the latter – is to compound his error. Harberger likens the economist to the engineer – a technician checking the drainage, the quality of the base, and so on. Just as the engineer has no professional skills in landscape design, the economist is said to have no professional skills in income distributional matters. The proper domain for both engineer and economist is said to be where precise performance standards exist, and where consensus might be forthcoming. Building a proper road is good science about which all engineers can agree; landscaping is for others to worry about. According to Harberger, counselling efficiency is good science about which all economists can agree; income distribution is for others to worry about.

Notice that the burden of Harberger's argument rests on *skills* and *consensus*. That is, he says that the economist has no skills in income distribution, just as the engineer has no skills in matters of landscape design. While skill can be taken to mean a number of things, it is difficult to imagine a social science that is as well equipped technically as economics to explore matters of income distribution as a dimension of public policy. On the matter of consensus, Harberger is on firmer but still shifting ground. True enough, there is no consensus among economists on what the distribution of income should be, though there is certainly the possibility of consensus on the impacts of certain policies on the distribution of income. Like the engineer, who can count on professional consensus codified over time into design standards regarding proper road construction, economists are claimed by Harberger to enjoy a consensus on determining what is efficient. It is this apparent consensus which legitimizes, to Harberger, efficiency as an objective truth rule. In terms of the ideology of a scientific discipline, Harberger is merely confirming that efficiency is part of the widely shared belief system in economics. The fact that belief in the objectivity of efficiency is widely shared does not make it so.[11] Harberger's appeal to consensus requires that we take this evidence of shared beliefs (ideology) as proof of the scientific credentials of efficiency. This is, I am afraid, not a very solid basis for something that claims to be scientific.

Several years later, Harberger - apparently to satisfy himself that his earlier position was unassailable - attempted to apply the idea of different distributional weights to analyze investment projects and to determine an optimal tax structure (Harberger, 1978). This was done, we are told, out of its appeal "to those nurtured in the grand tradition of economics" - by which we must assume he meant the material-welfare school of Pigou and Marshall. Upon concluding this effort with less than satisfactory results, Harberger argued that

> In the end, then, we cannot condemn as crass or unfeeling the idea [of] our profession's possibly moving toward a "consensus" based on the traditional criterion of efficiency. On the contrary, such a result might well reflect a greater and more sensitive understanding of the value systems of our citizens and our societies, as well as a more modest and realistic appreciation of our own professional role. (Harberger, 1978, p. S119)

To suggest, as Harberger does here, that a professional consensus on sticking to efficiency analysis reflects a correct reading of social mores, simply on the basis of his unsuccessful attempt to discover proper distributional weights for certain public programs, may charitably be thought of as a conclusion that overreaches both his model and his data. Still, Harberger has ample company. Many economists will insist that it is not a value judgment to assume that income is properly distributed and they can therefore ignore distributional concerns in their efficiency analysis. The rationale for this position is as follows: the current distribution of income *must* be the appropriate one for otherwise the politicians would change it.[12] This rather surprising declaration of faith in politicians is the only time that an economist will admit to any confidence in the outcome of the political process. On all other matters politicians are said to cater to the special pleadings of all manner of ne'er-do-wells. Why, in this isolated instance, do we suddenly regard politicians as having made the correct choice? The answer, I regret to suggest, is found in the fact that it manifestly serves our special interests to make that assumption. More specifically, the assumption then allows us to proceed with the delusion that we are being objective analysts, and that we are thus acting consistently with prevailing social preferences. This is precisely the conclusion that Harberger reached after (or was it before?) his "unsuccessful" attempt to find proper distributional weights.

The putative scientific objectivity of efficiency fails in terms of consistency and coherence. But what of concordance with the external world? Is Harberger correct that we do the citizenry no great disservice – indeed that we confirm their values – by counseling efficiency? Are policy makers, and the citizenry at large, impressed with our alleged objective truth rule?

3 POLICY ANALYSIS RECONSIDERED

The concept of Pareto optimality and the associated concept of PPIs [Potential Pareto Improvements] *should* not be confused with theorems of positive economics. If this emplies that economists must give up the notion that there are purely technical, value-free efficiency arguments for certain economic changes, and indeed that the very terms "efficient" and "inefficient" are terms of normative and not positive economics, so much the better; immense confusion has been sown by the pretense that we can pronounce "scientifically" on matters of "efficiency" without committing ourselves to any value judgments. (Blaug, 1980, pp. 147–8)

The voluminous writing in welfare economics over the past several decades has concerned such issues as the various surplus measures, and the reliability of indicators of gain from moves to new social states. On surveying this literature one is reassured to learn that: (1) efficiency, via the Pareto test, lends itself to rather precise measurement; and (2) economic efficiency seems to require the fewest value judgments on the part of the policy analyst. Less reassuring is: (1) the persistent debate over which welfare criterion is appropriate – Kaldor, Hicks, Scitovsky, Little, Mishan, or various combinations thereof; and (2) the Boadway paradox, in which the ability of the gainers to compensate the losers does *not* lead to an unambiguous improvement in social welfare (Boadway, 1974). More seriously, in all this prodigious elegance, rarely is there recognition that the Pareto test remains what it has always been – an analytical construct (inconsistent and incoherent at that) with no special claim to legitimacy beyond the tautological domain out of which it arose. Only Mishan, it seems, has concerned himself with the very real problem of whether or not there is a discernible social consensus for economic efficiency via the Pareto test (1980). He finds that there cannot be such a consensus for the very same reasons elucidated by Arrow some forty years ago.

Having failed on consistency and coherence grounds, we still may inquire as to whether efficiency nonetheless accords with the world into which it is imposed. The central issue, then, is whether the Pareto test comprehends what the public and its decision makers *need and expect* from economists engaged in policy analysis. The record of economic input into many public decisions over the past forty years does not indicate that the public sector is especially enamored of the efficiency advice offered by economists.[13] There are a number of others who have reached the same conclusions (see Buchanan and Tullock, 1975; Dorfman, 1976; Mishan, 1975, 1980; Nelson, 1987; Tribe, 1972). It seems safe to argue that Congress, when it first called for an assessment of the benefits and costs of public works projects, had rather more in mind than an analysis of potential Pareto improvements. Yet, policy analysis over the years has evolved under the influence of those who imagined that welfare economics could bring a satisfactory reductionist decision rule to something as complex as collective choice. Dorfman argues that the history of benefit–cost analysis demonstrates the futility of a simple economic criterion for guiding political choice (1976). If benefit–cost analysis is no broader than the Pareto test then, in the interest of intellectual honesty, we ought to refer to it as *potential Pareto improvement analysis*. Otherwise, the term benefit–cost analysis is an elaborate pun.

Bogus Science, Bad Advice

Curiously, the identification of benefit–cost analysis with efficiency via potential Pareto improvements has come despite overwhelming evidence from within economic theory of the logical fallacies inherent therein. These theoretical problems are thought to be minor in comparison with the loss of putative scientific objectivity should the Pareto test be abandoned. Still uncomprehended, apparently, is the quite obvious fact that *it is a value judgment* for the economist to claim that economic efficiency *ought to be* the decision rule for collective action. In the absence of a clear social consensus for the Pareto test, efficiency via this metric is advocated by economists quite without support from the collective unit onto which it is being imposed. In Dorfman's terminology, benefit–cost analysis has evolved as an effort to impose an economic approach onto a political problem. Economists who have persevered in this tradition seem content to overlook the logical inconsistencies in welfare economics, this obduracy apparently being justified on the grounds that a little economic analysis – even if indefensible on theoretical grounds, and therefore bogus – is better than a political process left to its own devices. Bad economics is offered up as being superior to politics. While the disciplinary imperialism is not surprising, it is more than a little disconcerting in view of the large number of pressing social phenomena on which economists – as objective scientists – are said to be unable to comment. We seem to have developed a refined capacity for selective perception concerning when it is acceptable to be normative.

Toward Policy Analysis

What then is to become of policy analysis if it is freed from the false objectivity of economic efficiency by means of the Pareto test? A reasonable place to start is with a simple word – analysis. Somehow, over time, this word has come to be associated with at least two possible connotations. The first, as in *analytical*, conveys the idea of rigor and precision. Analytical thus becomes a code word for good or solid, and it is used to invite scientific respect. The other usage, as in benefit–cost *analysis*, has come to mean a directed search for a decision rule by which good decisions might be demarcated from bad ones. Progress in policy analysis would seem to follow from an understanding that the term *analysis* does not mean that the economist must produce an objective truth rule for identifying good decisions. To undertake *analysis* is to elaborate and to study the different parts of something – in this instance a proposed policy change. To *analyze* something is not to reduce all its components to dollar estimates of surplus, or to changes in net national income. While these measures may clearly be *one part* of a complete benefit–cost analysis, to analyze a proposed policy is to attempt to understand who the gainers and losers are, how they regard their new situation *in their own terms*, and what this means for the full array of beneficial and harmful effects.[14]

If the issue of drinking-water safety is under consideration it seems most unlikely that the policy maker wants to be told the willingness to pay for certain levels of risk, or the compensation demanded to be free of certain levels of risk. The economist ought to elucidate the full array of impacts arising from different risk environments and let the political process determine, on the basis of economic analysis and other input, what will be done about Atrazine, or Aldicarb. An economic analysis along these more inclusive lines can be informative in that choice, but it cannot expect to drive the choice. In the domain of preservation of unique habitats it would seem that the Pareto test is the last place one ought to look for guidance on particular policy choices.[15] The public policy problem here is concerned with perceptions of entitlements across generations – a problem addressed in chapter 5. But reductionist analysis, in which economic surpluses are conjured up, would seem to comprise but a minor part of the necessary information in this policy problem. In the matter of soil erosion, little serious misallocation would seem to result from the fact that a collective decision through the political process, rather than via the potential Pareto test, mandates that greater efforts to reduce sedimentation ought to be undertaken. Once that decision is taken, there is ample scope for economists to advise on the most efficient means whereby that objective might be attained. We know this approach as cost-effectiveness analysis. That this particular policy initiative is undertaken in the absence of proof that the potential economic surplus therefrom will be positive is interesting, but hardly decisive. The collective has always undertaken actions for which the monetary benefits are unclear, but thought to be large enough to justify action.

I used, immediately above, a phrase *in their own terms* with reference to the effects of policy alternatives impacting individuals and groups. This phrase will no doubt be troublesome to some, and yet it goes to the heart of policy analysis. It is tautological that benefits and costs have no meaning without reference to a specific objective function, whether that objective function is explicitly stated or merely assumed. When economists advocate efficiency as measured by the potential

Pareto test, the implicit objective function is one that regards benefits and costs in terms of willingness to pay for something, or willingness to accept compensation to be deprived of something. While some situations may indeed fit this assumption, it is by no means clear that this is so for all settings. Relying on the potential Pareto test rules out the possibility that individual utility is independent of this revealed measure.[16] There is no empirical basis for this assumption. When I say that we must begin to assess policy impacts in terms that are relevant to those affected, I mean only that we must begin to expend more effort to ascertain exactly how individuals regard the benefits and costs of certain policy alternatives. This would stand in contrast with the current approach which regards pertinent benefits and costs to be those that we, as economists, happen to be proficient in measuring.[17]

Some will no doubt argue that to abandon efficiency and the narrow quantification (in monetary terms) of benefits and costs is to lose control of the policy process – an argument that presumes that economics was ever "in control" of that process. Many economists, in spite of a professed desire to avoid the normative position of indicating what ought to be done, do not hesitate to suggest the decision rule that ought to be used in differentiating good policies from bad. It is to be expected that economists engaged in policy analysis will be reluctant to abandon the high-priest role of passing praise or scorn on policy choices. Some will declaim that without the discipline of efficiency the government will enact all manner of controversial and "inefficient" policies and projects, as if that has not been happening all along, in spite of almost half a century of scorn and advice by economists (Dorfman, 1976). The second response, perhaps more serious, will be that the burden of developing a new evaluative paradigm lies with those with the impertinence to criticize received wisdom. And until such time as the critics come forward with a superior alternative high scholarship consists of continuing to practice the status quo, and to pass it along to our graduate students.

There are, it would seem, two quite distinct alternatives open to economists in the matter of public policy analysis, or what I call policy science. The first is to hunker down, to press ahead with the current intellectual agenda, and to become ever more shrill about the inscrutability of the political process. On this tack we would continue to explore alternative surplus measures, and to insist that the potential Pareto test represents an objective truth rule regarding what the public sector should be doing. The other tack would be to admit that the collective interest transcends the reductionist Pareto rule. Once this threshold has been crossed, we would be free to harness the impressive intellectual heritage of economic analysis to the task of designing an evaluative approach that reflects the concerns of public decision makers as opposed to one that reflects what we *think ought to concern them*. This task of building an alternative and intellectually legitimate paradigm does not belong only to the critics of received wisdom. It is a shared burden made more compelling by the simple rules of intellectual honesty.

But change never comes easily. The economist concerned to make a contribution to policy science faces an awkward problem. There remains a persistent belief that adherence to efficiency, variously defined, constitutes the necessary condition for an objective and value-free approach to policy science. This means, among other things, that policy analysis that does not emphasize efficiency will run the risk of being regarded as unworthy of serious economic notice. In western society, where there is *a priori* political support for market-like processes, the social and economic processes and outcomes of that framework are thought to be, for the most part, beyond question. However, to deny the existence of an objective truth rule in science is not to preclude scientists from operating in an exemplary and well-intentioned manner.

The implications of this will vary depending upon the nature of activity being pursued. In economics, it seems reasonable to consider this realization within two broad classes of research. I have elsewhere called the first of these *theory science* and the second *policy science* (Bromley, 1989a). Those engaged in theory science work between the real world and received theoretical wisdom. Some are more concerned with one direction than the other, but the essence of this activity is to pursue a closer correspondence between the postulates and conclusions of orthodoxy and its ability to characterize the world. Some economists are less interested than others in modifying or adding to theory, but most are still concerned with this problem of correspondence between the real world and our mental abstraction of it (a model or theory). The problems of individual objectivity and replicability are central here since it is important that the world be perceived and interpreted in a way that independent researchers might duplicate each other's work. Of course different individuals will choose different segments of reality to study, but the work is ultimately prescriptive in that one is prescribing modifications in theory (received wisdom or orthodoxy) to ensure that it more closely accord with reality. Those doing theory science want to be neutral and unpremeditated in order that the growth of science will reflect that reality. *Theory science in economics is about discovering what existing theory needs in order that it might more accurately model human interactions*. The objectivity of the scientist lies in the extent to which independent investigators can reach similar conclusions about the correspondence of theory and reality.

On the other hand, *policy science in economics is about discovering what individuals and groups want (or need) such that they might more easily fulfill their goals and objectives*. The theory scientist wants to adopt a research program that will maximize the probability that the end product (a theory) is the best possible abstract representation of what goes on in daily life. The policy scientist, on the other hand, wants to adopt a research program that will maximize the probability that the policy recommendation to result from the exercise corresponds exactly to what the individuals affected by the policy problem want to achieve. This view of policy science is a departure from policy analysis as currently practiced within economics.

Language and Concepts

It seems appropriate here to comment on an issue of language and concepts in policy analysis. Many economists will insist that they do not advocate any particular policy but merely indicate to the decision maker(s) what would be *efficient* to do. If the decision maker then decides to do otherwise, then it is obviously a political choice in which distributional issues dominate and the economist has done her/his job as an honest and objective scientist. This subtle delusion is without logical support. To suggest to a decision maker the course of action that would be efficient is to load the debate in an unsavory way. No-one, not even the much-maligned public decision maker, knowingly wishes to be inefficient; the problems arise in defining efficiency. Welfare economists ought to be the first to understand that any particular distribution of endowments – including property rights under competitive equilibrium – carries with it a unique efficient outcome. This is, after all, the second of two fundamental theorems of welfare economics. The public decision maker is generally seeking an efficient way to modify the status quo. The economist, on the other hand, counsels efficiency as the best thing to do, and feels content to indicate the magnitude of "efficiency costs" should the decision maker choose otherwise. The problem is in comprehending what efficiency means to the two parties.

Decision makers, and politicians, understand that most public policy is about either reallocating economic opportunities or redistributing economic advantage, a distinction developed in Bromley (1989a). When the economist suggests that something would be efficient, it is probably understood by the decision maker to be that policy change which will effect a certain reallocation of opportunity or advantage in an efficient manner. The economist, of course, means something quite different by efficiency. When economists use efficiency it is generally understood to mean that it would be wise (or unwise) to adopt the contemplated policy. For the economist to suggest the efficient option, and to demur on the other dimensions of the mooted policy choice, is to abdicate full responsibility. Hicks has commented on this stance by the economist who is allowed (even encouraged) to argue that if he

> has shown that a particular course of action is to be recommended, *for economic reasons*, he has done his job . . . if he limits his functions in that manner, he does not rise to his responsibilities. It is impossible to make "economic" proposals that do not have "non-economic" aspects, as the Welfarist would call them; when the economist makes a recommendation, he is responsible for it in the round; all aspects of that recommendation, whether he chooses to label them economic or not, are his concern. (Hicks, 1959, pp. x–xi)

In theory science, the economist is being both normative and positive. That is, the economist engaged in theory science is attempting to observe and describe reality in an unbiased manner (being positive) and then to prescribe how theory *ought to be* structured (being normative) in order to reflect that observed reality. In policy science the economist would be positive, but only *conditionally normative*. That is, in policy science the economist must first ask (or determine) the goals and objectives of those affected by a policy, an activity that requires the greatest possible level of objectivity, and then objectively draw on theory to propose which avenues will maximize the chances of attaining those objectives. Objectivity in policy science is concerned with independent researchers reaching similar conclusions with respect to what the target population says it wants to accomplish. Notice that it is *not* the science, nor the conclusions, that are objective but rather the economist who stands between theory and the individual(s) who must make a decision with economic content and implications. This critical difference between the objectivity of the *scientist* and the *science* has been muddled in much of the literature on research philosophy in economics.

Of course the policy scientist is dependent upon the success of the theory scientist, for the very essence of policy science is the received orthodoxy that is the domain of theory science. But the policy scientist is not an apologist, nor an advocate, for the dictates of theory science. That is, the objective policy scientist should be the last to denigrate those objectives of the citizenry that do not happen to accord with the economist's view that people should do what is efficient. Simply put, it is logically inconsistent to venerate individual preferences as expressed through volitional choice in markets, but to denigrate and to discount individual preferences as expressed through collective action.[18] The economist as policy scientist is concerned with problem solving and helping to do what is desired by those affected by the particular event under consideration, not with advocating what is said to be right by the postulates of welfare economics.

Substance *and* Process

This proposed view of policy science should not be confused with the triumph of process over substance. The policy process is still *end-result oriented* in the terminology of Lawrence Tribe (1972), but the end results pursued are not necessarily (nor restricted to) present-valued net benefits via the Pareto test to the exclusion of other results. Rather, the end results to be pursued are those defined as important by individuals involved in the process. Hutchison comments that the majority of economists are not necessarily

> completely devoted to exclusively materialist goals but rather that they are inevitably tempted to focus on measurable, quantitative objectives rather than qualitative non-measurable ones, and measurable goals inevitably tend to be somewhat materialistically conceived. As is well known, qualitative elements . . . largely elude indices of production or consumption. (Hutchison, 1964, p. 155)

The tradition in benefit–cost analysis is to maintain that the objectives to be pursued are not the proper domain of either the decision maker or the analyst. Rather, it is said that the proper objectives are given by the conceptual foundation of welfare economics and the criterion of a potential Pareto improvement. In this approach the economist rejects the view that a decision maker has the right to determine what constitutes social welfare. The norm is for economists to admit the difficulty in determining universal ethical propositions that will guide investment programs and thus to settle for the one that permits them to reach a decision on only one dimension – that of economic efficiency. Those effects that happen not to have the aura of scientific respectability are disregarded in a process that commits the fallacy of misplaced concreteness. Viner has recognized another logical fallacy in this regard:

> to reach final conclusions upon the basis of consideration of a single value, or of a very limited set of values, is liable to result in what has been called "the fallacy of the unexplored remainder". (Viner, 1961, p. 230)

The evaluative stance advocated here would see the role of the economist as centrally concerned to assist the decision maker in selecting choices that are consistent with the latter's objectives. The decision maker, by providing the policy objective that will guide the analysis of a particular collective choice, also ". . . provides the value judgements upon which a particular cost–benefit analysis is constructed" (Sugden and Williams, 1978, p. 236). This approach substitutes the value judgments of the decision maker for those of the economist, an event not without suspicion among many economists. Here, it is not the economist's place to challenge the objectives of the decision maker(s). The economist adopts the following position: "given that your objectives are this, here is the best thing to do." As in the earlier example of the firm, the economist is engineer cum accountant. The decision maker(s) implicitly decides what course of action to follow when the objectives are stated, and it then becomes the economist's task to develop the implications of this particular path. As pointed out by Sugden and Williams, once the decision maker's objectives are paramount in the evaluation process, all other valuations are irrelevant. This means that notions of costs and benefits will have meaning only with respect to the objective function of the decision maker, a point discussed previously.

Consider these differences in more detail. Under the traditional approach there is only one objective, economic efficiency. It is usually reckoned in two different ways. Sometimes efficiency will be in terms of the potential increase in net national income from a proposed change. Or, if nonmarketed goods and services are involved, efficiency will be reckoned as a potential Pareto improvement. For mixed undertakings, both conditions will be used. A particular project – or portfolio of projects – is economically acceptable only if there is a surplus of present-valued benefits over present-valued costs.[19] If economics is to be relevant to the policy process, it seems more appropriate to approach policy analysis in a manner such that the objective(s) of the undertaking can be whatever the decision makers want it (them) to be. Then benefits derive their definition from the stated objective(s). The latter approach has been called the *decision-making approach* by Sugden and Williams. While the conventional view of benefit–cost analysis has the appearance of scientific objectivity, and the decision-making approach appears to be subjective, it should now be obvious that these claims are ill founded. The value judgments in the conventional approach are several, although now so much a part of the convention of economics that their ethical content is easily overlooked.[20]

4 A NEW EVALUATION PROGRAM

I have argued in this chapter that efficiency via the potential Pareto test fails the test of consistency and coherence within economic theory, and that it fails to accord with what the citizenry asks of economic analysis applied to the policy arena. On this evidence, its claim as an objective truth rule is undermined on two counts. The remaining question concerns the nature of the legitimate role for economics in policy science. Before addressing that, let me note that economists adopted logical positivism just as it had been discredited by philosophers of science. The positivist's dream of a clear demarcation between the meaningful and the metaphysical was soon to be regarded as a false dichotomy. The idea of an objective *scientist*, as opposed to an objective *science*, however, can still be regarded as pertinent to economic theory and economic policy. Economics should require no less than principled adherence to high standards of observation, interpretation, and synthesis. But the persistent belief that economists who advocate efficiency are being objective scientists is simply wrong. If one seriously believes in consumers' sovereignty then it follows that the analyst must become concerned with the goals and objectives of individuals and groups, even when those goals and objectives are expressed in terms other than those of the Pareto test or of improving the net social dividend as measured in monetary terms.

This concern for objectivity in assessing the relationship between theory and reality will require that more attention be paid to the nature of cost and benefit incidence of the status quo; it is, after all, the bearing of unwanted costs, or the perceived opportunity for individual gain, that animates most individuals in their daily lives. Significant progress on air and water pollution turns critically on the distribution (incidence) of different kinds of benefits and costs, not just by income class, but by job category, by location of residence, by education level, and by a number of other variables rarely pondered in economic analysis.[21] Once freed from the false belief that to worry about the incidence of benefits and costs, or the distribution of income, is to abandon the rigors and purity of the detached and objective analyst, economists are then liberated to address the pressing problems of collective action and public policy with renewed interest, and with justified intellectual legitimacy. That inquiry into collective action, and the process of helping to decide what is best to do, will necessarily proceed from a clearer understanding of the way in which the status quo magnitude and incidence of costs and benefits is an artifact of the prevailing

institutional arrangements. It is these rules and conventions that determine what is a cost, who must bear those costs, and who will gain
from an alteration in the institutional arrangements that define individual
and group choice sets (Bromley, 1989a).

The economist as policy analyst will continue to face a difficult task.
It is not always easy to maintain a sharp distinction between policy
objectives and policy instruments. To the extent that this distinction
seems to offer a safe haven for the policy scientist to choose instruments
while avoiding objectives, we may be misled. This distinction presumes
that decision makers first choose policy objectives, and only then begin
to search for policy instruments to achieve those objectives. Blaug
reminds us that decision makers often will start with existing activities
and gradually define and formulate objectives in view of experience
with policies. That is,

> decision makers do not try to get what they want; rather they learn to
> want by appraising what they get. Means and ends are indissolubly
> related, and evaluation of past decisions, or technical advice about future
> decisions, searches in vain for a social preference function that is not
> there. (Blaug, 1980, p. 151)

The feasible thing for the policy analyst, it would seem, is to become
involved in the policy process in a way that will facilitate the dialectic
evolution of both policy objectives and policy instruments. In some
instances productive efficiency will be the objective, while in other
settings economic opportunity will be purposely reallocated. Yet other
situations will see conscious efforts to redistribute income. An objective
scientist can further the cause of economic rationality given the evolved
policy objectives of the collective and the decision makers therein. This
neither suggests, nor requires, that false notions of scientific objectivity
hamper or delude the economist. Collective choice situations are most
properly modeled as situations in which individuals and groups of
individuals have interests in particular outcomes. Those interests can
be manifest in a variety of ways, but the essence of collective action
is that individuals will attempt to have their interests translated into
claims on some new economic opportunity or situation of economic
advantage, and then ultimately transformed into recognized entitlements
by the state. It is this process, whereby interests become transformed
into entitlements, that is the essence of collective action and institutional
change (Bromley, 1989a). By *interests* I mean that someone (or a group
of individuals) has some strong feeling about a particular situation;
they have a *stake* in the situation at hand. That interest could be about
the plans of the government to store spent nuclear fuel in the vicinity,

it could be about the polluted river that serves as a sewer for an unfettered paper manufacturing industry, or it could be about the inability to compete against Brazilian soybean producers.

The reality of policy analysis resides precisely in these very circumstances. Economic input into the policy process will be enhanced to the extent that this reality is comprehended, and not dismissed as irrelevant.

NOTES

1   For a treatment of ideology in this vein see Appleby (1980).

2   George Stigler, no doubt speaking for a number of economists, has declared that "Economics as a positive science is ethically neutral" (Stigler, 1959, p. 522). From this one can reach two quite distinct conclusions. If Stigler meant by "economics" the entire body of economics embodied in, say, the accepted textbooks of the day then he should have said: "economics *is* a positive science and therefore it is, by definition, ethically neutral." Alternatively, if Stigler meant that there is a part of economics that is "positive" then he should have said "that part of economics which is a positive science is, by definition, ethically neutral." Under the first interpretation *all* of economics is declared to be ethically neutral, while under the second definition only a subset of economics – the "positive" part – is ethically neutral. Either way Stigler is offering us either a tautology – a definition – or his personal views; neither is compelling for there are no external criteria to which Stigler can turn for proof of his assertion.

3   In this regard, Peter Hammond has observed that: "Many succeeding welfare economists completely misinterpreted Robbins and took a particularly unfortunate step that proved to be a major handicap throughout the ensuing thirty years. In an entirely misguided attempt to be 'scientific', in Robbins's sense, many welfare economists saw fit to exclude even the slightest possibility of making interpersonal comparisons" (Hammond, 1985, p. 406). See Ng (1983) for a discussion of different types of interpersonal utility comparisons – not all of which are value laden. Hammond has earlier shown that ". . . if interpersonal comparisons of a certain kind are introduced, it is possible to construct a generalized social welfare function (GSWF) satisfying appropriately modified forms of the Arrow conditions" (Hammond, 1976, p. 799).

4   For a good discussion of the conflation of productivity with efficiency in economic history research see Saraydar (1989).

5   The potential Pareto improvement test has been met if the gainers from a change are *potentially* able to compensate the loser and still have some retained surplus. Notice that the compensation need not actually occur; it is only necessary that it be capable of occurring. See Boadway and Bruce (1984).

6   Hammond (1985) reminds us that full Pareto efficiency is not even a necessary condition for a true welfare optimum since Pareto efficiency ignores incentive constraints.

7   In spite of what Friedman claims about being a positivist, he is actually a methodological instrumentalist. See Caldwell (1982) for a discussion of Friedman's position on positivism.

8   One may ponder the precise language used by Arrow in this first sentence. To say that *social choices* can be made in the political arena by voting or in the economic arena by markets gives a rather new meaning to the term "social choices." It would seem that when one talks of social choices one has in mind rather conscious and explicit acts of choosing particular courses of action. For instance, a social choice is whether to prohibit Alar and other insecticides, whether to stiffen the legal liability for oil spills, or whether to subsidize agricultural producers in the interest of soil conservation. But to say that the market will make decisions about whether to prohibit Alar, or to stiffen legal liability for oil spills, or to subsidize agricultural producers is nonsense. The market does not make social choices; rather it reflects the outcomes of millions of individual choices. Hence, Arrow cast the argument in a somewhat specious manner.

9   Early in the Reagan era the White House issued the executive Order 12291 which called for a benefit–cost analysis of all government regulations. Those favoring the requirement reflected the prevailing ethic of the day that held government to be "interfering" in the private business of firms and families. If such meddling (regulation) could be found to be inefficient via benefit–cost analysis there would, presumably, be a strong case for eliminating such interference in individual "freedom."

10 D. H. Robertson, early on, laid down the gauntlet in terms of urging that economists "stick to one's last" – meaning, of course, that efficiency to the economist was like a bootmaker's last.

11 There are millions of adherents to the world's dominant religions and received truth – consensus – to one group surely differs from consensus to another.

12 There is a crucial difference between a distribution of income that is merely appropriate and one that is optimal. To say that income is optimally distributed is to suggest that the marginal utility of income across all individuals is equal. For a treatment of the impossibility of separating efficiency from its distributional dimension see Azzi and Cox (1973).

13 There is one contemporary exception to this claim, in which, interestingly enough, economists have been openly exploited by politicians for the latter's own ideological agenda. I have in mind Executive Order 12291, mentioned in note 9, requiring a benefit–cost analysis of all government regulation. Many economists, in the grand tradition of wanting to believe that we had something useful to offer the public policy process, took this as evidence of the belated acceptance of efficiency among politicians. In

fact, it was a cynical opportunity to use economists, and economics, to "prove" what the political right had been claiming since Barry Goldwater rose to national prominence, namely that the economy was over-regulated.

14   I have been told, for instance, that without reference to the Pareto test in benefit–cost analysis one has mere analytical mush. Exactly what is meant by analytical mush was not made clear. It seems safe to conclude, however, that the speaker had in mind an absence of rigor (or of theoretical content or of sophistication), and possibly the absence of a bottom line in terms of economic surplus by which the economist would be able to declare a particular policy as efficient or otherwise.

15   I note with interest a recent report from the New York Botanical Garden suggesting that the economic product from the Amazonian rain forests is higher in their natural state than if the trees are removed. This form of efficiency analysis was met with sighs of relief from those looking for ways to justify preservation, and with contempt from those intent on timber exploitation. Which will prevail over the long run cannot be foreseen.

16   For comments on revealed preference theory as it relates to individual choices see Bromley (1989a) and Sen (1982).

17   There can be no better contemporary (early 1990) illustration of this issue than the controversy surrounding the use of bovine somatotropin (BST) injections to induce greater milk yields. Economists appeal to efficiency gains in the dairy industry, drug manufacturers appeal to evidence from the Food and Drug Administration that BST is a naturally occurring compound in milk and hence there is no health risk, and scientists appeal to the need to continue technological innovation (including genetic engineering) so as to remain competitive. Consumers, meanwhile, remain unimpressed. A number of food processors and dairies have announced that they will not accept milk from cows that have been injected with BST. While economists and dairy scientists condemn the rise of neo-Luddism, consumers seemingly could care less. How this particular issue will be resolved is not clear. But it is clear that economists are not viewing the benefits and costs of BST in a manner that is consistent with perceptions by consumers in their own terms. As long as this dissonance continues, the general population will simply ignore the "economic" analysis of BST. I suspect that other areas involving unfamiliar risks show a similar pattern.

18   Some will object that at least markets force individuals to reveal their true preferences since they will have to pay for what they receive, while in the public arena people can demand what they may not have to pay for. It is, of course, a value judgment to say that "true" preferences are revealed through markets – they are only true as constrained by the current distribution of income. Additionally, measures now exist (that is, Groves mechanisms) for insuring that choices unmodulated by unit prices can be reliable indicators of true preferences.

19   This would include a positive surplus in the case of the potential Pareto improvement test.

20   An example of a value judgment is: "I believe that Alpha should be made better off at the expense of Beta." An example of an untestable proposition that is *not* a value judgment is: "I believe that this program will make Alpha better off at the expense of Beta." Ng (1983) and Sen (1970, 1967) regard these as examples of, respectively, nonbasic value judgments, and subjective judgments of fact.

21   Boadway (1976) has made an interesting attempt in this regard. His work departs from the convention of weighting the gains and losses according to the groups that experience them. Rather, he uses a "distribution characteristic" from Feldstein (1972) to attach distributional weights to goods and factors instead of to groups of persons.

Bibliography

von Albertini, Rudolf 1982: *European Colonial Rule: 1880–1940: The Impact of the West on India, Southeast Asia, and Africa.* Westport, CT: Greenwood Press.

Alchian, Armen and Harold Demsetz 1973: The property rights paradigm. *Journal of Economic History*, 13, 16–27.

Anderson, Glen D. and Richard C. Bishop 1986: The valuation problem. In Daniel W. Bromley (ed.), *Natural Resource Economics: Policy Problems and Contemporary Analysis*, Boston, MA: Kluwer, 89–137.

Appleby, Joyce O. 1980: *Economic Thought and Ideology in Seventeenth-Century England.* Princeton, NJ: Princeton University Press.

Arnold, J. E. M. and J. Gabriel Campbell 1986: Collective management of hill forests in Nepal: the community forestry development project. In National Academy of Sciences, *Common Property Resource Management*, Washington, DC: National Academy Press.

Arrow, Kenneth J. 1951: *Social Choice and Individual Values.* New Haven, CN: Yale University Press.

Azzi, Corry F. and James C. Cox 1973: Equity and efficiency in evaluation of public programs. *Quarterly Journal of Economics*, 87, 495–502.

Backhouse, Roger 1985: *A History of Modern Economic Analysis.* Oxford: Basil Blackwell.

Baden, John and Richard L. Stroup 1981: *Bureaucracy vs. Environment.* Ann Arbor, MI: University of Michigan Press.

Bagehot, W. 1885: The problems of English classical political economy. *Fortnightly Review.*

Baker, A. R. H. and R. A. Butlin (eds) 1973: *Studies of Field Systems in the British Isles.* Cambridge: Cambridge University Press.

Baker, C. Edwin 1975: The ideology of *The Economic Analysis of Law*. *Philosophy and Public Affairs*, 3, 3–48.

Batie, Sandra 1984: Alternative views of property rights: implications for agricultural use of natural resources. *American Journal of Agricultural Economics*, 66, 814–18.

Bator, Francis M. 1958: The anatomy of market failure. *Quarterly Journal of Economics*, 72, 351–79.

232

Baumol, W. J. 1972: On taxation and the control of externalities. *American Economic Review*, 62, 307–22.

—— and Wallace E. Oates 1975: *The Theory of Environmental Policy*. Englewood Cliffs, NJ: Prentice-Hall.

Becker, Lawrence C. 1977: *Property Rights*. London: Routledge and Kegan Paul.

Bentley, William 1984: *The Uncultivated Half of India: Problems and Possible Solutions*. New Delhi: Ford Foundation.

Bhatia, B. M. 1964: Disintegration of village communities in India. In B. N. Ganguli (ed.), *Readings in Indian Economic History*, London: Asia Publications House, 88–101.

Blaug, Mark 1980: *The Methodology of Economics*. Cambridge: Cambridge University Press.

Boadway, Robin 1974: The welfare foundations of cost–benefit analysis. *Economic Journal*, 84, 926–39.

—— 1976: Integrating equity and efficiency in applied welfare economics. *Quarterly Journal of Economics*, 90, 541–56.

—— and Neil Bruce 1984: *Welfare Economics*. Oxford: Basil Blackwell.

Braden, John B. 1982: Some emerging rights in agricultural land. *American Journal of Agricultural Economics*, 64, 19–27.

Brewer, Marilynn B. and Roderick M. Kramer 1986: Choice behavior in social dilemmas: effects of social identity, group size, and decision framing. *Journal of Personality and Social Psychology*, 50, 543–9.

Bromley, D. W. 1978: Property rules, liability rules, and environmental economics. *Journal of Economic Issues*, 12, 43–60.

—— 1982: Improving irrigated agriculture: institutional reform and the small farmer, Staff Working Paper 531. Washington, DC: World Bank.

—— 1983: Public and private interests in the federal lands. In Peter Emerson (ed.), *Public Lands and the U.S. Economy*, Boulder, CO: Westview Press, ch. 1.

—— 1985: Resources and economic development: an institutionalist perspective. *Journal of Economic Issues*, 19, 779–96.

—— 1986a: Markets and externalities. In Daniel W. Bromley (ed.), *Natural Resource Economics: Policy Problems and Contemporary Analysis*, Boston, MA: Kluwer, ch. 2.

—— 1986b: Natural resources and agricultural development in the tropics: is conflict inevitable? In Allen Maunder and Ulf Renborg (eds), *Agriculture in a Turbulent World Economy*, Oxford: Gower, 319–27.

—— 1989a: *Economic Interests and Institutions: The Conceptual Foundations of Public Policy*. Oxford: Basil Blackwell.

—— 1989b: Entitlements, missing markets, and environmental uncertainty. *Journal of Environmental Economics and Management*, 17, 181–94.

—— 1989c: Property relations and economic development: the other land reform. *World Development*, 17, 867–77.

—— 1990: The ideology of efficiency: searching for a theory of policy analysis. *Journal of Environmental Economics and Management*, 19, 86–107.

—— and Richard C. Bishop 1977: From economic theory to fisheries policy: conceptual problems and management prescriptions. In Lee Anderson (ed.), *Economic Impacts of Extended Fisheries Jurisdiction*, Ann Arbor, MI: Ann Arbor Science Publications.

—— and Devendra P. Chapagain 1984: The village against the center: resource depletion in south Asia. *American Journal of Agricultural Economics*, 66, 868–73.

—— and Michael M. Cernea 1989: *The Management of Common Property Natural Resources: Some Conceptual and Operational Fallacies.* Washington, DC: World Bank.

Brubaker, Sterling 1984: *Rethinking the Federal Lands.* Washington, DC: Resources for the Future.

Buchanan, J. M. 1962: Politics, policy, and the Pigovian margins. *Economica*, 29, 17–28.

—— 1972: Politics, property, and the law: an alternative explanation of Miller et al. v. Schoene. *Journal of Law and Economics*, 15, 439–52.

—— 1973: The Coase Theorem and the theory of the state. *Natural Resources Journal*, 13, 579–84.

—— and William C. Stubblebine 1962: Externality. *Economica*, 29, 371–84.

—— and Gordon Tullock 1975: Polluters' profits and political response: direct controls versus taxes. *American Economic Review*, 65, 139–47.

Burke, Edmund 1910: *Reflections on the Revolution in France.* London: Dent.

Burrows, Paul 1980: *The Economic Theory of Pollution Control.* Cambridge, MA: MIT Press.

Cairnes, J. E. 1965: *The Character and Logical Method of Political Economy.* London: Frank Cass. Originally published in 1874 as *Some Leading Principles of Political Economy.*

Calabresi, Guido, and A. Douglas Melamed 1972: Property rules, liability rules, and inalienability: one view of the cathedral. *Harvard Law Review*, 85, 1089–128.

Caldwell, Bruce 1982: *Beyond Positivism.* London: Allen and Unwin.

Cernea, Michael M. 1985: Alternative units of social organization sustaining afforestation strategies. In Michael M. Cernea (ed.), *Putting People First: Sociological Variables in Rural Development*, Oxford: Oxford University Press.

Cheung, Steven N. S. 1970: The structure of a contract and the theory of a non-exclusive resource. *Journal of Law and Economics*, 13, 49–70.

Chipman, John S. and James C. Moore 1978: The new welfare economics 1939–74. *International Economic Review*, 19, 547–84.

Ciriacy-Wantrup, S. V. 1963: *Resource Conservation: Economics and Policies.* Berkeley, CA: University of California, revised edition.

—— and Richard C. Bishop 1975: Common property as a concept in natural resource policy. *Natural Resources Journal*, 15, 713–27.

Clawson, Marion 1983: *The Federal Lands Revisited.* Baltimore, MD: Johns Hopkins University Press.

Coase, R. H. 1960: The problem of social cost. *Journal of Law and Economics*, 3, 1-44.

Commander, Simon 1986: Managing Indian forests: a case for the reform of property rights. *Development Policy Review*, 4, 325-44.

Commons, John R. 1961: *Institutional Economics*. Madison, WI: University of Wisconsin Press.

—— 1968: *Legal Foundations of Capitalism*. New York: Macmillan.

Cooter, Robert and Peter Rappoport 1984: Were the ordinalists wrong about welfare economics? *Journal of Economic Literature*, 22, 507-30.

Cruz, Maria Concepcion 1984: Population pressure, migration, and markets: implications for upland development, Working Paper 84-05. Los Banos: University of the Philippines, Institute for Development Studies.

Culhane, Paul J. 1981: *Public Lands Politics*. Baltimore, MD: Johns Hopkins University Press.

Dahlman, C. J. 1979: The problem of externality. *Journal of Law and Economics*, 22, 141-62.

—— 1980: *The Open Field System and Beyond*. Cambridge: Cambridge University Press.

Dasgupta, P. S. and G. M. Heal 1979: *Economic Theory and Exhaustible Resources*. Cambridge: Cambridge University Press.

Demsetz, Harold 1967: Toward a theory of property rights. *American Economic Review*, 57, 347-59.

Desai, S. S. M. 1980: *Economic History of India*. Bombay: Himalaya Publications.

Dick, Daniel T. 1976: The voluntary approach to externality problems: a survey of the critics. *Journal of Environmental Economics and Management*, 2, 185-95.

Dorfman, Robert 1976: Forty years of cost-benefit analysis, Discussion Paper 498. Cambridge, MA: Harvard Institute of Economic Research.

Dowdle, Barney 1984: Why have we retained the federal lands? An alternative hypothesis. In Sterling Brubaker (ed.), *Rethinking the Federal Lands*, Washington, DC: Resources for the Future, 61-73.

Easter, K. William 1977: Improving village irrigation systems: an example from India. *Land Economics*, 53, 56-66.

Einhorn, H. J. and Robin M. Hogarth 1987: Decision making under ambiguity. In Robin M. Hogarth and Melvin Reder (eds), *Rational Choice*, Chicago, IL: University of Chicago Press.

Fairfax, Sally and Carolyn K. Yale 1987: *Federal Lands*. Washington, DC: Island Press.

Feldstein, Martin S. 1972: Distributional equity and the optimal structure of public prices. *American Economic Review*, 62, 32-6.

Fleishman, John A. 1988: The effects of decision framing and others' behavior on cooperation in a social dilemma. *Journal of Conflict Resolution*, 32, 162-80.

Francis, John G. and Richard Ganzel (eds) 1984: *Western Public Lands*. Totowa, NJ: Rowman and Allanheld.

Freeman, A. M., III 1984: Depletable externalities and Pigouvian taxation. *Journal of Environmental Economics and Management*, 11, 173-9.

Friedman, James W. 1986: *Game Theory with Applications to Economics*. Oxford: Oxford University Press.

Friedman, Milton 1953: *Essays in Positive Economics*. Chicago, IL: University of Chicago Press.

Fukazawa, H. 1983: Agrarian relations: western India. In Dharma Kumar (ed.), *The Cambridge Economic History of India: 1757-1970*, Cambridge: Cambridge University Press.

Furubotn, Eirik and Svetozar Pejovich 1972: Property rights and economic theory: a survey of recent literature. *Journal of Economic Literature*, 10, 1137-62.

Gardner, B. Delworth 1984: The case for divestiture. In Sterling Brubaker (ed.), *Rethinking the Federal Lands*, Washington, DC: Resources for the Future, 156-80.

Geertz, Clifford 1963: *Agricultural Involution: The Processes of Ecological Change in Indonesia*. Berkeley, CA: University of California Press.

Gordon, H. Scott 1954: The economic theory of a common property resource: the fishery. *Journal of Political Economy*, 62, 124-42.

Gupta, Sulekh Chandra 1964: The village community and its disintegration in Uttar Pradesh in the early nineteenth century. In B. N. Ganguli (ed.), *Readings in Indian Economic History*, London: Asia Publishing House, 102-13.

Guttman, Joel M. 1978: Understanding collective action: matching behavior. *American Economic Review*, 68, 251-5.

Hallowell, A. Irving 1943: The nature and function of property as a social institution. *Journal of Legal and Political Sociology*, 1, 115-38.

Hammond, Peter J. 1976: Equity, Arrow's conditions, and Rawls' difference principle. *Econometrica*, 44, 793-804.

—— 1985: Welfare economics. In J. Feiwel (ed.), *Issues in Contemporary Microeconomics and Welfare*, London: Macmillan, ch. 13.

Hanke, S. H. 1982a: Privatize those lands, *Reason*, March.

—— 1982b: Grazing for dollars, *Reason*, July.

—— 1983: The privatization debate: an insider's view, *The Cato Journal*, 2, Winter.

Harberger, Arnold C. 1972: Three basic postulates for applied welfare economics. In Arnold C. Harberger et al. (eds), *Benefit-Cost Analysis, 1971*, Chicago, IL: Aldine, ch. 1.

—— 1978: On the use of distributional weights in social cost-benefit analysis. *Journal of Political Economy*, 86, S87-S120.

Hardin, Garrett 1968: The tragedy of the commons, *Science*, 162, 1243-8.

Hart, H. L. A. 1961: *The Concept of Law*. Oxford: Clarendon Press.

Hawaii Housing Authority v. Midkiff, 55 U.S.L.W. 4673 (U.S. May 30, 1984).

Hicks, John 1939: Foundations of welfare economics, *Economic Journal*, 49, 696-712.

—— 1959: *Essays in World Economics*. Oxford: Clarendon Press.

Hill, Polly 1970: *Studies in Rural Capitalism in West Africa*. Cambridge: Cambridge University Press.

Hodge, Ian D. 1989: Compensation for nature conservation. *Environment Planning A*, 21 (7).

Hoebel, E. Adamson 1942: Fundamental legal concepts as applied in the study of primitive law. *Yale Law Journal*, 51, 951–66.

Hohfeld, W. N. 1913: Some fundamental legal conceptions as applied in judicial reasoning. *Yale Law Journal*, 23, 16–59.

—— 1917: Fundamental legal conceptions as applied in judicial reasoning. *Yale Law Journal*, 26, 710–70.

Hughes, Jonathan R. T. 1977: *The Government Habit: Economic Controls from Colonial Times to the Present*. New York: Basic Books.

Hutchison, T. W. 1964: *'Positive' Economics and Policy Objectives*. London: Allen and Unwin.

International Monetary Fund 1984: *World Economic Outlook*, Washington, DC: International Monetary Fund.

Jevons, W. S. 1970: *The Theory of Political Economy*. Harmondsworth: Penguin. Originally published 1871.

Jodha, N. S. 1986: Common property resources and rural poor in dry regions of India. *Economic and Political Weekly*, 21, 1169–81.

Kahneman, Daniel and Amos Tversky 1979: Prospect theory: an analysis of decision under risk. *Econometrica*, 47, 263–91.

Kahneman, Daniel, J. L. Knetsch, and R. Thaler 1986: Fairness as a constraint on profit seeking: entitlements in the market. *American Economic Review*, 76, 728–41.

Kaldor, Nicholas 1939: Welfare propositions of economics and interpersonal comparisons of utility. *Economic Journal*, 49, 549–52.

Kamien, M. I., N. L. Schwartz, and F. T. Dolbear 1966: Asymmetry between bribes and charges. *Water Resources Research*, 1, 147–57.

Keynes, J. N. 1917: *The Scope and Method of Political Economy*. London: A. M. Kelley.

Knetsch, Jack and J. A. Sinden 1984: Willingness to pay and compensation demanded: experimental evidence of an unexpected disparity in measures of value. *Quarterly Journal of Economics*, 99, 507–21.

Leman, Christopher K. 1984: How the privatization revolution failed, and why public land management needs reform anyway. In John G. Francis and Richard Ganzel (eds), *Western Public Lands*, Totowa, NJ: Rowman and Allanheld.

Leopold, Aldo 1949: *A Sand County Almanac*. Oxford: Oxford University Press.

Libecap, Gary 1981: *Locking Up the Range*. Cambridge, MA: Ballinger.

McCay, Bonnie and J. A. Acheson 1988: *The Question of the Commons*. Tucson, AZ: University of Arizona Press.

McCloskey, Donald 1983: The rhetoric of economics. *Journal of Economic Literature*, 21, 481–517.

McKean, Margaret 1986: Management of traditional common lands (Iriaichi) in Japan. In National Academy of Sciences, *Common Property Resource Management*, Washington, DC: National Academy Press.

Marchand, J. R. and K. P. Russell 1973: Externalities, liability, separability, and resource allocation. *American Economic Review*, 63, 611–20.

Marshall, Alfred 1890: *Principles of Economics*. London: Macmillan.

Marwell, Gerald and R. Ames 1981: Economists free ride, does anyone else?: experiments in the provision of public goods IV. *Journal of Public Economics*, 15, 295–310.

Mill, J. S. 1967: *Collected Works, Essays on Economy and Society*, vol. 4 (J. Robson, ed.). Toronto: University of Toronto Press.

Mishan, E. J. 1971: The postwar literature on externalities: an interpretative essay. *Journal of Economic Literature*, 9, 1–28.

—— 1974: The economics of disamenity. *Natural Resources Journal*, 14, 55–86.

—— 1975: The folklore of the market. *Journal of Economic Issues*, 9, 681–752.

—— 1980: How valid are economic evaluations of allocative changes? *Journal of Economic Issues*, 14, 143–61.

Nash, C. A. and J. K. Bowers 1988: Alternative approaches to the valuation of environmental resources. In R. K. Turner (ed.), *Sustainable Environmental Management: Principles and Practice*, London: Bellhaven Press, 118–42.

National Academy of Sciences 1986: *Common Property Resource Management*. Washington, DC: National Academy Press.

Neale, Walter C. 1969: Land is to rule. In Robert Frykenberg (ed.), *Land Control and Social Structure in Indian History*, Madison, WI: University of Wisconsin Press, ch. 1.

Nelson, Richard R. 1981: Assessing private enterprise: an exegesis of tangled doctrine. *Bell Journal of Economics*, 12, 93–110.

Nelson, Robert H. 1987: The economics profession and the making of public policy. *Journal of Economic Literature*, 35, 49–91.

Netting, Robert 1976: What Alpine peasants have in common: observations on communal tenure in a Swiss village. *Human Ecology*, 4, 135–46.

Ng, Yew-Kwang 1983: *Welfare Economics*. London: Macmillan.

Norgaard, Richard B. 1981: Sociosystem and ecosystem coevolution in the Amazon. *Journal of Environmental Economics and Management*, 8, 238–54.

North, Douglass C. 1981: *Structure and Change in Economic History*. New York: Norton.

—— 1984: Transaction costs, institutions, and economic history. *Zeitschrift fur die gesamte Staatswissenschaft*, 140, 7–17.

—— and Robert Paul Thomas 1977: The first economic revolution. *Economic History Review*, 30, 229–41.

Okun, Arthur M. 1975: *Equality and Efficiency: The Big Tradeoff*. Washington, DC: Brookings Institution.

Ostrom, Elinor 1986: Issues of definition and theory: some conclusions and hypotheses. In National Academy of Sciences, *Common Property Resource Management*, Washington, DC: National Academy Press.

Pigou, A. C. 1912: *Wealth and Welfare*. London: Macmillan.
—— 1920. *The Economics of Welfare*. London: Macmillan.
Randall, A. 1972: Market solutions to externality problems: theory and practice. *American Journal of Agricultural Economics*, 54, 175–83.
—— 1974: Coasian externality theory in a policy context. *Natural Resources Journal*, 14, 35–54.
Rawls, John 1971: *A Theory of Justice*. Cambridge, MA: Harvard University Press.
Raychaudhuri, Tapan (ed.) 1982: *The Cambridge Economic History of India: 1200–1750*, vol. 1. Cambridge: Cambridge University Press.
Rhoades, Robert E. and Stephen J. Thompson 1975: Adaptive strategies in Alpine environments: beyond ecological particularism. *American Ethnologist*, 2, 535–51.
Robbins, Lionel 1932: *An Essay on the Nature and Significance of Economic Science*. London: Macmillan.
Runge, C. F. 1981: Common-property externalities: isolation, assurance, and resource depletion in a traditional grazing context. *American Journal of Agricultural Economics*, 63, 595–607.
—— 1984: Institutions and the free rider: the assurance problem in collective action. *Journal of Politics*, 46, 154–81.
—— and Daniel W. Bromley 1979: Property rights and the first economic revolution: the origins of agriculture reconsidered, Working Paper 13. University of Wisconsin-Madison, Center for Resource Policy Studies.
Samuels, W. J. 1971: Interrelations between legal and economic processes. *Journal of Law and Economics*, 14, 435–50.
—— 1972: In defense of a positive approach to government as an economic variable. *Journal of Law and Economics*, 15, 453–9.
—— 1974: The Coase Theorem and the study of law and economics. *Natural Resources Journal*, 14, 1–33.
—— 1981: Welfare economics, power, and property. In Warren J. Samuels and A. Allan Schmid (eds), *Law and Economics*, Boston, MA: Martinus Nijhoff.
Samuelson, Paul A. 1950: Evaluation of real national income. *Oxford Economic Papers*, 2, 1–29.
Saraydar, Edward 1989: The conflation of productivity and efficiency in economics and economic history. *Economics and Philosophy*, 5, 55–67.
Sax, Joseph 1983: Some thoughts on the decline of private property. *Washington Law Review*, 58, 481–96.
Schlatter, Richard 1951: *Private Property: the History of an Idea*. London: George Allen and Unwin.
Schmid, A. A. 1987: *Property, Power, and Public Choice*. New York: Praeger, 2nd edn.
Schotter, Andrew 1981: *The Economic Theory of Social Institutions*. Cambridge: Cambridge University Press.
Scitovsky, Tibor 1941: A note on welfare propositions in economics. *Review of Economics and Statistics*, 9, 77–88.

Scott, Anthony 1955: The fishery: the objectives of sole ownership. *Journal of Political Economy*, 63, 116–24.

Scruton, Roger 1982: *Kant*. Oxford: Oxford University Press.

Sen, A. K. 1967. The nature and classes of prescriptive judgments. *Philosophical Quarterly*, 17, 46–62.

—— 1970: *Collective Choice and Individual Welfare*. Amsterdam: North-Holland.

—— 1977: Rational fools: a critique of the behavioral foundations of economic theory. *Philosophy and Public Affairs*, 6, 317–44.

—— 1982: *Choice, Welfare, and Measurement*. Oxford: Basil Blackwell.

Senior, N. W. 1836: *An Outline of the Science of Political Economy*. London: London School of Economics Reprints.

Shubik, Martin 1982: *Game Theory in the Social Sciences*. Cambridge, MA: MIT Press.

Smith, R. 1981: Resolving the tragedy of the commons by creating private property rights in wildlife. *Cato Journal*, 1, 439–68.

Steiner, Hillel 1977: The structure of a set of compossible rights. *Journal of Philosophy*, 74, 767–75.

Stigler, George 1959: The politics of political economists. *Quarterly Journal of Economics*, 73, 519–27.

Stroup, Richard L. 1984: Weaknesses in the case for retention. In Sterling Brubaker (ed.), *Rethinking the Federal Lands*, Washington, DC: Resources for the Future, 149–55.

—— and John Baden 1982: Endowment areas: a clearing in the policy wilderness? *The Cato Journal*, 2, Winter.

Sugden, Robert 1984: Reciprocity: the supply of public goods through voluntary contributions. *Economic Journal*, 94, 772–87.

—— 1986: *The Economics of Rights, Co-operation and Welfare*. Oxford: Basil Blackwell.

—— and Alan Williams 1978: *The Principles of Practical Cost–Benefit Analysis*. Oxford: Oxford University Press.

Swift, Jeremy 1977: Pastoral development in Somalia: herding cooperatives as a strategy against desertification and famine. In Michael Glantz (ed.), *Desertification: Environmental Degradation in and Around Arid Lands*, Boulder, CO: Westview Press, ch. 11.

Tawney, R. H. 1948: *The Acquisitive Society*. New York: Harcourt.

—— 1981: Property and creative work. In C. B. Macpherson (ed.), *Property: Mainstream and Critical Positions*, Toronto: University of Toronto Press, 135–51.

Thomson, James T. 1977: Ecological deterioration: local-level rule making and enforcement problems in Niger. In Michael Glantz (ed.), *Desertification: Environmental Degradation in and Around Arid Lands*, Boulder, CO: Westview Press, ch. 4.

Tribe, Laurence H. 1972: Policy science: analysis or ideology. *Philosophy and Public Affairs*, 2, 66–110.

Tversky, Amos and Daniel Kahneman 1981: The framing of decisions and the psychology of choice. *Science*, 211, 453-8.

—— and —— 1987: Rational choice and the framing of decisions. In Robin Hogarth and Melvin Reder (eds), *Rational Choice*, Chicago, IL: University of Chicago Press, 67-94.

United Nations 1983: *Statistical Yearbook*, New York: United Nations.

Viner, Jacob 1961: Hayek on freedom and coercion. *Southern Economic Journal*, 27, 230-6.

Wade, Robert 1986: Common property resource management in South Indian villages. In National Academy of Sciences, *Common Property Resource Management*, Washington, DC: National Academy Press.

—— 1987: The management of common property resources: collective action as an alternative to privatisation or state regulation. *Cambridge Journal of Economics*, 11, 95-106.

—— 1988: *Village Republics*. Cambridge: Cambridge University Press.

Williams, Howard 1977: Kant's concept of property. *Philosophical Quarterly*, 27, 32-40.

World Bank 1984a: *World Development Indicators*. Washington, DC: World Bank.

—— 1984b: *World Development Report*. Washington, DC: World Bank.

—— 1985: *Ivory Coast: Second Forestry Project*. Washington, DC: World Bank.

Index

242